Catch

A Discovery of America

Catch

A Discovery of America

By Nick Hartshorn

MacMurray & Beck   Denver/Aspen

Photograph of Anne Sadler by John Kendall. All other photographs in this volume were taken by the author.

Copyright © 1996 by Nick Hartshorn
Published by:
MacMurray & Beck, Inc.
1649 Downing Street
Denver, Colorado 80218

Printed and bound in the United States of America

Library of Congress Cataloging-in-Publication Data
Hartshorn, Nick, 1969–
     Catch : a discovery of America / Nick Hartshorn.
          p.   cm.
     ISBN 1-878448-71-4
     1. United States—Description and travel. 2. United States—
Social life and customs—1971–   3. Hartshorn, Nick, 1969–   —
Journeys—United States. I. Title.
E169.04.H385   1996
917.304'929—dc20   96-23010
                                                                                              CIP

Catch designed by Susan Wasinger.
The text was set in Goudy by Pro Production.
Project management by D&D Editorial Services.

2 4 6 8 10 9 7 5 3 1
First Printing

FOR MY PARENTS

C o n t e n t s

ACKNOWLEDGMENTS

Many companies and individuals were integral in getting me down the road: Gene Taylor's Sporting Goods for the baseballs; George Fabian at Mizuno for two gloves; Jordan Campbell at REI for camping equipment; Denise Lebeaux-Becker at Fuji for the film; Mike's Camera for the photo work; City Market for the Top Ramen; The Sound Company for the recorder and cassettes; and Karen Piel at Five-Ten for the shoes. In addition, I'd like to thank Hank Ellison, Peter Slayback, Greg Vickers, Skip Behrhorst, John Reid, Pete Simon, and Concept Restaurants for their support.

In helping to get my words from the road onto the page, I am deeply indebted to the following: Fred Ramey, Robin Obermeyer, and my sister, Beck, for their guidance in shaping the manuscript; Gray Behrhorst and Stephanie Murray, for their unwavering enthusiasm; Ed Bradley, for introducing me to Central Park; and Bob and Randy Costas, for their constant support. Though his interview is not included here, I would like to thank Pete Collins of Stinnett, Texas, for the use of his photograph on the cover.

Most importantly, I would like to thank all the people who took time to throw the ball with me and talk about their lives. I am forever grateful.

INTRODUCTION

"YOU CAN GET IT—" he yelled as the ball arced fifty feet over my head and flew toward the barn "—you can get it!" My feet scampered over the loose gravel as I tore down the driveway to cradle the ball before it hit the ground. Glove outstretched, I lunged and felt two things at once—the ball slapping into my webbing and my side lighting up with heat as I skidded to a stop on the hard-packed dirt. Rolling over on my side, I turned toward him and thrust my glove skyward, the bulging pocket wrapped tightly around the ball.

"Yeah!" he howled, both of his hands pumping in the air as he came barreling toward me. I curled up as he landed on top of me, his arms squeezing the air out of my lungs in celebration. "You got it!" he yelled, smothering me in a victory tackle. "You got it!"

I had made the finest catch of my eight years. The ball was thrown by my brother.

During summer vacation after third grade, I went to stay with Opa—my grandfather—who had emigrated to the United States in 1938. With words couched in a softly spoken Bavarian accent, he consoled me for having been cut in recent tryouts.

"Sport isn't life," he said. "It only reveals what we can do." He arced the ball easily into my mitt. "Like playing catch, Nick. We don't throw the ball to win, but there's success in it anyway."

Six months later, Opa succumbed to cancer. I sent the ball to be buried in his hand.

The game of baseball has been described as five minutes of action stuffed into three hours. Playing catch is similar. It's not nonstop excitement but rather a rhythmic motion that sometimes delivers a pinnacle: a slicing curve-ball, an outrageously loud pop into the webbing, or a glance at the long shadows cast as the deep orange sun surrenders to the horizon.

Like driving down a highway, playing catch isn't constant sensory overload. Behind the wheel, you put in four hundred miles only to remember that one dead snake on the road and that one dust-covered blond woman who held a SLOW sign in the construction zone. After a hundred tosses, you remember this complete stranger telling you about getting high in Vietnam, and how once, out of nowhere, he threw a knuckleball. And the seams froze.

Last May, I pulled out of Grand Junction, Colorado. Three months later, I arrived in Calais, Maine, having logged over 12,000 miles on America's back roads playing catch. I didn't go in search of just philosophy, or God, or religion, or men, or women but of all these things. I went in search of a conversation. And while people may believe themselves to be vastly different from one another, the words that emerge as soon as the ball pops into the well-oiled webbing of the mitt weave the diverse voices into a common fabric.

Just after noon, I put the car in first gear, the tires crackling over smooth-stoned gravel in the driveway. They are the same rocks I tore through as an eight-year-old speeding toward the catch of my life. Only this time, as I pulled past the barn, it wasn't for sport.

I turned left out of the driveway and the tires hummed on the asphalt as I headed due south through town and into America. Not to seek pinnacles, as Opa would have said, but to listen—to uncover the roads, their character, and the people whose words define this country.

COLORADO HIGHWAY 50

Doing fifty-five just north of Delta on Colorado Highway 50 southbound, I cranked the radio. Top forty music pumped from the speakers; the sun broke from behind a cloud and poured light through the small sunroof. It was a glorious May eighth.

On the backseat rested a red Converse All Star gym bag, its zipper half-closed. Inside it were three right-handed baseball gloves, one lefty, three baseballs, a spiral notebook, a tape recorder, and my camera. In back I'd packed spare film, spare batteries, a heap of blank cassettes, a camp stove, and enough Top Ramen and frosted Pop-Tarts to last through August.

As I passed Cerro summit, the radio succumbed to the altitude, hissing and crackling as it searched for an FM band. I turned it off and drove in silence, the engine purring as I crested Blue Mesa summit. The road climbed again to Lake City, then gradually sloped downward into southeast Colorado. A chain of small mountains tapered to the south past Del Norte while the Sangre de Cristos carried along to the north, their deep blue silhouette towering into the sky.

I camped overnight at Sand Dunes National Park and then drove through a dense morning fog into Walsenburg, Colorado. There, the weather was too lousy to have breakfast outside, much less play catch with anyone. I ended up eating my Pop-Tarts in the driver's seat while parallel-parked on Main Street.

Later that morning, I entered New Mexico on Highway 87, two rippling lanes of road dotted with trailer homes and pinyon pine clusters until Des Moines, New Mexico, then a lonely expanse of asphalt linking a mesquite wind to its source in Texas. When I crossed the Texas border, the afternoon wisps of fog cleared to reveal a landscape marked with piles of lava rock. I spent the balance of the day on straight ribbons of road pulled tight over the horizon.

After a night in Dumas, I drove through light rain onto Highway 207 south of Stinnett. Merle Haggard's voice twanged from the speakers as I motored through the changing landscape, one where sandstone mesas stand guard over the slow erosion of deep red soil. Emerging from one of the canyons, I watched blood-red walls give way to immense flatness.

Such was the southward journey through the Texas panhandle, a corridor of arterial canyons and damp pinyon air. My gloves rested on the backseat, waiting for the weather to change as I passed through the tidy brick streets and wide alleys of Panhandle, Silverton, and Floydada.

Torrents of rain greeted nightfall on the outskirts of Lubbock, and people scurried out of a Little League park to get home. The rain alone was left to play under the lights, collecting in small pools around the plate and in a small divot on the pitcher's mound. After finding shelter at a Hardee's and scribbling down some notes, I pulled into an RV campground and slept in my car. A five speed. Deep metallic gray.

Texas rain.

When it starts to pour, the entire fury of the storm vents its rage at one sunroof. Yours. Maybe you did something wrong. Perhaps you forgot to signal. If your car survives the worst of it, the sheets of water taper to a steady stream, which fades to intermittent pops from late-coming droplets. God has moved the fury elsewhere, to hammer another.

On State Highway 84, which heads south from Lubbock toward Post, I must have committed three driving sins. The car was soaked in turn for each. By the time I slowed down on the main drag of Post, however, columns of sunlight fell haphazardly on the glistening street.

It was the first sunshine I'd seen since crossing into the state three days ago. The red brick buildings along Main Street glowed a moment in the new light as buttery pancake breezes from the cafes drifted over the wet asphalt. Stuffed under an awning that ran the length of the block stood a little barbershop next to a vacant store that was being gutted. The slowly spinning barber pole drew me in like a magnet.

I entered and met the proprietor, an older man reclining in a spare chair, his figure outlined against the sanitary hospital-green walls. On a small table to his side rested a pad of paper with a letter, half-written, in precise print. An AM country station popped out tinny tunes from the transistor radio on the sill, while in the background a blue light buzzed over the scissors, clippers, and combs. I introduced myself, told him about my trip, and did my best to explain why—without planning—I'd ended up in a barbershop in Post, Texas. He took on trust quickly and smiled at the notion. I asked if he had a few minutes to play catch.

"Haven't thrown a ball in a long time," he said with a smile, his words delivered in a clipped Texas twang. He folded his newspaper, set it aside, and rose to move outside. He stepped evenly and softly, his shoes scarcely registering a sound on the polished floor. Checking around to see that the shop was in order, he raised a freckled hand to turn down the radio. He turned back just as softly and moved toward the front of the store. When we reached the covered sidewalk, I handed him a glove—my old MacGregor.

"How's that gonna fit?" I asked.

"I guess I can git it on." He stuffed his fingers down through the leather and slapped his fist into the palm. A pickup revved up and headed down the street westward, the driver nodding his head at the barber as the tires hissed in the freshly fallen rain.

"How long have you been the barber here?"

"Twenty-five—no—twenty-six years." He inched his left foot forward and with his right hand let the ball go. It passed under the awning into my waiting glove, landing in the webbing with a soft thud. "Name is Mathews. Miriam T. Mathews. I'm the only male barber in town. We got women barbers, but I'm the only male—and I got one helper." I returned the toss, and he wrapped his glove around it. He fingered the ball from the webbing and smiled. "Haven't played in years." He let it fly again. "It's been years.

"I'm from Morton, Texas," he continued. "Lived forty-one years out there. Morton's a hundred miles west of here—Cochran County—sixteen miles from the state line. 'Bout sixty miles west of Lubbock." A careful man, he shaped his words into clean, quick strings—except for the more meaningful syllables, which he stretched out as long as the horizon. "Miles" became "miiiles." "Years" became "yeeears."

"I was born there in Morton in 1925. My grandpa was the first county commissioner out there; they came out in January '23 and he laid those streets off with a walking turn-in plow—'fore that there wuddn't a buildin' on town site. And my dad, well he was the first mail carrier there in Cochran County. I went to the public schools there and barbered out there for sixteen years after I got out of the Navy." Pop. Back into my glove.

"How was growing up there?" I carried my hand over in an arc and the strings rolled off my fingers.

"When I was a kid in Morton—back in the '30s—well it was durin' the Depression. I shined shoes, cost a dime a shine. I always had good money from that—good spendin' money. Other kids didn't have any money, so they'd come borrow a nickel or a dime from me. Course I give it to 'em just as a gift, they didn't have any way of paying me back. Back then, you got a Coke for a nickel, a hamburger for a nickel—six for a quarter—big ones, nice ones . . . bananas a nickel a dozen." He flipped the ball into the air, caught it, and tossed it my way.

Miriam threw the ball tenderly, much as he walked. Shuffling his left foot lightly over the concrete, he started his body slowly rocking while holding out his gloved left hand to target the throw. At the end of the motion, his right arm delivered the energy to the ball, which traveled in gentle arcs.

"Course that was back then; shoe shinin' has faded out quite a bit since. But in Lubbock now they've got shine boys out at the mall and at car washes and they gettin' four and five dollars per shine—some of them gettin' as much as I do for a haircut." He stepped and tossed the ball.

"I'd be better off if I was up there shinin' shoes than I would be down here cuttin' hair for six dollars—tell you th' truth I would. Little ole can of polish, don't have to buy a license or shop permits or nothing. And you don't have to pay taxes." The ball sailed from my hand. "Here, by the time I get my shop permit, my license, and doctor's inspection and physical, it costs me ninety-five dollars. Ninety-five. Used to cost two. Two dollars. I tell you, it's hard to make a livin', it is." He released the ball and glanced down the street.

"Tell me about the Navy," I said.

"I was a first deck machine major in the Navy, World War II," he boomed, holding the ball and moving his hand to punctuate the words. "I went across the ocean and stayed over there four years, seven months, and twenty-eight days serving the country. I was aboard ship all the time. My first ship I was on board for nineteen months; come home for a forty-five-day leave and right back out there." He whipped the ball and it sailed on a line under the awning. "I went when I was seventeen years old. My dad went to World War I, I went to World War II, my son served four years in the Air Force, and now my grandson's in there. We've got a four-generation record and we're proud of it. We're all volunteers—didn't have to go but we're proud of serving the country. Course a lot of people wouldn't go to the service, they'd say 'that's not my cup of tea,' but I don't believe in that myself. I don't believe in somebody else havin' to go in their place or go for them." His arm slipped through the air.

"How were those days—in the war?"

"Well. . . . " He paused and we tossed the ball several times without speaking. "Hot."

"Hot?"

"Hot—heat rash, ringworms, and fungus all over me. Was hot all the time. I was in Guadalcanal and the Solomon Islands—buried three of my buddies over there. And it always was so hot—that's what sticks with me. Course I got away in pretty good shape. I think the people's prayers—my mother's, the church's—all brought me back home, really. I believe in prayer," he said and nodded his head. "Yessir, I do." The ball slapped into my glove.

"And after that?"

"Then I came back and went to barber college in January of '48—Amarillo. Those were good years. And I been clippin' my friends ever since." He laughed and rolled back his shoulder to throw again.

"And how's barbering?"

"Well you see, this shop's been here since 1926, been a barbershop ever since this buildin's built. First barber here in this building was a man by the name of Benny Sargee. But the first barber in Post was, oh, what's his name?" Slap. Into his webbing. "Oh yes, Ben Williams—he started out in a tent here, least that's what I understand. Gosh, as far as bein' a barber, it's been nice here, really has. I enjoy livin' here. People here are nice, wonderful people. Where I left out there got wonderful people, too—in Morton. We lived out there sixteen years after we married." He finished and threw.

"Why'd you move?"

"Too much sand out there for my wife, so we had to come down here to get out of it. Course she was born and raised here so it was a homecoming for her. She's retired as the activity director of the nursing home." We tossed the ball several times without words. The sun was beginning to warm the day.

"How big is Post?"

"Oh, I'd imagine 'bout thirty-five hundred people live here in Post, roughly. It's down a lot, since the mill closed." He threw the ball, the strings spinning sideways. "See, it had about four hundred people workin' down here. Started out a sheep mill in 1911 and they closed it here about ten years ago, I guess, and it sure put a crunch on the town." I'd thrown it back and his foot skidded softly into a return toss. "But fortunately, we've got a lot of oil down here; it's helped the town—heck, the whole area—survive." A door opened up from the building being gutted and a cool rush of dusty air gushed out. I released the ball and Miriam closed his glove around it.

"What do you think of the country?"

"Well, things are goin' pretty good—I'll tell ya. People are gripin' about everything goin' on bad bad bad, but I'll tell ya, hasn't nooo-body got a gripe comin' for the last fifty years." He tipped his head and threw the ball.

"I never been to a funeral here in this country where anybody starved to death yet. Everybody's eatin' jus' like wealthy people, poor people's eatin' like wealthy people. People're drivin' new automobiles—they're doin' it on credit, but they're still drivin' 'em and makin' payments on 'em and they haven't got nooo gripes. You go overseas and see some of them other countries over there—why, this is heaven. This is heaven on earth right here in America. That's right, this is heaven on earth." He shook his gloved hand. "And people ought to be thankful for what we've had . . . a wonderful country. Ever since I got out of the service, we've had a—well—it's been heaven on earth, like I say." He fished out the ball and tossed it.

"Had all we want to eat. The fattest people in the world are right here in America, including me." He patted his belly and continued, "I don't miss no meals. I owe lots of bills but I'm not going to miss any meals to pay 'em." I brought my hand down and tossed the ball.

"Course, along with that, I've personally been blessed with good health. I don't take no medicine and I'll be sixty-nine next month. You can't never tell, I may not live to get home tonight, but we don't ever know that." He tossed the ball through the columns of sunlight cutting onto the sidewalk.

"And we got our freedom, we got our rights because of the veterans. Nobody'd have any freedom, nobody'd have any rights if it wasn't for the veterans." He rolled the ball in his hand. "I fought for these big ranchers and these big farmers for their land—I don't own none of it, but I fought for it. I gave up the time of my life for it but I don't own a foot of it. I own my house and I own this building and I pay taxes, just like anybody else."

Slap. He held the ball and fingered the strings. "We've got some wonderful people here and there's wonderful people all over the world, I'm sure. Course I haven't been all over the world—been to Japan and China and all out in the Pacific Ocean, but I never been any further east than Texarkana, Arkansas." With a gentle step forward, he rocked into a toss. "But Post here is a wonderful town.

"And like I say, it's a wonderful country," he said, looking across the street as a woman and her daughter exited a cafe. Their forms were mirrored in pastel images on the still-damp street. Miriam turned his head my way, ready to throw. "And we are very fortunate to get this rain."

_____

Four hours later, I sat behind the wheel, listening to more country music and churning through the miles toward San Angelo. I stayed a night there with some friends of friends—the Martinez family—who fed me cornbread and beef fajitas until I could barely move.

Later that evening, I took in one of the most spectacular sunsets of my life: sitting in the back of a pickup out in Knickerbocker—southern Tom Green County—with Barney Jr., Chico, and Billy, all Martinezes, slowly draining Busch tall boys. The sun set among layers of red clouds as wild turkeys flew up into a stand of trees on the edge of the pasture.

As I was dodging in and out of rainstorms the next morning, Barney Jr.'s words echoed in my head: "I love West Texas," he said, "and I don't ever care to leave." After playing catch with an old Texaco station attendant in Barnhart and traversing the endless, arid prairie of Pecos County, I understood him.

NATHAN SMITH HIGH SCHOOL STUDENT – *Las Cruces, New Mexico*

By the time I pulled my car out onto the road north of El Paso, the great state of Texas had overwhelmed my senses. The previous night, I had thrown the ball with two top-less dancers west of town before ending up in the raucous streets of old El Paso, a mix of gaudy Mexico, big-time Texas, and—in my case—several rounds of tequila.

Morning began with the ball traveling between an appliance salesman and me, his career highlights spilling onto the running cassette as my head floated in a mix of ache and regret. He shook my hand firmly and returned to watching his son's youth league soccer game as I gingerly placed myself behind the wheel and went in search of petroleum.

After gassing up, I eased my car north. My head was still cloaked in a light fog, and it was a great relief that the first road of the day was the soothing, shaded asphalt of the Pecan High-way in southern New Mexico—it felt like a Sabbath-day gift.

The Pecan Highway is New Mexico County Road 478, a two-lane wonder that parallels its city-slicker brother—Interstate 10—linking El Paso to Las Cruces. Whereas I-10 is a mass-transit, fume-belching speed corridor, the Pecan Highway is a lazy stretch of pristine oil and rocks, laid in black ribbons through countless acres of pecan orchards that ease any headache or heartburn the big city may have caused.

Along the road, I stopped and played catch with a forty-five-year-old woman working at a church sale. After extolling the virtues of her congregation and telling me about each of her three children, she fed me fresh muffins and orange juice as the midmorning sun splashed through high-canopied trees around the church. Then she sent me down the road with a fresh cup of coffee in a ceramic mug that she intended for me to keep. With precise rows of pecan trees zipping by on either side, I shook my head and felt no pain. It was that kind of morning.

Shortly after slugging down the last of the coffee, I pulled into the southern edge of Las Cruces in search of groceries. Within a few minutes, I had parked at the IGA Van Winkle's.

Van Winkle's is the kind of supermarket where the workers press fresh tortillas behind a glass partition at the deli counter. The tortillas are sold in bags of ten or twenty but the su-pervisor will give you one or two for the asking. After wrapping cold slices of turkey and some sour cream in a warm one, I went out to the parking lot to eat. The late morning was awash in a lazy desert light that hadn't yet turned aggressive—it was too early in the season. I took a seat on the hood of my car and—between intermittent bites of the makeshift burrito—watched the easy movements of Las Cruces: a squat Hispanic woman with a string of kids skipping behind her heading toward the store's entrance, a gray-haired woman with a pair of black shades wrapped around her temples getting out of a faded Nova, a teenager in lightning-white hightops pushing a long string of carts back to the store.

At the edge of the parking lot, three high school kids and a couple of adults occupied the shade under the awning of the store. Taped to a card table in front of them, a sign done in bold ink letters read: SUPPORT SUMMER LEAGUE BASKETBALL. From behind the table, a woman addressed me as I approached: "Care to help us raise money for the tournament?"

"Actually, I'm just looking to play a little catch before I head off." At this, the kids perked up and walked over.

The tallest of the trio came to the table and smiled. "If it makes for a break from this, we're all in."

I played catch with all three of them—first Jermaine, then Luke. The third was Nathan Smith. He was of medium height; his long, thin arms flowed in wavelike motions as he grabbed the glove and slipped it onto his hand. His dark brown hair was piled loosely atop his head and shaved short on the sides. With a tug on the leg of his baggy shorts, he moved away from the table, ready to start.

"I'm a junior—I go to Oñate High School," he began. "I've been here in Las Cruces most of my life." He moved the ball behind his ear, then pulled his arm downward in a fluid movement, sending the tight sphere on a line. His feet scarcely moved. "I was born in El Paso, Texas, about forty miles down the road. I moved once, when I was young, to Missouri, and lived there for a year. But outside of that, I'd consider myself to be from here."

"What about your parents?" I cocked back and threw.

"My parents are still together." The pop of the ball echoed off the sidewalk.

"Rare enough these days."

"That's true," he smiled. "My dad is a meteorologist at White Sands and my mom is a re-altor and an artist. She's a realistic artist, works mostly in pencil and pastels—she's real good but doesn't have much time to do it; she spends most of her time in realty."

"What do you think of them?" Nathan caught the ball and then turned his head a moment to watch a group of young kids scurry past the sale table.

"Well, they're human, of course—but I wouldn't change anything about either one of them." Smiling frequently, Nathan made his comments in soft-spoken strings. Between tosses of the ball, his eyes scanned the parking lot. And the sidewalk. And the street. I had the feeling that he knew the position of every car in the lot and what the people were doing, in front and in back of him. He fixed his eyes on mine for the next question.

"So your high school days are over soon."

"Yeah." He gloved the ball and held it in his right hand.

"Then what?"

"I want to get a scholarship to the art school in Denver, Colorado. They have an art institute there." He rolled the strings onto his fingers and flung the ball. "That's a ways off, and for right now I don't have any money to pay for college. So the only way I'll go is if I get a scholarship. It seems a little challenging but I don't know; somehow I'll get to school—if I have to get a job and pay my own way or whatever the deal is." Pop. Into his pocket. "Maybe my parents will help me out. Somehow they'll find a way to get me to college."

"Can you use sports to get a scholarship?" The ball rested in his mitt.

"It doesn't look good. Unfortunately, the basketball program I'm in has no discipline, so it's tough to get any recruiters around to take a look at us." Bringing his hand down, he tossed the ball. "A lot of our varsity players are hoods and druggies—it kind of makes the team get overlooked." I pulled the ball from my pocket and tossed. "Me and that other kid over behind the table are the rare straight ones."

"The 'golden kids'?"

He laughed. "Yeah, I guess you could say that, though I don't know that everyone would agree."

"You're an artist, too?"

"Uh-huh." The strings whispered off his fingers. "I do a lot on my own. I don't talk much about my feelings and stuff so that's kind of how I express myself—through art. Like I did this basketball picture for the program and it became the logo for schedules and T-shirts and all of that. I've won art contests and other kinds of stuff but that's the first time I've ever done anything like that." He snatched my toss from the air.

"I mostly work in pencil—I haven't had the chance to try other things—in art classes, because of sports. I've been in track and basketball all through high school, so it's kind of kept me from taking many art classes and stuff."

"So what do you see yourself doing in the world?" The ball arced into his glove.

"Well, I've thought about that." He released the ball again as he paused between words. "I feel like there's something I want to do for people in general—you know, something positive. I've always thought I needed to do something that didn't just serve me." Pop. Again, the ball arced into his mitt. "I mean, God has blessed me with so many talents and stuff that I want to give back to people, you know. I'm not really sure what I'm gonna do yet, I just figure I'll kind of let God show me the way He wants me to head and go with it, I guess." With a rare step forward, he started into a toss.

"Are you religious?"

"I guess you could say I'm a pretty religious guy—I mean, not so much going to church all of the time—we go as often as we can, but mainly it's just a personal thing. I base a lot of my life on Christ. Although sports get in the way of Sundays quite a bit."

"Church is important to you, then."

"Well, my uncle is probably my biggest role model, as far as morals and that kind of stuff. But to tell you the truth, I don't respect much of the way people are today; it's just totally different than the way I was brought up to be, you know, with my family and all. Around here especially, morals are not very—how should I say it?" He caught the ball and fingered it out of the webbing. "You don't find them—morals—much in many of the teenagers around here. The drugs and alcohol, for instance, are getting way out of hand. Like, I have a ton of friends who are already pregnant. . . . It's really scary." In a fluid motion, Nathan brought the ball from behind his ear and sent it zipping under the awning. "Scary and kind of sad at the same time."

"Are you pretty clean compared to most of your friends?"

"I'll go to a party and have a good time, but I don't drink and I don't smoke—it's a personal thing. I mean, of course I've had the speeches from my parents about drugs and all that, but it's really just a personal choice. I take pride in not doing that kind of stuff." The ball popped into my mitt. "But as far as that being popular, I don't know how they could get everyone to catch on. I mean, they've tried everything—or at least it seems like it—and I don't know exactly what will turn it all around." He gloved the ball and held it. "I suppose education, mainly. I mean, if you look around, there's a lot of uneducated people right now—uneducated not just about school but about how to live a life of quality. For me, if my family wasn't as tight as it is and we weren't as close as we are with each other, I don't think I'd be the person I am. The education I got at home is like the real lessons of life." Nathan threw the ball several times. "So that's about it," he said.

"If you got invited to the White House and the president asked you for your advice, what would you tell him?"

"Somehow the people in charge of the whole show—from the country as a whole down to the local schools—have got to get respect for teenagers, because so many teenagers look up to those people." Pop. Into his glove. "Sometimes, it seems like the people who are out here trying to help kids haven't experienced what it's like—or at least not recently—so the kids don't really have anybody to look up to. They need role models, real ones." He tossed. "A lot of my friends and even some of my cousins don't have anyone to look up to like I do. I mean sure, the celebrities—Michael Jordan and stuff—are good, but I think real role models are found in someone close who the kids can talk to. Like my uncle, the one I told you about—someone who's been there and understands, someone who can help the kids out with what they're going through." The ball slapped into my webbing.

"But what about the kids who are in trouble—gangs or whatever—you think that they want to make good?"

"I think they do. I think everybody does. Something inside of them does, you know?" He held the ball and looked up under the awning, then back toward me. "They just get side-tracked from what they feel and get a little confused."

"Confused by the world?"

"Yeah, or maybe better said, the speed of it."

"The speed?"

"I mean, hey, for teenagers—as far as the stuff they're doing—they're looking for some kind of happiness and they're just kind of looking for it in the wrong places. They just don't realize the long-term effects of what they're doing. I mean, I have friends who are getting girls pregnant now, and by the time they're older and are finally *really* ready to start a family, they're already gonna have kids who are five years old." His hand cut through the air. "I mean, I think happiness is in a family and in being close. But being a parent to a child can come way too early." Again, the ball slapped into his glove and Nathan held it. "We should spend our time on other things when we're young: playing sports, making grades, learning, exploring.

And on the human side of things, we've got to create friendships, you know? Things that count for something."

"And what do you want?"

"I just want to be happy. And I'm happiest doing art. So that's what I want to do. Ultimately, I'd like to do what I would tell other people if they asked me: Surround yourself with good people and do what makes you satisfied."

"How old are you, Nathan?" I tossed the ball and he tucked it into his glove.

He turned his head back to look at the sale table, and I didn't know if he'd heard the question. Then he turned back to me and released the ball in one fluid motion, a smile lighting up his face. "In July, I'll be seventeen."

That afternoon, I picked up Interstate 10 and was zipping along westbound toward Arizona. The sky had clouded over and wind gusts sent sandy fingers reaching across the vacant highway. Past the exit for Akela, I spotted two women hesitantly sticking their thumbs out for a ride. I pulled over and asked if they could use a hand.

Turns out the daughter—about fifty—was en route to drop off her mother at the airport in El Paso when their car broke down. They maneuvered their way into the limited confines of my Honda and off we went, the mother wide-eyed with excitement about the first hitchhiking experience of her life. The daughter seemed less enthralled, a worried furrow stitched across her brow until I dropped them off at a gas station in Deming. The daughter raced to the phones and began dialing hurriedly while the mother stayed, leaning against the open passenger-side door and thanking me profusely.

After shaking my hand a final time, she turned toward the phones. I headed back to the highway, still thinking of the women as my tires tallied miles toward Arizona. I was grateful to the road—it had delivered the women, giving me the chance to pay it back for the muffin and coffee I'd received this morning. Just as it had given me the pecan orchards and Nathan Smith to clean the cobwebs from last night. "I can tell you," the mother concluded before I drove away, "and you just proved it again today—you really can make a difference just by being out here."

I still think about the optimism and hope that Nathan embodied. I remember vividly the shadows cast on the soil of the pecan orchards. And the mother has written three times to thank me for the lift to Deming.

POOKIE & K-NUT
SGT. COLLINS & JACKIE

Inglewood, California

Southern California. Talking with one person, or fifty, or a thousand seemed not nearly enough to capture the essence of the area. I was barely into the state when I started up a chat with a construction worker eating dinner at Carl's Jr. in El Centro. As we played catch at dusk in the parking lot, he gave me his best advice: Balboa Park in San Diego.

Two days later, I was there. From the school buses of kids visiting the museums and the gays parked in their cars to the Latino prostitutes sprawled out on the grass and the graying elders rolling polished spheres at the lawn bowling club, the park was a microcosm of the culture: young and old, seamy and stately—all reveling in the same space. My gloves got a workout there, as they did when I headed up through Palm Desert and Joshua Tree National Monument.

But Southern California came most alive for me when I stopped the car and let someone else do the driving. On my third day in Los Angeles, after tossing the ball with young investment bankers in downtown, hulking musclemen and musclewomen on Venice Beach, and a music teacher in Beverly Hills, I hopped into the passenger's side of squad car 20 of the Inglewood Police Department.

Behind the wheel, Sergeant Amy Collins adjusted the radio knob. "Do you copy, 20?" The static-ridden dispatcher's voice crackled, "23 is on scene at Tamarack—he's going to need a backup."

She fingered the receiver. "10-4, I'm en route—210 West Tamarack, correct?"

"Affirmative. They're near the garage area." My head jerked back as we lurched out of the parking lot, the tires squeaking. Between us rested the blue steel of a gun. As we hurtled through intersection after intersection, I attempted to make small talk.

"What kind of gun is that?" I ventured.

"A shotgun," she answered. Rounding the corner, she stuck the accelerator; the transmission whined into a higher gear.

"How long have you been in the force?"

"Twelve years," she said.

"Where are we going?" I asked.

"We've got an officer on the scene at a domestic disturbance and I'm going over there to back him up." She delivered her words in curt, businesslike strings, leaving spaces open to hear anything of importance that might come from her radio. After two minutes of crisscrossing anonymous city streets, she pulled up hard in front of an apartment building and whipped open her door. "C'mon," she said as she approached the building.

Adrenaline surging, I turned off the tape recorder and took up the chase. As I closed in behind her, I remember wondering to myself what would constitute a safe distance. Should I be right next to her, so she could cover me? Or should I stay back, so that I could run to the car?

She motioned me to her side as we came up to the apartment, where a dispute was in full swing. Sergeant Collins told me to stay outside against a stucco wall while she joined the officer inside the house. I listened tensely as, over the next several minutes, she and the other officer eased a man and woman from screaming threats to softly spoken concessions and faint sobs. Moments later, a man eclipsed the doorway, clothes stuffed under his arm, and brushed by me as if I wasn't there.

The officers followed shortly and Sergeant Collins led me back to the car. We climbed in and she pulled back out onto the street. The whole incident left me trembling. Sergeant Collins, by contrast, glanced around the streets with seeming nonchalance.

A few days before arriving in L.A., I had called the Inglewood Police Department and asked the best way to get into the inner city while incurring the least risk. After hearing about my project, they had arranged for me to do a ride-along with Sergeant Collins. The ride-along had begun with a jump start.

"Was that typical?" I asked.

"Yeah," she answered. "Usually when a couple breaks up, there's one person who isn't hurt by it and one who is. And if the situation looks bad enough, we get called in to make sure it doesn't go through the roof." She drummed her fingers on the steering wheel and turned right.

"How is it being a cop in Inglewood, California?"

"Interesting."

"Do you like it?"

"Oh yeah, I like it. It's different." Her voice broke from its businesslike meter. "I mean, this area isn't a hellhole—you just don't get to hear about the nice guy or woman who goes to work every day and has two children. Instead, you hear about the bad element—which is really a small percentage—that seems to be sensationalized by the press. But certainly the majority of the people here are nice, hardworking people."

"Are you from this area?"

"No, I'm from New York," she said, "Long Island." She laid a hand on the blinker and turned left.

"Where are we headed now?"

"Well, you're going to be out here with me for a couple of hours, so we'll try to give you a look at some of the things around." I nodded. The more we spoke, the more animated her voice became. "Have you spoken with any prostitutes?" she asked.

"No."

"Would you be interested?" she asked. Again, I nodded. "Well, let's try to find one," she said as she grabbed the radio. "I'm looking for a 647-B. Did you copy?" The grainy voice of the dispatcher responded and we headed in a new direction. After crossing several streets, we turned onto one with more boarded-up windows than usual and a host of other dilapidated structures. "We have a lot of prostitutes that hang out up and down this street," Sergeant Collins said. "We've been doing a lot of prostitution sweeps, so they tend to avoid us." Scanning the street with her eyes, she spotted a woman seated on a cement step and pulled up in front of her.

Stepping out of the car, I sat down next to her as another squad car pulled up. Sergeant Collins began talking with the other female officer back at the cars. I turned my attention to the woman beside me: Her wild smattering of red and gray hair framed a face dominated by squinting, bright blue eyes. Whereas I had envisioned being dropped at a row of stunningly made-up Las Vegas hookers, the street was instead lined with seedy two-level motels and vacant patches of weeds. It was one of the most quiet and lonely places I'd seen.

"My name's Nick Hartshorn," I said, pulling a ball from the duffel.

"Nice to meet you," she said, extending a hand. "Jackie."

"Jackie, what do you do here in the big city?"

"Uh, sleep a lot."

"Are you homeless?"

"No, I live in a board and care home." As her eyes wandered over my face, she strung her scratchy words together with a slight slur.

"Where are you from?"

"Conego Park—that's Ventura."

"How did you end up here?" The ball rested in my hand.

"I made it through my twelfth year of school and then I flunked math so I didn't end up graduatin'. Lived with a musician after that." She looked down the street, then back at me, "Band's name's Whiskey Jones—you ever heard of 'em?"

"No, never heard of 'em." She cackled at my response, shaking her head slowly side to side. "Have you done any kind of work?" I asked.

"Yeah, I used to do soldering and makin' speakers. I also cooked and worked for an optometrist."

"What happened?"

"Well, they laid me off 'cause I was late gettin' to work 'cause I had to take the bus one day when my car broke down, but I had planned on taking up optometry." Her eyes shifted from my face to the ball and she stuck out her hand. I placed it in her palm.

"How long ago was that?"

"It's been about ten years, now. I've been sick since then—you know—my thoughts and such." I nodded.

"Are you clean?"

"I drink beer, but not a lot." She kneaded the ball in her fingers.

"How do you make a living?"

"On my SSI."

"SSI?"

"Social Security. I get $739 a month, but rent's $660."

"How do you live?"

She cackled, her vocal cords coughing out laughter. "I don't."

"What do you think of living in America?"

She looked up the street again before speaking. "I'd prefer to be out of town, up in the mountains."

"What'd be better about the mountains?"

"Better atmosphere." Behind me, Sergeant Collins had stopped talking to the other officer.

Turning to Jackie, I continued. "If you lived your life again, would you do anything different?"

"Yeah, change my style of life." She stared at her feet. "So I don't come back like this."

Sergeant Collins came up alongside Jackie and me and said we should get going. Jackie looked up from where we sat, squinting her eyes at the sergeant, then stared over at the backup squad car pulling away from the curb. I put my hands on the straps of my duffel and started to stand up when I felt Jackie tap me on the arm. She handed me the baseball and looked at my face, her eyes fixing on mine. "God bless you," she said. "The Lord's looking out after you." I took the ball from her.

"Thanks," I said, smiling. As the moment passed in slow motion, I was hoping my smile would somehow mean something to her. "Don't get in trouble, okay?"

"I won't," she cackled, running a hand through her frazzled hair. "I can't afford it."
I shut the door, my eyes still fixed on Jackie. She waved as we pulled away.

"Why do they hook?" I asked Sergeant Collins as we pulled out onto a main thoroughfare.

"Oh, lots of reasons," she said. "Drugs, money, groceries—they're people who've hit the bottom." As we passed slowly through an intersection, she beeped her horn at a carload of teenagers who began reaching for their seat belts in exaggerated motions. "Nice try," she yelled at them with a smirk. Turning to me, she explained: "They all just put their seat belts on. We have a law, so whenever you pass people, they put them on."

I looked down and pointed out that she wasn't wearing hers. "Yeah," she said, "one time, I had mine on and I was shot at. . . . It didn't hit my car or anything but I couldn't get out so I'm a little leery of wearing it on patrol. But outside of work, I wear it all the time."

"After something like that, do you think to yourself, 'Maybe I should switch professions, maybe I'll go open a bakery in Idaho or something like that'?"

"No, because if you open a bakery in Idaho, you can get burnt, you can cut your arm off—whatever, you know. I do consider my job more dangerous—I'm placed in more dangerous situations more often, more life and death situations, I guess, than your average person, but every line has its bad parts."

"Do you worry day to day about getting killed?"

"Sure I do, I have to. I have to constantly be on my toes and be aware of what we call officer safety. Because if I'm not, I could get hurt out here. But again, it's part of the buy-in for the job. Hold on a sec—" She picked up the radio. "What's that—do you think he wants to play catch with a chicken?"

A male voice came through the radio: "He'd probably see a lot of things on that corner."

She smiled. "Some of the officers on patrol have heard that you're out with me so they're keeping their eyes out for things you may find interesting—that call was from an officer who passed by the Church's Chicken mascot. It's a pretty colorful area." The more we drove around, the more comfortable our conversation became. She got another dispatch from her radio, then asked, "You said you wanted to talk with some gang members?" I nodded. "I think we've got some waiting over on Lawrence," she said as she flipped her blinker.

"If I weren't here with you, what would you be doing?"

"I'd be doing the exact same thing."

"You just wouldn't have to answer so many questions, right?"

"No, I'd be talking to myself." After a couple of turns, we entered a section of the city that seemed empty; few people were on the sidewalks and all porches were vacant. High walls surrounded apartment complexes and small businesses alike.

"Is this a rough section of town?" I asked.

"Yeah," she responded. Turning onto Lawrence at Woodward, Amy radioed in our location. The entire street was empty except for two figures. We pulled up in front of them and Amy asked them a few questions before turning to me. "Here are your gang members," she said. We hopped out of the car as a backup unit arrived, the other officer getting out as Amy frisked them both. "They're all yours," she said.

Their eyes studied me casually as I grabbed my duffel and walked over to them. I shook hands with both, then asked if we could play catch. They agreed, hesitantly, the larger of the two stepping forward. His right arm was in a sling, the biceps bandaged in a fresh, white dressing. "My catchin' hand ain't nothin'," he said.

"That's okay, we'll just toss without the gloves—if that's okay."

"Awright," he said.

"Your name?"

"Pookie," he said. "P-O-O-K-I-E."

I dropped the gloves into the bag and stood about ten feet in front of him. "What happened to your arm?"

"I got shot with a .380 a couple months ago—two bullets. Broke the bone, hit me in the chest." The ball arced into his bare hand with a slap.

"How old are you?"

"Seventeen." With a jerky motion, he tossed the ball. "This ain't my normal throwin' hand," he said with an apologetic smile.

"No problem," I said. "What gang are you in?"

"Crenshaw Mafia." His voice was soft; the words issued slowly from his lips.

"How many people are in the Crenshaw Mafia?"

"A lot. Hundreds, I'd say."

"How long you been in the gang?"

"Since I was eleven . . . that'd be '88."

"Why did you get into gangs?" He raised his eyebrows. "Don't worry," I added, "I'm not going to get you into trouble."

"Oh no," he smiled and waved a hand at me. "I ain't trippin' like that, I'm just thinkin'." The ball rainbowed between us occasionally, slapping into our palms. "Well, you know, it was just like around me and everybody I knew was in it and my mentality was like, you know, it gave me somewhere to go—people to hang with. You don't really think about the reasons, it just happens." Behind Pookie, the other kid leaned his bony shoulders against the wall, his eyes following the ball as it arced between us.

"Tell me about your life."

"Life out here?"

"Yeah."

"Lately, it's been kinda slow. Like, back in the days though, it was kinda rough out here."

"When was 'back in the days'?" I held the ball.

"I'd say like, when I got shot. Not too long ago, two months ago."

"Wasn't there a truce going on?"

"The truce is over within Inglewood, man. Only place it's still goin' is Watts."

"Who calls a truce?"

"It's like the older people from the other sets, the ones in Watts for this particular truce."

"How old is 'older'?"

"Like thirty, thirty-two—the old fellas that's been in for a long time."

Stepping forward, I lobbed the ball softly over the three squares of cement that separated us. "What do you do, day to day?"

"Weekdays, I go to Morningside High School. I'm a junior. I'm in a special program— 'School with a Purpose.' I go for four periods from 8:15 to 12:25. Then I wait for my ride to come—you know—and they take me back to my house. Then on the weekends—like today, you know—I just come out, kick it, chill out." The ball rested in his palm.

"Do you want to make it out of here?"

"Ain't nothin' wrong with it," he said, shrugging his shoulders.

"What do you want to do with your life?"

"When I turn eighteen, I'm going to get a job and stuff. Right now, I'm just goin' to finish school." He tossed, the motion becoming smoother.

"What kind of work do you want to do?"

"Right now, I'm still debatin'—pipe fittin' or something is what I'm interested in."

"Will you stay in the area?"

"What do you mean by in the area? In the city or somethin'?" I nodded. "Ain't nothin' else out there, nothin' that'd interest me, really. I imagine I'd stay here."

"Do you like it here?"

"Uh," he hesitated, "yeah, yeah. I ain't gonna say I get a bang out of it, it's just where I live, you know, where I ended up. I know everybody here."

"Do you have family?"

"Just my mom. My father died when I was like real young. He got beat to death saving his brother over in the Jungles—you heard of the Jungles?"

"No."

"Over there by King and Crenshaw, he was tryin' to save his brother 'cause his brother was in trouble, fightin' with some fools. He ran over there to help him and told his brother to go get help but when his brother came back, he was dead."

Sergeant Collins interrupted us and said if I wanted to talk with both of them, I needed to speed it up.

"What do you have to say to America?" I asked. He broke out in laughter—a youthful laugh—and tossed up his hand.

"Tell the world?" He stepped into a final throw as his tone became thoughtful. "That life here ain't no joke. It's like people watchin' TV see this and that happen in the 'hood but for me, you know, this is life. This is *my life*. And it ain't no joke bein' down here."

"Thanks for playing," I said.

"Yeah," he nodded, drawing out the syllable. "Awright."

Walking toward the stucco wall, Pookie turned his head to the other kid and flipped him the ball. I tossed him a glove out of the duffel as he positioned himself about five squares of cement away. He stood tall and thin, his boyish frame not yet filled with the muscle and weight of Pookie's. He pushed his hand into the glove easily and stepped into a toss.

"Name's K-Nut," he said, the ball lighting out from his fingers. "K-N-U-T."

"And are you guys in the same gang?"

"Yeah."

"You're seventeen?"

"Yeah, I'm seventeen—go to Centennial High School." K-Nut's voice was sharp, cutting cleanly through the space between us. His words were honeyed with an urban drawl.

"Did you grow up in this neighborhood?"

"Yeah, right down the street." He turned his shoulder and pointed down the silent sidewalk.

"When did you get into the gang?"

"About '89, when I was twelve."

"Why?" My hand cut slowly through the air.

"Family members—my brothers and uncles were in it and you know—just bein' out here with the homies. You know what I'm sayin'—we all young, runnin' around, doin' the same stuff so when we want to do somethin', we all doin' it together, so we all just came in it together." His smooth voice seemed years older than his slender frame.

"Are you scared of dying out here?" I asked.

"Yeah, I'm scared of dying, you know, but if somebody come with a gun, I'm gonna try to run, try to get away. But if I really got up in it, you know, that's the chance you got to take—of dying. So I ain't gonna lie, you know. I'm scared of dyin' but at the same time, I'd do anything to avoid that situation." He placed his fingers across the strings.

"Are you going to make it out of here?"

"Really, I don't know 'cause what the coaches tellin' me—my basketball skills is lookin' good but it's just, by me gettin' arrested, that's what's messin' it up."

"Messin' up your chances?"

He held the ball, his body motionless. "Messin' up my shot outta here."

"Have you been arrested more than once?"

"Yeah, a couple of times. I just came out of camp on Thanksgiving."

"Camp?"

"Yeah, you know—jail, Younger County, as some people say. Really all I gotta do is, you know, I've got a seven-month-old daughter so I've gotta chill, you know?"

"Are you taking care of her?"

"Yeah. I'm doing good so far. I was with her and her mom all last night, so I'm hangin' in there." He nodded his head to the side. Behind him, Amy walked toward me and said we had to go. K-Nut pulled off his glove and tossed it to me.

"Sorry to cut it short," I said. "Thank you."

"Awright, man," he said as Amy fired up the squad car. "Awright."

As we pulled away, I watched the two lone figures crossing the cracked asphalt. Pookie's arm stayed close at his side while K-Nut strode out with a confident swagger. I could still tell one from the other a hundred yards down the road, Pookie's thick frame contrasting with K-Nut's vertical silhouette. They grew smaller and smaller in the mirror until I couldn't see them at all.

Amy and I headed over to Club Drive just east of the Forum, where the Lakers play. After pulling into a parking lot, she killed the engine. "We're supposed to wait," she said. "We're doing a stakeout in conjunction with the L.A.P.D. and we've gotta wait here until the subject makes a move." Except for an occasional string of information from the radio, it was quiet. Amy kicked a knee up near the steering wheel and put her head back against the rest, her eyes still leveled at the street.

"Are you going to stick with the force until you retire?"

"Yeah, I'd like to get to lieutenant level. . . . I imagine I'll stay in Inglewood about nineteen more years."

"What would you like to be remembered for after you retire?"

"That I had integrity."

"What would make the biggest difference in your job out here?"

She placed her foot back on the floor of the car and turned to answer me. "Find out who the good people are and let everybody know that they're not alone—that there's a lot of other good people out here and that if they all band together, they can overcome the bad. There's a lot of good people, they're just the quiet ones. You don't hear from them." The cellular phone rang and she beeped it on, exchanging information with another officer.

"Was police work your only calling?"

"No," she said, checking the rearview mirror. "I could have taught. . . . I mean, I like what I'm doing, but I could've been a teacher."

"Do you get to see positive outcomes from your job?"

"Oh yeah."

"The majority of the time?"

"No, but finding a lost kid, you know, or catching a criminal, or helping a woman who's been beaten for years, arresting the husband. Those are good things."

"Is it demoralizing to deal with those sorts of issues—wife beating, et cetera—on a day-to-day basis?"

"You know," she said, raising her eyebrows, "it's just what we do. We deal with society's ills, we deal with what people don't want to deal with. When people don't know what to do, they call the police, you know?" Just as she finished, a dispatch came over the radio. Then a call on the cellular. More words blurted from the radio as Amy fired the engine and blasted onto the street.

In an instant, we were converging with three other squad cars on a sedan pulling out of a nearby cemetery gate. Whipping into a U-turn, we led the others in pursuit of the sedan, which pulled over within five blocks. Squad cars pulled up on either side of ours and officers jumped out, leveling shotguns at the sedan's occupants.

"Stay here," Amy said to me as she took position behind one of the other cars. From the car to my left, an officer got on a loudspeaker and ordered the people out of the car. The driver was the first to get out, holding his hands behind his head and walking backwards until an officer cuffed his wrists and led him to the curb. Then, slowly, the short figure in the passenger's seat scooted over toward the door. The officers tensed their hands on the shotguns.

As he moved on the seat, he seemed to match the description of the suspect—short and squat. His head was barely visible above the headrest. When he finally got out of the car and walked sluggishly backwards with hands above his head, however, it became apparent: He wasn't a he at all. The short, stubby frame belonged to a grandmother in a black dress, trembling mightily. The officer with the loudspeaker ceased barking commands as two others wrapped the old woman in embraces and seated her on the curb.

Across the street, a group of about eight blacks dressed in brilliantly colored traditional African dress stood in front of their church and watched the scene intently. After the officers had finished questioning and apologizing, the young driver and the grandma headed back to the sedan. On the way to the car, the driver raised his fist to the onlookers across the street. Resplendent in robes of orange and green, they raised their fists in response.

Amy returned to the car as the sedan pulled into the street, shaking her head in a mix of anger and disgust at the mistake.

Six hours had passed since I arrived at the Inglewood Police Department and hurtled off with Amy in the squad car. As she slowly navigated the intersections back to the station, I studied the streets that are her workplace: Like many small towns, they are lined with a mix of solidly established homes and businesses. Unlike small-town America, however, the clean, tidy structures are indiscriminately erected beside tracts of neglect.

Her eyes scanned the streets without bias, looking for the seams where the bad spills over into the good. My fascination as we started out in the morning had a lot to do with contacting people whose lives are spent on the seams. Their passions, I came to see, mirrored my own: wanting stability, wanting to talk.

We pulled up to the station and I asked Amy if she had time to throw the ball. "I couldn't," she said. "My supervisor'd kill me if I did that during work hours." She asked if I wanted to talk with someone else in the station but I didn't. We shook hands near the lot where I had parked and walked in opposite directions toward our cars. As she opened her door, she turned to me. "Send me a copy of the book, will you?" she asked. I nodded. Amy fired up the squad car and signaled left, heading out through an intersection as the afternoon sun began to pale. Within a few seconds, her car disappeared into a maze of buildings and people.

I started up the Honda, putting it into reverse and taking a right out of the lot. After several turns, I merged onto a freeway headed north, away from the seams that separate the city.

As night approached and I counted the miles north of Los Angeles, my thoughts were on the city. I thought about Amy and her safety. I wondered whether the night would find K-Nut home with his daughter. And I kept my eyes open for Jackie, in case she was hitchhiking up to the mountains.

PAUL SAUNDERS INVESTMENT ANALYST – *San Francisco, California*

After Los Angeles, I needed a retreat. Highway 1 north of San Luis Obispo delivered it. I didn't play catch with much of anybody the whole day. I just drove, stopped to take pictures of the deep blue Pacific, and listened to the tape from the previous day over and over again. With regret, I realized how much more information I could have gotten and how much more I may have seen had I not been scared as hell.

One of Opa's favorite sayings was, "We fear what we do not know," and listening to the tapes from Inglewood confirmed it. Unlike other times I had played catch, the strangeness of L.A. changed my meter. I had let three teenagers from Duncan, Arizona, rattle on at length about their upcoming senior class trip but had nervously cut short the words of Pookie and K-Nut. Words about their survival. Words about their hopes and how their dreams paralleled everyone's. Next time, I told myself as I closed in on Monterey, I'll know more. I'll fear less.

I stayed in Monterey overnight and woke up ready for the journey to continue. While tossing the ball with me, an anesthesiologist who was planning to retire on April Fool's Day mentioned two words that changed my plans: Reggie Jackson.

Turns out Reggie lives near Monterey and the doctor knew how to get there. After scribbling down the directions and winding through the streets to the gate of his wooded estate, I prepared for what I figured would be one of the biggest thrills of my life. Taking a deep breath, I rang the bell. One of the house workers got on the speaker and told me, "Mr. Jackson is not available." She said the same thing half an hour later. And again fifteen minutes after that. Then I got smart.

Instead of ringing the bell frequently, I walked around the neighboring streets, taking in the serenity, and returned to the gate at broad intervals with a new voice and new tack on getting to see Mr. October. Unfortunately, they weren't taking visitors, no matter how important. Just before I figured the Monterey police would come to detain me for a different, less comfortable night's stay in town, I gave up and headed north.

As I headed out of Santa Cruz, keeping pace with the thick rows of traffic, I was thankful to have spent most of the day in the trees outside Monterey. I felt cleansed.

––––––––––––––––––––

I had never square-danced with an unemployed investment banker. Until San Francisco.

First, he moved his right foot sideways and sank it softly into the grass. His body continued the motion up through his hips to his arm, which swung down slowly and sent the ball arcing into the spring air. Between tosses, his arms hung loosely at his sides. I returned the toss and he pulled it from the webbing.

Again, he rocked his right foot—only this time forward—and delivered the ball. Pop. It slapped into the leather. I returned the toss and he repeated his motion once more, this time stepping to the left. "You're thirty-eight?" I asked.

As he released his fourth toss, his foot retreated to its point of origin. "Exactly." He stepped to the right and let the ball fly; it slapped dead on target into my mitt.

The sun was at that place in the sky between day and night and cast an orange-gold light on the rows of white homes and apartments clustered on a ridge far behind Paul Saunders. Still farther behind the ridge, the skyscrapers of San Francisco stood in a hazy grayness that would soon envelop the city. The breezes kicking up from the bay lifted his light brown hair once and again and tossed it from its part. The sunlight struck his eyes, lighting them as he stretched out a gloved hand to catch my toss. He released the ball and spoke.

"I was in public schools through high school and then went to Stanford—both for an undergraduate and a master's in engineering, between which I took a year off to work for a while and then travel around the world."

"And then?" I threw the ball and it lit up after passing from under the shadows.

"And then, let's see . . . " His feet remained planted. "I worked in Silicon Valley for about five years as an engineer for a couple of start-ups. Actually, they were a couple of small companies, and I went to them with the thought that they were going to become, you know, big successes and that I would in turn become wealthy." He stepped into a throw.

"In neither case did that pan out, however, so I decided to go back to biz school at UCLA. I guess you could say I'm sort of a professional student, really." He smiled and set a spin to his next toss, the strings rotating sideways. "At any rate, I was down there for two years getting an M.B.A. It was great fun, actually, but as soon as it was over I moved up here because L.A.'s just not my cup of tea."

"And now?"

"Well, I've been up here since getting my M.B.A., mainly working in marketing for technology firms. Right now I'm unemployed." He stepped back, threw, and continued, "By choice. I quit in January, I think it was, looking to make a career change, and it's actually not working out as I had planned. I've been pursuing a career in investment management to no avail, so I'm sort of changing focus on that a little bit now."

"But still looking for work?"

"Well, I have lots of free time on my hands, which gives you a lot of time to think about stuff that you don't think about if you're working all the time." He stepped back as his arm moved forward. "It's almost like work is a distraction from dealing with major issues in life."

"Like what?" The ball cut across the copper silhouette of the apartment buildings on the horizon and slapped into his webbing.

"Like, you know, the meaning of life, heady sorts of things." He stepped to the right. "In a way, I'd love to have a job just to have that diversion again, because it's difficult, you know, to have that stuff in your head all the time. I mean, for the most part, it's been a good thing to go through. It's sort of turned out to be, you know, a midlife evaluation."

"How's that?" The ball slapped into my glove and I fished it out, cocking to toss again.

"Well, the whole issue of trying to decide what I want to do, and then not being successful in getting a job that I want, despite being, in some cases, overqualified." The ball rolled off his fingers. "And as I said, I went for years—I mean, these issues would sort of come up, but it's not that big of a deal when, you know, you're working eight to ten hours a day and you go home and eat dinner and watch TV for an hour and then go to bed." He fingered the strings. "Then the next day, you get up and do the same thing again. Now, I've got a lot of time on my hands to think about other things."

"What 'other things' do you think about?" I stood, my glove empty.

"A lot of my thoughts revolve around this sort of Western societal notion that money equals happiness equals success. I pretty well bought into that at a young age, despite the fact I'm convinced it's not the route to happiness." He shuffled his foot to the right, adding care to his words. "But at the same time, it's a pervasive notion in this culture." I gloved the ball and threw it back.

"You know, the high-paying careers are sort of what all my friends do. So if they're at one end of the spectrum and moving to India to work with Mother Teresa is at the other—I guess you could say I'm caught in the middle of the two, frankly." He set his fingers against the strings and brought his hand down. "What I'm finding in thinking about it is that I'm really grasping onto the security of all the trappings of Western materialism, while knowing that's not the end-all, be-all to life. Those are the issues I'm trying to deal with."

"What are you doing about money?" I placed my fingers with the strings and tossed.

"Financially, I'm not strapped yet. I managed to tuck away some savings. But the issue for me is not so much paying the mortgage as it is defining my sense of self-worth based on having a job—which seems ludicrous." He fingered the strings. "You know, I'm not what my job is, and yet when I was working, those sorts of questions didn't arise." He pulled the ball from the oiled leather. "Because most people *are* working, you know, most sort of middle class-ish people who've gone to college are working. But if you step out of that, then the issues that come up are things that, you know, I had no idea would. I just figured I could get a job easily and have this sort of career transition, and what's really happened is—as a result of not getting a job right away—I find myself in a struggle.

"One of the big problems, the way I see it, is that noble pursuits, et cetera, don't pay that well—and it's not an issue that I'm proud of. At all." Stepping back, he raised the ball to his ear. "But I just can't see myself, at least right now, making what to me appears to be that drastic a sacrifice. And as I said, in some ways that realization is the most disturbing for me because it speaks to a belief that money buys you happiness." Pop. "As I said before, you know, while I don't think that's necessarily true, I'm so conditioned—I've bought into that whole notion so thoroughly—that I'm having a hard time shaking it, despite having some notion, you know, that I think it's very fundamentally flawed." Rocking a foot to the right, he sent the ball in an arc.

"I think a noble way to spend one's life is to have a job that has some meaning." Paul gloved my toss. "Something fairly tangible is assisting people who are less fortunate, for instance. But, as I said, I have a hard time thinking I would actually do that, again because of this perceived sacrifice that I see." Extracting the ball, he fingered the strings. "And yet a lot of people do it and find their calling and it's the best thing ever. I don't know . . . " he said, shaking his head.

"In the last three to four weeks of dealing with this on a fairly frequent basis, certainly daily, you know, those are the issues that come up." We threw four or five times as a large black Labrador darted between us, trying in vain to snatch the ball in its mouth. Paul moved his foot to the left and threw the ball in a high rainbow as he returned to his thoughts.

"I do fundamentally believe that all of this existential angst that I'm dealing with will have some value, but 'I'll deal with it later' is what I feel like right now." On a line, the ball slapped into his webbing. "And yet, it doesn't really go away. Sooner or later, I'll have to deal with it. For some people it never arises as an issue, and maybe ignorance is bliss for them, I guess." Retreating with his right foot, he flung the ball.

"If you could find the perfect job, where would you be in a year?"

"I don't know, I suppose with my interest in Europe and the Far East, if I could just magically make it happen, I'd probably go overseas. . . . Just because I have a stronger sense now, I guess I should say, of life being finite and short, as the cliche goes." I laid my fingers with the strings and sent the ball spinning. "You know, I'm now reaching thirty-nine—in a couple of months—and I do have a sense of it being very much midlife-ish. And you know, I was aware of the raw numbers and how two times thirty-five is seventy and seventy is about the average life span, but the other thing, you know, is that I could die on the drive home to my house, so who knows?" The ball flew to my glove, never breaking free from the shadows.

"And if you died on the way to your house, what's the last thing you would want people to hear from you?" Timed with my question, the ball flew.

"You know—and the message is not unique to me, I've heard and read versions of it elsewhere—I've never regretted doing something, but I've certainly regretted not doing things." He held the ball, letting his arm hang at his side. "So I guess my message would be if you had any notion of something that was of some adventure or some romantic adventure in particular—like a dream—I would say, find a way to make it happen because I don't think you'll regret it, and in fact—" he stepped back as he released, the ball now a black sphere cutting across the gray-blue sky—"later on you probably will regret it if you don't."

The next morning, I spent several hours in Golden Gate Park, tossing the ball and talking with different people about their dreams in life: a guy who swallowed swords for a living and wanted to direct films someday, a kindergarten teacher who wanted both her kids to grow up safely, and a Ukrainian couple, Lyudmila and Leonid Dunduchenko, who had already realized their dream. Two months ago, they said in broken English, they had emigrated to the United States. They lived with their son and his family in a small San Francisco apartment.

After a solid day's driving north of the Bay Area, I passed through Phillipsville, where I played catch with a construction worker while his sons got ready for their Little League game. He sent me up the road a ways to the "Avenue of Giants," where redwood trees wider than my car and towering hundreds of feet into the air created a wooden canyon. I pulled off the road and got out there, staring in awe.

I wish I could have brought Paul Saunders with me. And the sword swallower. And the teacher. Because standing among the redwoods, the construction worker had told me, you can let your dreams loose. They bounce up between the trees, ricocheting higher and higher, until they slip past the last green canopy and into heaven. Then heaven watches out for your dreams, he said, and brings them to life.

WAYNE CHANDLER

HIGH SCHOOL JANITOR – *Langlois, Oregon*

By the time I reached the Greasy Spoon Cafe in Langlois, Oregon, I had played catch with nearly fifty people since Texas. I threw the same ball with every one, and its once white and shiny surface had seasoned to a light brown with grit and dirt worked into the holes around the strings. After pulling off Highway 101 and parking, I snagged the ball from the passenger's seat. My feet crunched on the fine pebbles as I approached the cafe entrance. A bell rang when I pushed open the door, and most of the diners looked up from their plates.

Holding the ball in my right hand, I walked down the aisle of the restaurant between the two rows of tables and asked if anyone was interested in playing catch. A snicker or two registered as I moved toward the back of the restaurant. On a wall near the bathrooms hung a bumper sticker with a rendering of a spotted owl perched and ready to use toilet paper. Under the cartoon it read: "Owl + Trees = Imported Toilet Paper, Five Dollars a Roll." I turned back around and was halfway to the cash register when a guy in a Cat Diesel baseball cap motioned to a neighboring table and said, "He'll do it."

I flipped the ball to a small man whose eyes hid behind smoke-gray lenses, the kind that get darker in the sunlight. It seemed a natural fit in his hands; his stubby fingernails were lined with grit. "Sure, I'll play," he said. The other diners chuckled and returned to their lunches. He snubbed out his cigarette and pushed aside a cup of coffee, walking out the door with me to a patch of grass behind the cafe.

The thirty-by-twenty-foot plot of grass on which we stood was a sort of oasis, tamed by a lawn mower, while the surrounding coastal field grasses grew waist-high. Though the shore was a good distance away, a constant wind kicked up from the ocean and nestled our conversation in the whispering of the grasses. He stepped forward and tossed. An eighteen-wheeler motored past on the highway, gearing up as it crested a small rise in the road. He stepped forward again, producing his second, third, and fourth tosses with the consistency of a metronome.

Wind hissed. Twenty tosses back and forth. A car whooshed by. He stepped into the throw and delivered the ball, the motions coming smoothly to his small frame. From behind the now-darker lenses of his glasses, he focused his eyes on my delivery.

"What's your name?"

"Wayne." The ball flew between us. "Wayne Chandler."

"Tell me about yourself, Wayne."

"Well, I grew up in Sacramento, born in 1959, come from a pretty good-size family. I got a brother that's eight years older than I am, got two brothers that're six years older than I am, I have a sister that's four years older than I am, and got a twin brother that's eight minutes older than I am. So I'm the youngest." The baseball was like a meter. It rested two seconds on his half of the mown plot, three seconds on mine. He didn't use his tosses to punctuate his words like most people, but to keep them flowing.

"I was athletic. Played Little League as a kid, played baseball in high school, went to college for two years at American River College—a junior college in Sacramento—and played baseball there." Wayne had the ball for two seconds. Pop. Into my glove. Three seconds. Thud. He gloved it. "Then I went in with a stepbrother I had there and we owned a janitorial service, and I worked for a school district at the same time down in Roseville, which is just north of Sacramento." The wind cutting through the tall grass muted any sound of the ball in flight. There was only the pop of the gloves. In metered time, Wayne continued.

"Then Prop Thirteen went through—I think it was about '81—and I lost my job at the school district. The prop cut state and local jobs—school district jobs and such. I still had the business, but I got kind of tired of Sacramento so I sold the business and moved up here with my grandparents. It was '82. I must have been about twenty-two at the time. In fact, no, I'd just turned twenty-three and my grandmother had cancer real bad and my grandfather wasn't doin' too well, so I just came up to help them out. Figured I'd only be around for about six months and I ended up staying here." I was hesitant to hold the ball as I had with other people, worried that it may damage the ease with which he was unfolding his life. "I met a girl here, married her, and had three kids by her—she had one when we got married." Thud. "Then, about five years later, we got a divorce."

"Oh," I said, "that must've been a drag." Another truck buzzed up 101, the driver grinding the brownie box to find third.

"Yeah, it was a terrible thing. You know—it got ugly."

"How's that?"

"Well, I had the girls livin' with me here in Langlois." (The "Lang" rhymes with "dang"; the "lois" with "show us.")

"Anyway, she—my wife—was born and raised just north of here in Bandon, and one day she decided to take off with my kids to Montana, and a good friend of mine and I went back to Montana to try and get the kids back, which we couldn't do." He stepped and threw. "So a couple of months later, my attorney wrote her a letter and she came back but left the girls with a friend back there."

"Back there?"

"In Montana."

"Oh."

"Anyway, I got a phone call at four-thirty in the morning that she had come back into town, so I caught Amtrak and went up to Spokane, rented a car from Spokane, drove through Idaho halfway into Montana, picked up the kids, and brought 'em back home. And that was about that—I've had 'em back here ever since." Two seconds had passed and the ball closed on me.

"And how old are they now?"

"My oldest one's eleven—Marisa. She's biologically not mine but she's the oldest. I raised her since she was a baby. My second oldest is Sheena, she's eight; Courtney is seven years old today—just turned. Then I have a daughter named Fallin, she's five, and I have a new daughter, Jordan, she's ten months old." I tossed the ball. "It's been since 1990 that I've had 'em back and I have a new wife now—Samantha. She raises the girls."

"How long you been married?" A flurry of wind rippled through the long stalks of bright green grass.

"We got married a year ago last February."

"And how's it going?" Pop.

"It's going great."

"So you've surrounded yourself with women." Two seconds, too quick to see how he laid his fingers on the strings.

"I suppose I was always a little more partial to women than guys," he said, letting out a chuckle. "It's worked out well." Pop.

"That's just the way it goes, you know. I come from a family of five boys and one girl and I guess it's my turn to have the girls. I was the last one in the family to get married, the oldest one to get married—when I did—the first one to get a divorce, and I'm the one with the biggest age split between wife and husband—I'm thirty-five and my wife's twenty-three." He smiled and we tossed several times, the meter of the ball remaining constant.

"So what do you do now?" Two seconds. Pop.

"Well, I'm a custodian at Pacific High School. You must've passed it on the way up here."

"Does it have something about one of the running teams on the sign?"

"Yeah, the girls' cross-country team won the state championship. I work there at nights as a custodian and that's just about it. I've just gotten my contractor's license to paint houses. I've been paintin' houses during the day when I'm not workin' and then I go to the high school."

"Sound like long days."

"Well, my shift goes from three to eleven-thirty so I don't get to see my kids a lot—maybe an hour in the morning and then on weekends." The whine of a semi engine muffled the thud of the ball into Wayne's glove. "My ex-wife takes them every other weekend.

"When the kids are around for the weekend—you know—I spend most of my time with them, and when they're down at their mother's, I generally work—you know—paintin' houses on the weekends and such." I crunched my fingers and tried to throw a knuckler. Wayne didn't notice. "Sundays I take off and spend with my wife because she has them off, too."

"What does she do?"

"She's a waitress up in Bandon at the Station Restaurant. It's a good place to eat if you're goin' up there."

"Oh yeah?"

"You bet." The ball continued. "It's great 'cuz she actually makes more money than I do. We're doin' good and with what I do—you know—we have benefits. We're not gettin' rich—you know—but we're gettin' along okay. We're hoping to be buying a house within a year."

"What do you figure for your daughters' futures?" I released the ball.

"As far as my daughters, I don't really care what they do as long as they do it well—that's the main thing. I think they'll all eventually go to college. I've told my oldest daughter that if she keeps her grades up—she's got a three-point-eight right now—and gets a full ride to school, I'll buy her a brand new car."

"That's quite a deal."

"Well," he laughed, "it's a lot cheaper than having to go out and pay for college. I can see my daughter Sheena doing something with animals—a veterinarian or something. Marissa could be a teacher. And Courtney, she could be an athlete. She's the tomboy. Fallin could be a nurse or something. And the baby, anyone's guess what she'll be." The meter of his throws continued. "But whatever they do—within the law, you know—I hope they do it well. That's all I ask. My parents never forced me to do anything. They always said just do what you want to do and enjoy it. And I enjoy my job. I really like it, you know. I work around high school kids and I'm more of a friend to them than I am their custodian. We get along great. We can tease each other, joke with each other. It's a fun job."

"Is it a big school?" The wind gusted through the grass, matting down the more limber stalks.

"Well, I think the graduating class was twenty-two."

"And you stop by here on your way to the school?"

"Yeah, I eat at the Greasy Spoon almost every day I go to work. I stop and at least have coffee. It's good food; Evelyn's a good cook. Also, I like the company; a lot of my friends are in there—'most everybody I know around here."

"How big is the town?"

"Langlois used to be big, the way I understand it. During Prohibition, they did a lot of moonshinin' here and it was a real good-size community, about six hundred people living in it. Lot of logging, too—they had mills everywhere around here, small mills. But the timber industry has suffered. We've had mills close down; there's not as much logging going on. And we've had problems in the fishing industry—not enough salmon, they claim." His fingers closed around the ball.

"We have cranberries, too. They grow 'em mainly for the color out here, not for the sweetness but for the cranberry color. I work on a bog with a guy."

"A bog?"

"Yeah, the bogs are where they grow the cranberries. The growers around here do okay. They sell most of them to Ocean Spray, mostly for their color. Wisconsin, back east and whatnot, they grow for the sweetness."

"So this a pretty small place."

"I would guess there are a couple hundred people here now, give or take." The polished tank of a milk truck caught the sunlight and shimmered as it flew past.

"What appeals to you about living here?"

"Well you know, the most important thing is your family and your kids. You gotta raise your kids—you know—proper. You just gotta raise 'em to be good people. And in a town like this, you can do that. You know, we've got too many problems in America now with youth not having the family life, and I think that's where it all starts is with your kids. You gotta spend the time with your kids and teach 'em to respect people and teach 'em to be honest and educate 'em—not necessarily in school but in everything." He threw hard. "You've gotta teach your kids right from wrong because they can't teach themselves.

"I raised my kids the way I was raised. I come from a loving family. My parents always took time out for us kids and they always cared. They were strict with us, but hey, there's not one person named Chandler out of our family that's turned into a bad person. And I think with six kids, that's something." Wayne's words paused but he kept throwing. Clockwork. Every two seconds.

"Anyone ever tell you that you've got a good arm?"

"Oh yeah, I had a friend of mine, Tom Chandler—no relation—but he always told me I was a natural. It was when I was four years old. I grew up right across the street from him. He was an older guy, close to my parents' age. I used to play catch with him and you know, I was never afraid of the ball. If it hit me, I'd just pick it up and throw it right back." Pop. "Hey, it's America's sport, and I tell ya, I'd quit my job just to play baseball."

"Well, at the rate the big leagues are going, you may get the chance."

"I would. I would pay to play in the major leagues. Course obviously I'm too old now, but when I was younger, I tell ya." The ball slapped the leather. Then it was back in the air.

"Pete Rose was always my big idol, just the way he played. I don't know the guy personally, obviously, but I just liked the way he played—hustle all the time. That's the way I played, you know. I never walked out to the field, I ran. That's the way I live, too. When I work, I'm the same way. I mean, I'm not in a reckless hurry, but I try to take pride in my job, in my work. That's the way I was raised, you know. No sense in doing somethin' twice." Three seconds. Pop. The wind gusted again through the grass.

"Well thanks, Wayne."

"You bet," he said and stepped back. For the first time since we walked onto the mown plot behind the Greasy Spoon, he held the ball still in his hand. With his index finger, he pushed his glasses up on his nose.

"Thank *you*," he said.

———————————

By late afternoon, I pulled into Coos Bay and spent time down by the waterfront. I ended up meeting an officer aboard the U.S. Coast Guard ship *Citrus*, who after playing catch invited me aboard the ship for dinner. He was unusually thoughtful for a man in his mid-twenties, a trait he ascribed to having lost his father at a young age and his mother just two years ago. Work had become his passion, and in the absence of his parents, he longed for the day when he would stay put on land and have a family of his own.

After eating, I followed his directions to the gradual beaches that slide into the Pacific Ocean. It was a stunning sight: seagulls darting down over the water as the sun played out in brilliant colors over mild waves. I stood with my feet in the cool ocean, skipping shells over the thin film of water and relishing my last hours on the coast.

The following morning, I ran through a rainy parking lot to have breakfast at a diner in Reedsport. After a double order of hash browns and a few cups of coffee, I was back out on the road, heading first inland to Eugene, then north toward Seattle. The inclement weather stuck with me for the next three days, soaking my car and my gloves in towns like Port Townsend, Bremerton, and Chimacum. After a last rainy night in Seattle draining beers at Kell's Pub with an old roommate, I decided it was time to head east.

As I lay on my back in an upper room at the Annapurna Inn in Port Townsend, the woman dug her thumb into the bottom of my bare foot. "Did you have red meat for dinner last night?" she asked. I nodded. "I can tell," she said. "There's a real tight spot right here." I squinted my eyes in pain as she again pried her thumb near the ball of my foot. "I can tell from the tightness in people's feet what sort of toxins they have in their bodies—it's reflexology." She nodded to herself and sounded convinced. I agreed.

The woman holding my foot in a death grip ran the inn, a retreat that catered to holistic healing and living in a natural balance, mentally and physically. After playing catch, she had asked if I wanted a foot rub. Ten minutes later, I lay supine on a hardwood floor, being told what I'd eaten for the last several days and how precious little of it was good for me.

The conversation eventually shifted to my trip and the plan to head into the open skies of eastern Washington and Montana. I asked if she knew any particularly good roads. "The road you're looking for," she said, bearing down on my arch with her palm, "is Highway 2. It's got to be one of the most scenic stretches in the state." Two days later, I was on it. She was right.

East of Seattle, the two lanes of Highway 2 rippled into dense evergreens and fresh air, leaving the city behind. In Startup, a dot of a town, I pulled over at a rest stop and played catch with a man who was just starting on a bicycle tour across the country. "Be in Atlanta in about four months," he said. "This is my first day."

The road climbed through the mountainous Wenatchee National Forest before descending into the scenic tourist sprawl of Leavenworth, a town that looked as though a little bit of Switzerland was misplaced and left to flourish in west central Washington. But it wasn't until I'd passed through the sleepy towns of Quincy and Ephrata in the middle of the state that I came to see why the woman back at the Annapurna had sent me this way.

After hours of twisting through forests and small cedar mountain towns, Highway 2 exploded into the east. Past Coulee City, the sky parted from horizon to horizon, and for an hour or more of driving I felt as if I was in a small rowboat paddling through a boundless sea of wheat. Unlike the flat farmlands in Texas, however, the fields were composed of small, rolling hills, linked together into contoured oceans of cultivation. I drove the next sixty miles looking out the side windows, with an occasional glance at the blacktop.

I had pulled onto the highway looking to head east and instead had been delivered into a different part of America. At a small cafe in Dunbar, retired farmers sat around a large linoleum counter playing dominoes, while outside the sun beat down on the wheat, making it glow down on the wheat, making it glow. Later that evening, I parked out near an old farmhouse and watched the sunset. Behind me, to the east, the sky had turned a rich blue and was inked darker with every passing moment. Under those skies, where stars began to twinkle, were people who've grown accustomed to the wide open spaces. And people, I hoped, who would grip the baseball's deep red strings and tell me about themselves.

About ten miles west of Helena, Montana, I studied an old, beat-up Gremlin as I slowly passed it. The windows were rolled down, revealing a Latino couple in front and their toddler crawling around on the backseat. The rear windows, where the child's head would occasionally pop up, were smudged with playful lip- and fingerprints. The car, its deep blue paint mixed liberally with patches of rust and primer, was puttering along at about 45 mph.

After stopping for breakfast at a cafe in Townsend, I got back onto Highway 12 and within ten miles saw the family again. They waved. Later, when I stopped to take pictures of the sprawling ranch valleys and crystal blue sky, they passed by a third time and honked their horn.

I passed them a final time after I'd stopped to play catch with a female diesel mechanic in White Sulphur Springs. They smiled and yelled something to me from the window, but I couldn't make out the Spanish.

Around noon, I pulled into Harlowton, the seat of Wheatland County. I had a good feeling about the place. As I had come to expect, one of the best ways to canvass a town of Harlowton's size is to go to the county courthouse and speak with the sheriff's dispatcher about who in town might be interested in throwing the ball. Moreover, as I'd learned from experience, it was best to try and visit just after 1 PM. At that hour, the dispatcher generally had returned from lunch before the sheriff and would have some time to help me out.

At the first mention of my purpose for being in Harlowton, Montana, on this bright and breezy afternoon, the dispatcher had the telephone in her hand. "Wait a sec," she said to me as she dialed in a number. "Yes," she said, turning her attention to the receiver. "I'm looking for Jim. Is he around?"

Following a brief chat, she hung up the phone and gave me the directions to the Harlowtown Federated Church. I thanked her and went to the door, which I held open for the sheriff. He tipped his hat, thanking me, and walked into the office. Crossing over the immaculately clean main street of town, I drove past several blocks of bright green lawns and neatly kept homes. After taking a final right, my car fell under the shade of the church.

I parked against the curb and entered the open door, walking lightly so as not to disturb the quiet purpose that seemed to occupy the pews. My hesitant "hello" cut through the calm, echoing softly off the far wall. I continued my search up a flight of stairs and finally to a corner office. Rapping lightly on the door opened it. The gentleman behind the desk looked up. I quickly related my reason for being there, and after looking at his watch he said he'd be more than happy to toss the ball.

"My shoulder's been really sore," he said. "Maybe this'll loosen it up."

We walked out on the grass, flanked on one side by a sidewalk and on the other by the church. He had no trouble pulling the glove onto his left hand and held it up, ready to receive. "I guess we should start with your name," I said. I threw the ball and he wrapped his glove around it in a natural motion.

"Jim, Jim Hovland." He spelled it out letter by letter, "H-O-V-L-A-N-D. It's a Norwegian name." He took his hand high above his head and then brought it down; the ball came sailing my way.

"How old are you?"

"I'm fifty-one." He spoke with a firm yet thoughtful voice.

"Tell me about the life and times of Jim."

"Well, I grew up in northern Virginia—the Washington, D.C., area—and so did my wife. I went to public schools back there, Annendale High School, and then went to college in West Virginia." As I put my fingers across the strings to throw, Jim rotated his right shoulder in its socket. "I got into the ministry out of college, went to a seminary in Richmond, Virginia, and since then I've been a lifelong Presbyterian minister." He caught the ball and rotated his shoulder again, loosening it.

"My wife and I moved from the Shenandoah Valley of Virginia four years ago to Fort Laramie in southeast Wyoming. I was the pastor in a small church. The congregation was pretty much all ranchers, and we bought horses, cows, a bull, and all of that and sort of settled in." He brought his hand down in a fluid motion and the ball took flight.

"Then last fall, we got to talking with people who were with the church up here. The time seemed right, so we sold our cows and moved up here right after Christmas. In fact, we just sold our bull two days ago." The ball returned to his glove. "We still have our horses and are looking for some land outside of town."

"Any kids?"

"Our children and grandchildren are back in Virginia. But my parents were originally from South Dakota." He lifted his gloved hand to his shoulder and rubbed it.

"So do you consider yourself a rancher—in spirit?"

"Well, my mother is from Custer, South Dakota, and if you move to a place like this, people expect you to have some connection. They don't want you to just come in from outside.

The ranching is really kind of a way of hooking into local folks. I mean, I could either meet the locals in the saloons or I could go out and help 'em ride and brand and do all of that stuff." An old Dart passed slowly by the church. "It gives me the chance to be with them in a little more legitimate situation."

"How's the new job treating you?"

"Well, it's a three-fourths–time job, even with the two churches together—this is a Methodist and a Presbyterian church in one. Of course, being new here, it's been about a hundred-and-fifty-percent–time job getting to know everybody. But it'll slack off. I mean, I can even come out and play ball sometimes." He laughed as he stepped easily into a toss. "I guess you could say I'm cross-dressing. . . . One week they have a Methodist minister and the next they have a Presbyterian. But we're also yoked with a church in Judith Gap just north of here that's a hundred percent Methodist."

"Do you hope to stay here for a while?"

"Well, they've had a lot of ministers pass through in a short period of time, so for the sake of the church I hope I'll stay for a while because they need some stability." His glove popped. "But what happens in Wyoming and Montana—since I've now been in both states—is that two and a half years is about the average stay. I think that's because most of the ministers don't try to really connect with the culture, and without any physical connection to the way of life out here, it can get really lonely. And a lot of wives of clergy have troubles with it. My wife loves it, though. She can't get enough of the agriculture and the connection people have to the land here."

"How's religion as a job?" He stopped his shoulder stretch in time to snag the ball from flight.

"Well, it's kind of like yours, maybe. It's getting paid for doing what you'd be doing anyway. I figure if I was going to be giving any thought to the life of the spirit and being a part of a worship service, you know, the best way to stay awake is to be the minister." He laughed while wrapping his fingers around the red seams. "And the older I get, I think maybe I've finally started to turn a corner. Here in the last five or six years, you know, I really do think there is something about a midlife change—it has been a very spiritual thing. It's a time when a lot of unnecessary things are up for grabs and maybe you're not spending so much time trying to prove yourself in the world but finally kicking back and figuring out who you really are."

"What do you mean by 'unnecessary things'?"

"Well, not just in the material sense but the whole business of trying to spend my time trying to do this or be that—you know, kind of being lost in an external world." Jim held the ball to his side. "The internal world gets a whole lot richer and it's something to look forward to. And unfortunately we don't have any models for how that works except for the guy who goes crazy and leaves his wife." He brought his hand down and the ball flew. "Women go through menopause, you know, but nobody ever talks about how those shifts are a spiritual life change, as well. It's exciting. It's really powerful."

"Is that what led you from Wyoming—a shift in your view of the world?"

"Well, that was important. There seems to be more spiritual receptivity up here. But actually, to answer your question, my wife and I never really talked to people about coming out West at all until we'd made a trip to Nepal four years ago. She was working with an outfit in Franklin, West Virginia, that was helping put in a conservation region around Mount Everest in Nepal and Tibet, and as a part of that job they decided she ought to go over and see what she was doing. They let me tag along on one of her trips, and I tell you, I sure got a different view of religion on that trip. I mean, Nepal is the only officially Hindu country on the planet, but most of the people we were around were Buddhists, so I got the opportunity to see two religions working together." He held the ball and rotated his shoulder.

"You see, one of the problems with religion in our country is that we not only treat Christianity like it's the only thing but, you know, if you're a Methodist then you just hang out with Methodists and if you're a Presbyterian then you just hang out with Presbyterians. We don't even get along with each other. And the fact is, if I've been spending my whole life as a religious professional, I ought to know a little more about the broader sweep of spirituality." I raised the ball to my ear and threw it back.

"So with our time over there, we really got to look at religion differently, and when we returned we wanted to seek out the opportunity for something different, more along the ideals of what we'd experienced in Nepal." A lone woman made her way under the shade of the trees on the sidewalk. "We couldn't really talk to people back East much about it, but out here it's different. The people are more connected with the land, with agriculture, and not so far removed from the homestead era when people lived not a whole lot better than they're living in Nepal right now." He brought the ball from the webbing and launched it. "So those were the shifts that led us first out West, and then from Wyoming to Montana."

"I've heard the analogy," I said, "about all of the different faiths in the world being like different sides of a pyramid: You can't see the other sides from your own, but they're all shooting toward the same peak." I threw the ball, working the knuckler.

"I think that's exactly what's happening. You know, I'm thrilled to be a Christian. I mean, I value the witness of Jesus of Nazareth, but I find Him saying the same thing that a lot of other people in other traditions are saying. And, you know, it's a fresh way to come back at what I've always believed and see it as a whole lot richer than I ever imagined it to be." The ball flew.

"What do you think about religion in America?"

"Unfortunately, religion in America bears the taint of culture in America: just not connected with the rest of the planet. You know, if it's not American, then it's not good. We end up kind of in the same boat as China back in the Middle Kingdom era—like we think we've got everything to give to the world and therefore we can't receive." Jim held the ball in his hand and highlighted the topics. "We don't receive religion, we don't receive culture, we don't receive information and education. And that's the Dead Sea scenario. It's the bottom point; we're self-sufficient but we're not really interchanging.

"It's really disturbed me because while we were in Nepal—just for the six weeks we were there—the country went from being an absolute monarchy to a constitutional democracy." He stepped forward and threw. "I mean, that's a huge change and it would be fascinating to know how they're working it out. But do you ever see anything about Nepal in the news? I mean, you could hunt all you want and you'll never see it. The whole world knows about us, but we don't know dink about the rest of the world." He gloved my next toss in frustration.

"Did you hear about the world parliament of religion last fall? Eight thousand people from all around the planet of different religious persuasions got together for a multiday conference and it didn't make the news at all." He threw with some zing on it. "And we don't care."

"What do we lose by that?"

"Richness. End up living in a world where you stop at any interstate rest stop in the country and it's all the same." A bird lit into chirps in a tree near the sidewalk as the wind gusted. We threw the ball back and forth several times without saying anything, Jim flexing and stretching his shoulder between tosses.

"Is it pretty conservative up here, religiously?"

"Well, that's hard to say because I would make a distinction between spirituality and religion. And I would make a distinction between cultural or political liberalism and conservatism."

"What is the distinction between spirituality and religion?" He caught the ball and held it in the webbing.

"If the quest of spirituality is really to lay hold of the divine spark that's within you and to unlock the potential that really has been intended for your life, well that doesn't impinge on any political stance, and it doesn't necessarily impinge on one or more personal habits." He held his glove open. "It's not like 'stop doing this and start doing that.' You know, anything—religious or otherwise—can be the addictive thing that's keeping you from connecting with your true self.

"Every person is a hologram of the whole creation. I mean, people have so much going on within them but generally speaking, we try to connect ourselves with external stuff and not really pay attention to what *we* are. Generally, religion in America is supposed to be self-denying and almost a codependent kind of thing—'don't think about *me* but love someone else'—when in fact, the best thing I can do spiritually is pay attention to myself and that immediately moves me into contact with others, with you."

The ball sailed between us again for several throws without words.

"What has made you the happiest in your life so far?"

"Rock climbing." I raised my eyebrows. "Oh yeah, I've been a climber and mountaineer for decades. Unlike anything else I've done, it really has forged some friendships that were kind of different and helped me address some fears—or at least have a model for what you do in a scary situation. Part of those friendships is just the time spent together. I mean, the time spent climbing is neat, but that's always accompanied by time getting to and from the rock, which may be days' worth of travel. And of course fishermen and other people do that, too, but there's also something about being together on a climb where you have to be inordinately sensitive and patient with each other.

"I mean, I've never done anything that requires you to pay attention to your fatigue and your partner's fatigue as much as climbing. You have to be kind and sympathetic to each other. And when you're in a frightening situation, it's almost like being in therapy with somebody. Like with my wife: We can do things that are terribly frightening at times and having worked through them, it gives us a shared experience, a shared sensitivity of how we handle tension, and another model for us of being sensitive to each other." He tossed.

"The rock climbing and mountaineering that we've done compresses stages of growing together that otherwise would have taken a long time. Like the first time my wife and I climbed Devils Tower, we stayed up to watch the sun go down, which means we came down in total darkness. Nobody had a flashlight or anything, so it was a challenge. It gave us an opportunity to overcome adversity together."

He described his climbing feats as if they were everyday activities. Descending Devils Tower at night. Summiting most major climbs on the eastern seaboard. Climbing Mount Makalu in Nepal. The climbs, much like the times he branded cattle, weren't a statement or a vainglorious pursuit. They were just something he did.

"What would you like to be remembered for, Jim?" I threw.

"Well, do you know the name of those mountains?" He motioned with his free hand to a chain of mountains to the west. "If you came from Helena, you came right over them—they're the Crazy Mountains."

"You've climbed them?" I asked.

"No, it's not that," he said, a smile parting his lips. "I suppose that, like their name, I'd like to be remembered for being just a little crazy."

Just as he finished his answer, I heard a car pull up on the street. I turned to look as the rumbling engine turned off. It was the blue Gremlin I'd jockeyed with all morning on the roads leading from Helena.

I stood back as Jim approached the car. The Latino couple got out and talked with him in quiet tones. After they spoke for a few moments, he walked back over and handed me the Mizuno glove he'd been wearing.

"They're looking for assistance," he said. "It happens quite a bit around here."

"Thanks for taking time out of your day," I said, shaking his hand. "What should I call you if I end up writing about today? Is it 'Pastor Jim'?"

"No," he responded, kneading his right arm. "Just call me Jim. And thanks for the shoulder workout."

I spent the rest of the afternoon racking up easy miles into Billings, where I ended up on the Rocky Mountain College campus. After I played catch with an alumni worker there, he let me use the showers at the school's gym. Feeling clean and refreshed after a day behind the wheel, I went out for a burger at a local steak house. Sitting back with a bellyful of food on wooden-slat bleachers, I spent the short hours before darkness watching local Little League players scurry across the diamond.

Following a night's slumber tucked in my sleeping bag under the awning of a building on the Rocky Mountain College campus, I was awakened by a gruff voice: "What's going on here?" Ten minutes later, I was playing catch with the owner of the voice—a security guard who was rebounding from a recent divorce. After a good half-hour of throwing the ball, he led me in his small pickup to his favorite bakery, where he bought me a cup of coffee and a jelly-filled bismarck.

Leaning against my open window the way the mother in Deming, New Mexico, had, he thanked me for playing catch. "Guess you never know what you're gonna find when you wake up a complete stranger," he said, shaking his head slowly. He stood upright and patted my car door as he looked down the street. "Sure wish I could just hop in and go with you, Nick," he said, chuckling to himself. Then, turning his head, he pushed a beefy hand toward mine and embraced it. "You're living my dream, too." He raised his body again and slapped the door with an open palm. "Now get on."

An hour later, I exited Interstate 90 in the middle of the Crow Indian Reservation and headed east toward Busby.

ROB PETERSON Bar Owner — *Alzada, Montana*

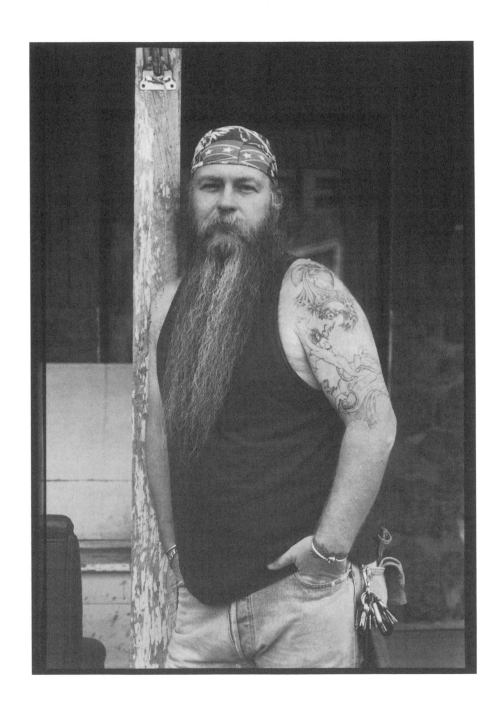

After steering along the curvy, often cracked asphalt through the lightly wooded hills of the Northern Cheyenne Reservation, I stopped outside Lame Deer. There, a sign read: "Birthplace of Ben Nighthorse Campbell, Member, United States Congress." Pulling into town, I stopped the car and started to play catch with a young girl who was overseeing her family's yard sale. Not two minutes after her first throw, however, somebody began browsing through some clothes hung on a tree and she dropped the glove, running over to help them out. She knew her priorities.

As I passed off the reservation on Highway 212, there were fewer and fewer hills. In the early afternoon, I stopped to make a sandwich and ate it on the bleachers at a Little League game in Broadus. The contest was pure magic, players scampering around in dust up to their ankles. Under the fiery sun, the local ten-year-olds held on in extra innings to take the game 8-7 over the visitors from Ekalaka. I talked with several of the players' mothers from Ekalaka and was astonished at their drive to the game this morning: three hours each way.

The closer I got to the southeast corner of Montana, the more I felt as if I was driving into the pliant heart of no-man's-land. It wasn't so much that the space was void of life, but that I felt completely lost in the enormity of the landscape. I had more or less hung up the gloves, planning to finish the miles through Montana and set up camp early at Devils Tower in Wyoming. The plan changed, however, a few miles north of Wyoming. That's where, in Alzada, Montana, I saw a sign that read: "Stoneville Saloon: Cheap Drinks, Lousy Food."

I went in and the place was empty. Walking back toward the kitchen, I kept my eyes peeled for the proprietor. Turning to the small window where the food came from the kitchen into the restaurant, I saw him. He looked like one of those bikers that you'd never mess with if you didn't have to: Long beard. Piercing eyes. Potbelly. Thick, flabby arms covered with tattoos. He probably had motorcycles, I figured, that could pull my car.

When I asked him to play catch, he looked at me as though I must be joking. Grudgingly, he went out to the big sand-and-gravel parking lot that stood between the facade of the saloon and Montana Highway 212. His name was Rob Peterson.

———————————

"So where are you from, Rob?"

"Long Beach, California. I've been up here two years. Used to live in Orange County, California. Before that, I lived in Huntington Beach." His words were terse, as though he planned to answer a few questions and then go back inside.

"So what brought you up here?" I stepped and tossed the ball to him. He caught it, a little uncomfortably, and put it in his meaty hand.

"Nothing in particular. A realtor found this place for us. We had just decided to sell our businesses and get out of California. I was in the security business for twenty-seven years—security and fire alarm systems in custom homes and businesses. I was born and raised in that area and lived in California my whole life." He swung his arm down in a jerky motion and the ball rainbowed toward me.

"Do you have a family?"

"I live with my wife, Diane, and I've got two daughters. One lives here—she'll be fifteen next month—and one lives in California." He wasn't giving yes-or-no answers but his curt, monotone responses had that feel.

"So was your wife in the business with you down in Huntington Beach?" The ball thudded into his glove.

"No, she was in a motorcycle parts business down there. She's a tattoo artist; she's working on this one." Rob tucked the glove under his left arm and pulled his sleeve aside to reveal a right shoulder dominated by a Viking warrior with a horned helmet.

"I went to the public schools out in California and then went to some college but decided I wanted to make money instead." He put his hand back in the glove and released another rainbow. "But I continued to get educated. I went to Long Beach City College, Mount San Antonio College, Cypress Junior College, Fullerton Junior College, Cal Poly Pomona, just bumped around and did what I wanted to do. Psychology was what I leaned towards. That would have been my major had I stayed in school."

"How do you like the change of life up here?" My eyes scanned the plains behind us.

"Kind of grows on you. You have to be a real self-sufficient person to live up here because there isn't anybody to call to fix things, so it's kind of like living on a sailboat—if it breaks, you've got to fix it." The ball popped in his glove and he stood, immovable.

"How old are you?" I was hoping for the essay answer.

"Forty."

The essay wasn't coming. "How's forty years old treating you?"

"'Bout the same as thirty." He held the ball and squinted his eyes. "This is some cornball way to interview people, man."

"You think so?" The ball arced.

"Well, been interviewed by experts."

"For what?"

"Oh, different stuff. I was interviewed by Steven Spielberg and asked to be in his movie *Hook*."

"The Peter Pan flick?" At last, a topic requiring more than one sentence.

"Yeah, I was the guy that made the hook—the blacksmith. There's a picture in the bar. And as a result of that, I was in one of Sawyer Brown's music videos. One called 'Some Girls Do.' They hired me and one of my bikes. That was when we lived down in California."

"How did you get into that?"

"It's a look, I guess, and people in Hollywood don't know how to make that look. I had sent a photograph in and they called up. Everybody involved with the picture had to be interviewed by Steven Spielberg."

"What kind of stuff did Spielberg ask?"

"Same kind of shit you're asking—had nothing to do with what you're doing. You know, it was just a put-you-at-ease kind of thing to see what kind of person you were, how you acted. That's all it really was." Rob's words were spoken with particular articulation and clarity.

"You're a biker?"

"Well, I ride Harley-Davidson motorcycles. I guess it depends on where you are in the country."

"What does it mean to you?"

"Well, I don't know. I guess if you ride a Harley and you look like I do, you're a biker. But there's a lot of people who ride Harleys who don't look like I do." He caught my throw. "There's a lot of them that look like you." His belly quaked as he spurted out a laugh.

"How long you been riding Harleys?"

"Oh, probably since before high school. It's kind of like joining a minority by choice, I guess—but that's slowly changing."

"Do you still get out a lot?"

"We don't get out of here for big weekend rides. This is our busiest time of the year. We do big days over the bar during the rally. Sturgis is sixty-two miles from here and the big Harley rally there has been happening for over fifty years. So everybody out of the Pacific Northwest and everybody out of western Canada comes by here. I guess this bar has always been a place to stop, but since we took it over two years ago the numbers have increased. An old couple owned it for fifteen years before we came in. We don't want to be here forever. Our plan is to stay here about five to ten years and then sell it to somebody else that wants to get out of the big city."

"And then?"

"Well, I'm planning to go to the Caribbean and stay."

"That's different."

"I suppose." He glanced at the road.

"What do the locals think of you?"

"I don't know. Probably a percentage of the people have formed an opinion of us so they don't come in—and yet they've never met us in two years. I'm not worried about it. I'm not trying to win a popularity contest because you can't make everybody happy." The ball traced a fat parabola through the air. "I mean, we tried for the first year to do things the way the local people expected it to be done, and all you do is basically get run over, you know. You have to realize that it's your business—not theirs—and run it the way you want to. If they want to be a part of it, that's fine. If not, it's sixty miles to the next bar that way and thirty-four that way." He motioned down the road in both directions. "This last year we've decided to just run this place the way we want to and they can fit in or not." Again, his thick arm sent the ball skyward.

"But the younger people around the area, you know, they all come in; we don't have a real problem with them. It's the older people, you know, fifty and over, that seem to have a problem with whatever they think we are because of what we look like."

"What do you think of that?" I returned the ball.

"My reply to that is I look this way by choice, you know. It's no big deal. The people that really piss me off are the ones that keep asking me stupid questions like 'Why did you come here?' I just tell them, 'Part of the witness relocation program' and then they don't have a clue 'cuz I might be right, you know, and they don't know for sure so they kind of back off."

"Why 'The Stoneville Saloon'?"

"Well, this area is reasonably historic. This was Stoneville, Montana Territory, in the 1870s and was a stage run between Deadwood, South Dakota, and Miles City, Montana. There were bad guys here and all kinds of stuff from back then." His glove wrapped around my toss. "The George Axelbee Gang was here and the gang that Billy the Kid rode with from New Mexico was in a big, bloody shoot-out right here in Stoneville. As far as the first place to drink out here, it was the Stoneville Saloon. I found that out from reading up on local history. I read just about everything.

"It was the Alzada Bar and Cafe when we bought it and we went with the Stoneville Saloon—it looks more appealing, I think. I'm not quite finished yet, but that's the way it is up here. You know, in California you could just make a plan, start a job, and do it until it's done. Because down there when things with a project go south, they have a way of getting taken care of. Up here, I'm the one who fixes it. But that's the part I enjoy—being able to fix everything and do that kind of stuff. And then to stand back and look at it. It's a feeling of independence, to a point." His trickle of words had begun to flow.

"Speaking of independence, what do you think of living in America?"

"I like this country. I don't like the government, I don't trust the government, but I don't think it's in need of being overthrown and changed with something better. It's just that you tend to begin to realize that everybody in politics is crooked in one form or another and it's bared out every day in the news." Rob lobbed the ball again, his arm taking on new expertise as the jerkiness faded. "There's graft, there's the take, you know, whatever you want to call it. When a person is younger, I think they perceive themselves to be pretty liberal minded, governmentwise.

"What I find to be happening with friends of mine and myself as we grow older is that we're becoming more conservative—if you have to put a tag on it—politically. The conservatives may be crooks, but they seem to be crooks for the betterment of the majority of the population, rather than the liberal Democrats, who are trying to stick it up everybody's ass." His eyes focused on the ball in midflight.

"I suppose it's pretty reactionary thinking, you know, but I think that the days of the United States being a savior for the world have long since passed. Unfortunately, there are people—not only in government but just people in the general population—who feel the United States should be the saving grace for all of the third world countries. That's a lot of the reason why this country's in the condition that it's in." The reticence was gone from his voice. "I would like to see it be more back to being concerned about the individual and, you know, block off the borders. I mean, I'm not bigoted by any stretch of the imagination, but it's pretty obvious that if you can get a free ride somewhere you're going to go take it. And a lot of people do that—I mean, they do it in a daily job situation, you know? If there's three people doing a job and two of them will carry the load, one of them will just kind of coast." The ball arced upward.

"I mean hey, I believe that people have the right to be helped when they need something—I don't care who they are. I'm an EMT up here and I never ask when I treat people. . . . Everybody gets the same equal chance with me. Because if you're an asshole, you're going to prove it real quick. It doesn't matter what color or whatever you are. There's an old rule that says, 'There's always one more asshole than you counted on,' so if you go out with that in mind, you'll know how to deal with them when you find them." He threw.

"But the government, it seems to me, has taken too much of a father figure role. And although there's a lot of common sense lacking in the country, I think the people are more capable than the government would have them believe they are." I sent the ball spinning sideways.

"If there's always one more asshole than you counted on, what do you tell your daughters about making it in America?"

"What I've told both of them is learn a trade. Go to school if you want to, but better to start a trade and work up through the field. Learn something that you can go get a job doing anywhere in the world, and then you'll be that much better for it because you did it on your own and it's exactly what you want to do." He spoke solidly as the ball picked up to an even meter between us.

"What will your obituary say?"

"Well, I don't know, man; that'd take a lot of thought. I pretty much just want to be cremated and spread. But when I say that to a lot of people I know, they get into these almost violent pissing contests about it and I go, 'Hey f____er, a hundred years from now, it isn't gonna matter.' And the people who have half a brain stop and think about that. The other thing is like, hey, we ain't here for a long time so let's just have a good time." The ball rainbowed between us a few times.

"I guess if I had to think of something right now"—he snapped his fingers—"it'd be that. Or it could be the title of a Jimmy Buffett song—'I'm the King of Somewhere Hot.' It's a double entendre and you can take it for what it is, you know—what's 'hot'? Just try and not get so caught up in the now, you know? If you take care of the little shit, the big shit just sort of rolls." The ball landed in his mitt and Rob held it there.

"An old guy, when I was fourteen, told me something that's stuck with me my whole life. He said if you have the opportunity to do something, don't put it off to a better time, because there will never be a better time to do it. Take into consideration your responsibilities, though." Rob raised the ball in his hand. "I mean, if you've got kids you can't just say, you know, 'F___ it, I'm going to the Caribbean.' But his point was well taken—don't wait until you're his age and still be saying, 'I wish I'd have climbed a mountain' or 'I wish I'd gone to Alaska' or whatever. Do what you want to do if it's within your realm of doing. Because if you wait until there's a better time to do it, it'll never happen." The ball moved between us. He was fully into his thoughts, rounding them to a conclusion.

"It's tough, when you think back on what you thought when you were a kid—you can't get hung up with this 'I've got to make a difference in the world' thing, because you are making a difference. Just by being here." He stepped and lofted the ball. "And I think you have to realize that. May not be a big deal but, like I said, a hundred years from now it won't matter." The sun tucked behind a cloud as a car made its way up 212. It was the first one I'd seen since we came outside.

"There are very few people who make an across-the-board huge difference in things. We read about them. They make movies about them. And the other people aren't going to matter." I returned the ball to his glove. "But that's not a sad thing," he concluded, staring me in the eyes. "It's all part of making it just turn forward, you know. It's all part of making it turn forward."

A dirt-road mile south of Alzada, I crossed into Wyoming on Crook County Road 112. Within an hour, I had set up my tent at the Devils Tower campground and was cooking Top Ramen with carrots and broccoli on my camp stove. As the sun set, the stone monolith of the tower sat dark against the pink sky.

I thought of Jim up there with his wife, climbing down the sheer rock columns in the darkness. And I thought of Rob, serving up a few drinks as night fell over Alzada. I was joined at my picnic table by Ingo, a German traveling across the western United States, who—after inviting himself to sit down—filled my mug with whiskey and the night air with stories of his homeland as well as recent adventures in Wyoming. After we tipped our cups a second time, I recounted experiences of the past day and highlights from weeks prior. The night air came alive—with stories both real and imagined.

Grandmother – *Almena, Kansas*

I awoke early as sunlight struck Devils Tower. After washing my face in the icy waters of a stainless-steel park service sink, I piled my things into the car and headed off on Interstate 90 through South Dakota. The miles that passed were a sidelight; I was more intent on the radio, searching the AM bands for anything that sounded perfect.

Around midmorning, I heeded the four to five hundred billboards that had started well before the Dakota border by stopping to visit Wall Drug. I spent a brief amount of time there before heading toward the east end of town to watch the regional high school rodeo finals.

There, mothers clung nervously to the metal crossbars of the arena fence while sons rode bucking bulls and daughters roped calves. I spoke with Pam Sheer, a mother of one of the bull riders, who turned her head away from the arena at frequent intervals. "Scares me to death just to watch it," she said. With a clatter, the gate swung open and a spotted bull burst into the ring, a young man tensing all his strength into his gloved right hand.

I moved to the pits behind the bull chutes and talked with some of the teens who were about to mount up. I tried to get a feel, through their words, of being strapped by one hand to a wildly gyrating beast. Of the four young men sitting there, three looked as though they were about to nod off to sleep.

After a night at the campground in Valentine, I played catch with a postal clerk in town and then drove south across Nebraska. A cold dose of lemonade served in a Styrofoam cup at a cafe in Ansley lasted well past Holdrege. The cup rolled around on the floor, empty, as I passed into Kansas on State Highway 283.

I came into Kansas in search of Highway 36, a road that the doctor back in Monterey, California, had grown up along and said epitomized the heartland. When I pulled into Norton, my path intersected with 36 and I decided to stay there for the night.

The following day, after a noontime cheeseburger at a dimly lit cafe in Almena, I got into my car and followed the thick clouds of dust kicked up by Ada Arford's Lincoln Continental. She was leading me to the farmhouse of her mother-in-law, Marjorie. I was given the names of both of them by Helen Bullock, a woman from Norton who was kind enough to suggest some people to track down as I traveled through the area. She also suggested a man named Abner Williams, but he was on vacation.

I cut my engine and hopped out as Ada rolled down her window. "She's expecting you," she said. As I rapped on the graying wood a few times, I heard the Lincoln fire up and turned in time to see clouds of powdery dirt billowing from beneath its tires.

———————————

Ten minutes later, I stood in Marjorie Arford's backyard. To my right, her old one-story farmhouse spread a partial shadow over the unruly blades of grass.

"Boy, you can't get them fingers in very far."

"Well, they don't go in all the way."

"They don't?"

"No, they just go up to here on the glove." I traced a line about halfway up the mitt.

She shook her head. "Well they've got to go further than that," she said, pushing her fingers into the leather holes. I reached down and pulled out a ball from my bag.

About twenty feet in front of me stood an old woman with tufts of wiry, brownish-red hair that fell haphazardly from her scalp. Her back was slightly hunched and her lean arms toiled busily with the task of securing the mitt on her hand. The breeze shifted through the cottonwoods and ruffled the long fur of the dog that lay napping between us. Finally, the glove found a place on her hand.

"Well, my dog's gonna be in your way." The dog lay motionless. "That's Ed." Ed slowly stirred and took to his feet. He lumbered over and looked at me optimistically, as if perhaps I'd stopped in Almena, Kansas, to play ball with him. Drool oozed from his sagging mouth as his eyes followed the ball in my hand. I raised it to my ear and tossed it softly toward Marjorie. He loped a few steps in her direction, saliva flopping in lazy streaks onto the unmown grass. She gloved the toss as Ed closed in on her. "Did you play baseball?" I asked.

"No, not really. I just played catch with the boys." She took the ball out and looked up into the sky. The sun glared down on her thin, white skin. "Let's get in the shade; you've got me out in the sun." After moving to stand under the cottonwood, Marjorie rotated her arm at the elbow and flicked the ball. Ed turned again and plodded a few steps in my direction.

"You throw well." The ball thudded softly into my mitt.

"Well, I have crooked fingers but they're pretty limber. I'm a pretty good typist. I got a gold pin for sixty words a minute in high school." The curveball she couldn't throw with the baseball was compensated by the one she just broke in the conversation.

"Where was that?"

"That was here, in Almena. Graduated from high school in 1928. I was the valedictorian." She pulled the ball from her glove and again flicked it into the air. "But I'm not too smart." Curveball. Ed looked at me, wagging his tail. "I'm a heck of a speller, though."

"How old are you, Marjorie?"

"I'm old," she said. "I hate to tell you—I'm 83. But I haven't got much of a biography. I was born in this house, my son was born in this house, and I was married in this house." I took care to return the ball softly.

"Did you have just one son?"

"Yes, I've had one kid, Johnny. He was the prettiest little curly-headed boy and then he lost all his hair—I can show you some pictures." Her tosses came regularly with the flick of an arm. The thoughts were less consistent. "Now Mr. Arford, my husband, was a farmer as well. We were married real young, at eighteen, and I was always, always crazy about horses." I tossed the ball and it glanced off the heel of her glove, falling to the grass. Ed, who had been tracking its flight, pounced on it instantly, taking it between his slobbery teeth. "I'm not used to catching with my right hand," she said. I called to Ed and wrestled the ball free, wiping the slimy leather on the grass.

"So I got married two years out of high school—I graduated when I was sixteen. I had a little scholarship to go to business college but my boyfriend wasn't interested in me leaving so we just visited and had fun for two years. And when we were courting, he gave me a bronco pony—a big one, stood about fourteen hands. It run like a deer."

"Tell me about growing up here." I lofted the ball into her patch of shade.

"This land where we're standing was the original quarter section that my dad bought in 1905."

"How much is that?"

"Hundred sixty acres. My grandparents homesteaded just a mile east of here in 1878 and my mother was born there. And then when Papa came out from Nebraska, he met my mother. They were married in 1908 and I was born in 1911 and went to the little country school over here about a half a mile east." The ball continued in soft arcs between us.

"How many people were in your class?"

"When I started, there was everybody clear up to the eighth grade—I'd imagine there was close to twenty, maybe. But when I graduated from the eighth grade, there was only two in my class—me and the neighbor girl up where Ada lives now, just a mile north as the crow flies."

With the ball between her bony fingers, she pointed through the pastures behind me. "Anyway then, my father farmed corn and a few cattle, but it was nothing big or anything like that. After my husband died, why I willed a quarter section to my grandsons—right south and a little northwest of here—so I don't own so much land anymore."

"When did your husband pass away?" She hadn't thrown a curve in a while.

"My husband passed away July Fourth, 1988. We were married in '30 so in March of '88 we'd had fifty-eight years. He was one of those people who smoked." She narrowed her eyes. "You don't smoke, do you?"

"No."

"I hope you don't. I think that's what helped kill him because he lost his breath." The ball arced above Ed's watchful eyes. "But he wasn't in too bad of shape. He didn't lose his mind or anything." I returned the toss.

"So I got awfully self-sufficient. I could do chores—in fact, I never even quit milking and giving my son and his wife milk 'til last summer. When we were first married, my husband and I, we'd milk about ten and then we'd separate by hand; then when we got electricity in '41, we had an electric separator. And an electric stove." She held the ball, which was nearly dry. "So now I'm having to buy my milk and cream and I just hate it. I finally sold the last horses two years ago."

"What sticks in your mind from living here all that time?"

"We just come through all the bad years, you know. 'Thirty was a very good year, we had good corn then and the national cornhusking contest was just a mile west and a mile north of here." Ed tired of following the ball and sprawled out to sleep. "That was one of the big deals of Norton County, anyway, and then come '33 where corn was ten cents a bushel and wheat about thirty, and then '34 come the grasshoppers and the drought, then the dust storms."

"Sounds rough."

"We didn't get too rich," she said, shaking her head. "Course we were still crazy about horses."

"Tell me about that."

The words came without a pause. "Well, we got started with this little old bronco that we'd race a little but he couldn't run quite as fast as a thoroughbred. Then about '32 we bought our first thoroughbred mare—she was awful silly and didn't run too much, and we had another beautiful horse called White Socks and we took her around to a few races at fairs— in Norton, you know—I rode races where you'd only get five dollars to win."

"How long were you a jockey?" Ed lay asleep between us.

"Well, I'd never seen a racehorse 'til I was married. I guess maybe the first time I ever got to ride in a race with any men or anything might have been about '35 or 6, maybe. It was fun and thrills for us and we could make our eatin' money." She tossed the ball as breezes rustled in the cottonwoods. "My son was born July 13th, 1938, and I was riding in races just a month later and taking him along. And when he was a year old, why we built a homemade trailer house and went to Cheyenne, Wyoming, and won a couple of races up there."

"When you'd win, what would a race pay out?"

"Oh, a big payout on a race back then—in 1940—was thirty dollars. That would cover a lot. Gas was maybe twenty cents a gallon, and you know what we lived on?" I shook my head. "Pork and beans and potted meat. You see, we lived with my folks out here, and my mother's brother lost his wife and they had a little girl—a year and a half old—so we raised her. She was just like a sister to me." She whipped out the details. "She was a wonderful baby-sitter and went with us in the trailer house when we raced.

"You know it's against the law to ride in the trailer house now? And we went through Cheyenne and Albuquerque and everything ridin' in that old trailer. Course I had lots of accidents on the horses and shoulda had a broken neck a couple of times but it didn't happen." The baseball traveled between us.

"Back then, I was one of the only women in the races it was all men. Well, Cheyenne was a ladies' race, but in general there weren't many races for us. And women couldn't ride in the parimutuels—that's where you bet, you know—like they have now. So I didn't get to ever win a race in the parimutuels."

"Were you fairly successful?" The breezes caught tufts of Ed's coat.

"Well, in the summer of '39, when my son was a year old, I think we won nineteen races without ever losing all through the bushes—county fairs, you know. I did it for a lot of years but it was tough to get away from the farming, you know. I raced from '39 up into the '50s." She gloved my throw. "All sorts of horses—Baby Lake, Sleepy John, and our prettiest horse was White Socks."

"Was it a job or a hobby?"

"Well, it was a gamblin' hobby, you know. I fed us and clothed us from bettin', nothin' big though." She lofted the ball high. "It's awful easy to be a gambler, some places. I mean, I've never bought a lottery ticket, but I made enough money to take care of the family with the racing and the gambling.

"We'd always bring home enough money in the fall to buy some hay and get the cows through the winter and things. We could've made more money if we'd raced through the winter, you know, instead of coming back to farm; the farming was tough and still is. I'm trying to talk my son into getting out of it." She flung a curveball into her thoughts. "They're in the junk business, too, as I call it. I haven't had to buy anything for years—they give me dishes and clothes, more stuff than I could possibly want." She shifted the ball from glove to hand.

"What are you happiest about in your eighty-three years?"

"Well, I can sure think of a lot of happy horse races, and I was awful happy when my son got married, he married such a nice wife." The ball rainbowed. "And I have a darling grandson that's in San Francisco now. It was great to baby-sit for both of the grandsons—one of them turned out to be a cheerleader at K-State." I braced for her delivery. "He can hold a girl up with one hand. I wish he could make a career of it but they don't get paid anything for that."

"What do you think of the world today?" Ed shifted his position on the lawn. I threw the ball and Marjorie held it in her glove.

"Well, you just can't believe how much different everything is now. When I was a girl, I never heard of a homosexual or lesbian or anything like that. Never had drugs . . . " She paused. "I guess there was some hanky-panky that went on—some of our neighbors'd run away with other neighbors and such—but it never touched you." She put the ball in flight. "But you wouldn't believe how much it's changed." I tossed the ball back and she held it, her thin arm dangling.

"I think, looking at life, I'd follow my mother's motto. She said we were put in this world to help others." She looked at me and squinted her eyes, her lips parting into a sly smile. "But she didn't know what the others were put here for."

After her last throw, Marjorie insisted that we go inside and have a snack. We sat together at her linoleum-topped table, eating angel food cake with white frosting and drinking sweet lemonade. She sifted through dusty photo albums, her fingers searching the pages and pointing to black-and-white pictures that chronicled her life. Pictures of her husband riding Roman astride two horses. Pictures of her thoroughbreds: White Socks and Sleepy John and many others I don't recall. She showed me a photo finish where she won the race by a head. She showed me a picture of her grandson, his hand supporting the weight of a bright and shining K-State cheerleader.

She introduced me to her cats and after sending them outside made me search my body for ticks. She packed me a bag of pretzels and gave me a handful of fresh carrots to eat on the road. In short, Marjorie had thrown me more "curveballs" that afternoon than any major leaguer could have. Then again, maybe I should've figured.

She was a lefty.

That evening, I attended the "dinner dance," a gathering of Norton's local guard at the golf course clubhouse. Out on the deck, as the sun peered red through a hole in the bank of clouds dominating the western horizon, a woman born and raised in Norton filled my ears with her tales: Travels to Germany. Her prizewinning jellies. How she knew a gentleman who owned his own plane and flew to a home in the Caribbean. And how, to the east, Highway 36 passed by the geographic center of North America.

"You'll know when you get close to it," she said, her fingers wrapped around a big glass of iced tea. "It's the place where the continent rests on God's fingertip."

B O B   C O S T A S   SPORTSCASTER – *St. Louis, Missouri*

Making an appointment with a celebrity is like trying to get five teenagers from separate families to a movie in the same car: twenty-three phone calls, seven changes of venue, two defections, and finally—if you're lucky—one agreement. Hooking up with Bob Costas was similar.

Four weeks before pulling up to his house, I was on a pay phone at a rest stop just off Highway 86 in southern Arizona, talking to Bob's assistant in New York City. "Could you fax us some information on your project?" she asked.

Fax. With a fax machine. I had a lot of things in my car. I had a camp stove. I had a gas-powered lantern. I had this handy little bamboo spatula with a handle that doubled as a butter knife. But I didn't have a fax machine.

"No problem," I said.

This wasn't the kind of "no problem" that was *really* no problem. It was the kind of "no problem" that meant, "If you were working on your first book and one of the leading sports announcers in the country gave you an opening, what would you do?"

So I found a way to send the fax. And Bob liked the idea. And we agreed to play catch. After stopping at the Pony Express museum in Marysville and grabbing a chocolate shake in Hiawatha, Kansas, I pressed on to St. Joseph, where I got on Interstate 29 headed south. My detour ran its course when, several hours later, I pulled into the western outskirts of St. Louis.

Four weeks after sending the fax from Ajo, Arizona, I sat in Bob's kitchen solving rebus puzzles with his wife. "He should be home any minute," she said, returning her attention to the task at hand. "Now what does this one mean?" She pointed her pen at an old classic.

"Saline over the seven seas." The words had no sooner cleared my lips than Bob swung open the door from the garage. His blond-haired son, an eight-year-old, scampered in from another room to greet him. Bob patted him on the head, asked him about last night's perfect game in the bigs, and then turned to me.

"Hi," he said, with that voice that sounds as if it just may cut to commercial. "You must be Nick."

We shook hands and I'm not quite sure what I said. Probably something like "yes" and "it's a pleasure" and "I'm glad I faxed." He crossed the room to see his wife and I got a good look at him: Two days' growth of whiskers shadowed his face and his hair was tossed somewhat, as if he'd been driving with the window down. He wore khaki pants and a short-sleeved shirt. His movements were swift about the kitchen and he turned to me again.

"Let me change out of these and I'll be down in a sec," he said and disappeared upstairs.

Ten minutes later, Bob led me out to the garage and fished around for his glove. He emerged with it on his left hand and walked out to the backyard where he paced off a good sixty feet between us. I put my MacGregor on my hand and pulled the ball from its webbing, placing my fingers across the strings. Bob stood waiting as I let my first toss sail.

At sixty feet, you've got to put a good deal of zip on the ball for it to travel and reach the other person's glove. I did so, and after hissing through the wind, the ball landed with a slap in Bob's mitt. I stood facing south, and the early evening sun, still high enough to clear the garage, shone golden on both of our faces. It occurred to me that I was here, after all, to interview this man. But I hadn't a question in the world to ask.

Bob simplified that by interviewing me.

"Where have you stayed, mostly?" He stepped toward me and flung the ball. It hissed through the air before smacking loudly into my mitt.

"Family and friends, plus camping out. I think tonight will be the first night in a hotel out of the last several weeks."

"Really?"

"Yeah, I try to keep costs to a minimum." I stepped into the throw.

"What are you doing foodwise? How often do you stop?" He threw the ball harder than anyone I could recall.

"I cook out of my car quite a bit."

"Really?" he asked, almost incredulous.

"Well yeah, I've got a camp stove so I eat off of that, mostly." I darted the ball back to him as his son, Keith, erupted from the house with his glove on.

"Back in the game is number fifteen!" Keith boomed as he ran between us. He took his place further back on the lawn and Bob tossed him the ball. He gloved it, pulled it from the pocket and arced it my way. I turned and tossed the ball to Bob, closing the triangle. As Bob stepped again toward Keith, I began.

"So tell me about your life, growing up and such."

"I was born in '52 in Queens but I grew up on Long Island, for the most part. We lived in L.A. for a couple of years in the early '60s, and then Connecticut for about a year and a half in the mid-60s, but more or less Long Island." He stepped toward Keith and the ball flew. "Then I went to college in Syracuse and did my undergrad there. I studied public communications." Keith caught the ball and rounded the horn, putting some pace on it.

"Tell me about growing up on Long Island."

"I was out in Suffolk County, not Nassau County, but it was pretty Long Island—lot of strip malls and fast food there and, you know, residential."

"And your family?" Keith gloved the ball again and whipped around, unloading it in the middle of a crucial double play.

"I have a sister who's two years younger than I and lives in Massachusetts. My father was an electrical engineer and my mother had some office jobs at various times but mostly was a housewife."

"Did you enjoy growing up in suburbia?"

"Well you know what, Nick—in my head, I always thought I lived in New York City. We had cousins and aunts and uncles that I visited there and the ball clubs were there; television and radio stations came from there, the newspapers I read were from there—so I remember thinking of myself as a New Yorker, really." His words were crisp, the syllables enunciated with a clarity and projection that I'd seldom heard in a one-on-one conversation.

"Were you in sports as a kid?" The ball traveled the triangle.

"Yeah, I played almost every sport except hockey—I never learned to skate. Baseball was always my favorite. I was a pretty good ballplayer as a kid. I remember hitting third in Little League, playing every position and pitching some." He floated a fly toward Keith. "A little bit like Keith, I had a precocious understanding of the game. I wasn't a kid likely to misunderstand the difference between a force and a tag play when I was eight or nine years old like most kids in Little League do, you know.

"I watched a lot of baseball, listened to a lot of baseball, had older cousins and friends in the neighborhood who knew a lot about baseball and played a lot of baseball. And it wasn't like what you hear people complaining about now where kids supposedly only play in organized leagues. I mean, we played every day. You'd go down to the sandlot or the schoolyard and you'd have a game, and if you didn't have enough guys for a game, you'd play 'catch a flies-up' or 'hit the bat.'" The ball zipped from my hand.

"If you were by yourself you took a rubber ball or a tennis ball and threw it off a wall or the stoop in front of your house and created a game in your mind. You know—I'd hear Mel Allen or Red Barber's voice in my head while I was going through this stuff; playing stickball, playing slap ball—or punchball.

"I kept playing on up through high school but from the time I was like fourteen, I knew that I wouldn't be big enough to be a really good player. I was like a lot of kids who were small—I was coordinated earlier than other kids, but by the time I was in junior high, a lot of them had caught up to me." Keith turned the ball at his corner with the urgency of someone in his first major-league start.

"Tell me about your days at Syracuse."

"Well, I left before I graduated. I had gotten a job broadcasting minor-league hockey and I cut back on my credits so that, you know, I could continue working and graduate in five years." I spun a curve. "And then I got the job broadcasting games for the Spirits of St. Louis in the ABA and I came here, back in '74, and forgot about school. I never did go back." He stepped toward Keith.

"Will you finish up some day?"

"No, I doubt it. I have an interest in furthering my education but more from the standpoint of reading books or sitting in on courses. I don't care about the diploma that much." Keith broadcast a description of the double play he was turning, sending the ball on a line for my chest. It slapped and he called the out.

"Tell me about your family."

"Married for thirteen years." He gloved my toss with a soft slap. "I went and spoke to my wife's third-grade class in 1980—almost like show-and-tell. One of the kids brought me in on a career day type of thing and she was the teacher and that's how I met her. Then we started dating. We have two kids. Keith is eight and Taylor will be five next month. Keith, as you can see, likes baseball quite a bit—likes all sports. He's pretty knowledgeable about baseball for an eight-year-old kid." Keith stepped at an angle and tossed.

"And it seems like your career's been on quite a roll since settling here."

"Well, I've been very fortunate; a lot of things happened that I didn't envision when I first signed with NBC." The ball popped. "One-thing-led-to-another kind of stuff."

"How long did you do 'Later'?"

"Ran from '88 to early this year and then I quit."

"Why was that?"

"I wanted to spend more time at home; the schedule was too demanding. Four shows a week to prepare for and you've got to give it your full attention." He tossed a floater to Keith. "I was satisfied that I'd done a good job, that by the end, it was much better than it had been at the beginning. You know, that I'd made some progress with it, and looking back on it, five and a half years is long enough to have been a significant run but not so long that people are expecting you to leave, you know? I think one of the keys is get off the stage before anybody wants or expects you to."

"How do you become successful in your business?" Keith quickly unloaded the ball.

"Well, you know, I think it's kind of subjective and it's very hard to evaluate yourself. I think clearly you have to know your stuff, but what does that mean? I can't *know* what happens down on the field when you're facing Nolan Ryan's fastball followed by his curveball. I can't know that as well as somebody who played the game. I can't know certain technical on-field aspects of the game as well as Joe Morgan or Tony Kubeck or Tim McCarver." He stretched out his glove and caught my throw.

"I can know them much better than the vast majority of fans by virtue of my interest in it and my access to information about it, you know, but I always respect the difference between someone who has acquired knowledge through study and someone who actually lived a situation." Again, Bob held the ball. "I think that one of the best things that a person can do in my position is respect that difference and have a healthy curiosity about it. And to be the person who facilitates—through asking good questions and gauging what will push the right buttons—getting the story from Joe Morgan or Tim McCarver or Tony Kubeck to the person at home who wants to hear it." He let the ball sail.

"So you've got to know your stuff, but you also have to respect what you either don't know or you can't know as well as the greatest expert. The other thing is the willingness to respect each assignment and prepare for it. I try very hard to be prepared for every game."

Keith gloved the ball and yelled, "Last out, coming home," before humming it into my glove. I made a tag on the grass as he ran between us toward the house. Our three-way had become a two-way and I flung the ball to Bob.

"Is there any magic left in baseball, as you see it?"

"Well, I think it's a game of rituals. It's a game of atmospherics, you know. I guess that's true of all sports—the sound of skates on the ice in hockey or the dribble of the ball and the squeak of sneakers on hardwood, an autumn afternoon in college football; but I just think it's more true of baseball." He took time with his motion and hissed the ball. "I think a sense of place matters in baseball. That's why the first run of new ballparks in the '70s were such an abomination, because they eliminated a sense of place—they had no character, no individuality.

"I think the everydayness of it is important. I think the *romance* of baseball can be and has been overstated, to the point where there's a backlash against it because, you know, a lot of intellectuals have overused baseball as a metaphor and as a means of communicating with a mainstream audience. But that doesn't mean that the romance of baseball doesn't exist.

"There's more romance in baseball than all other sports put together. There's more of a genuine feeling of nostalgia, and history matters in baseball much more than in any other sport. Generations are linked through baseball. Comparisons matter more in baseball, era to era, player to player, team to team. Context is everything in baseball. And I think there's a world of baseball that you enter." The ball zipped between us, slapping cleanly against the leather.

"I think where most other sports are a spectacle, baseball really is a pastime. It has rhythms: infield practice, batting practice, putting on the uniform in the clubhouse—you know—that's at the top level. But it even has rhythms out here having a catch, you know?" He closed his glove on the ball. "Again, without reaching too far for the meaning, it's just a pleasing thing. The sound of having a catch and the ball smacking into the leather sounds good. The sound of the bat hitting the ball, that resounding crack when somebody makes contact and how—even in a full ballpark at the major league level with 50,000 people in it—you can sometimes hear that crack of the bat. I think those things are all aesthetically pleasing. I'm not attributing to them any larger meaning, necessarily, except that they're pleasing." The ball sliced through the air.

"Certainly Wayne Gretzky skated around a pond when no one else was around. I'm sure he did that. And certainly there's the image—and it's a compelling one—of a kid on a farm somewhere or in the inner city by himself shooting at a basket that doesn't have a net on it. So I'm not saying that other sports don't have their solitary aspects to them, but it seems to me like the components of baseball can be broken off from the team game more easily." Pop. Into Bob's glove.

"You can just have a catch. You can just swing a bat. You know, you can play a little pepper. And I think also, especially as you get older, you realize that while size and strength are important in any athletic endeavor, baseball's a little more democratic than other sports. A smaller guy can still do pretty well in baseball." Bob threw it low and away and I lunged at it with my glove, snagging the ball in the pocket.

"Whoa!" he said, the voice from the broadcast booth filling the yard. "Great stab."

"Thanks," I said and hurled the sphere. After the catch, his eyes fixed on my mitt.

"How long have you had that glove?"

"Since I played back in high school."

"Well broken in," he said, holding the ball in his mitt.

"Yeah, you want to try it out? It's a bit sweaty but it's a helluva glove." He walked toward me and we swapped gloves before returning to our matted circles in the grass. He slapped his fist in the webbing of the trusty MacGregor.

"Where did you play?" he asked as he flung the ball.

"Same as you—Little League, then a bit in high school." I zipped the ball back. "Most of my athletic high points seemed to be when I was about fifteen years old."

"Yeah, mine too," he said, opening and closing my mitt. "This is a good glove."

"Yeah," I added, "it's a peach." I flung the ball and he wrapped the MacGregor's soft leather around it. We tossed without words, getting a feel for the new gloves.

"What are you the happiest about in your life?"

"Well, I'm happiest about my family, about my children, and about being able to do something which—while acknowledging that even on our best day we do it imperfectly—seems to reach people." He gloved the toss.

"You know, I get a fair amount of reaction from people where it seems like I've struck a chord with them. I mean, I think they know that my feelings about baseball are genuine. I'm also sure you could line up people with legitimate criticisms of me. But I get a lot of letters from people who share my feelings about baseball and I think I've been able, when I've had a chance, to occasionally say something beyond 'ball one, strike two' or beyond the score of the game. Sometimes that's been not just expressing my love of the game but also criticisms of the way it's presently being run, and I get a lot of favorable response to that—from people who feel like the institution is being trashed by people who either don't understand it or don't care about it, which is what I think." I closed my glove around a curveball tailing in.

"So I think the most gratifying thing is that, without overstating it, in my best moments I might have communicated something a little bit more than craftsmanship. I hope the craftsmanship is always there, because it has to be, you know. But in the course of doing that, I think there are times where I can get across something a little bit more, and people tend to respond to that. So professionally, that's been the most gratifying for me."

"What would you like to be remembered for?"

"Well . . . " He paused a few seconds and fingered the strings. "Of the public person, that my work was, at least in large part, an extension of who I am, that there was something truthful in it." The ball flew from his hand. "Some of what I do, like I say, is just craft. Inevitably, some of it is just giving scores or saying 'Let's go to Joe Blow in Seattle' and you hope to do that as pleasantly and capably as you can. But then there are other times when maybe you can get across something a little bit more than that, and I hope that's what people remember. I don't hope for anything much more than that." I returned the ball on a line. "I hope also that I'm able to use the visibility that automatically comes with this to occasionally do some good for people and help some people out."

Sometime during the last several tosses, the last of the sun's rays folded for the day. We continued to toss the sphere as dusk enveloped the neighborhood.

"What do you think the most positive qualities of people are?"

"The most positive qualities of people? Wow, that's a little bit deep." The world was silent, just the pop of the ball in the gloves. Four, five, six times the ball slapped into the webbing.

"I think that the aberrant tends to gain more attention now than ever before." He stepped into a toss. "The worst aspects of the human condition are more attention-grabbing and the media—even what used to be the mainstream media—tilts more and more now in a tabloid direction. Even the tone of the newsmagazines, gossipy stuff, celebrity stuff—celebrity as a virtue in and of itself rather than a recognition that grows out of merit, which is what fame used to be, or at least what you hoped it was." The ball slapped against leather. "Now, the difference between fame and infamy, the difference between appreciation and celebrity has been blurred, and I think that in that atmosphere we're liable to lose track of the fact that, in my view at least, the vast majority of people are decent and well-meaning. They're trying to do the best they can, and they're trying to live their lives in accordance with some sort of values." He focused his eyes on my outstretched glove as an accurate throw hissed from his fingers.

"What are good words to live by, as a dad to his kid?"

"Um . . . " Again, he threw the ball several times, in no hurry to answer. "Find something in life you believe in and that you can give yourself to, be it on a personal level or a professional level, and give yourself to it in an uncompromised way."

"Have you been able to live that, for the most part?"

"I don't think anybody attains their idealized notion of themselves one hundred percent, but like most people I try." The dusk deepened and would soon overpower the flight of the ball.

"What do you think it's all about?"

"What do I think it's all about?" Bob took a few slow tosses, then held the ball. "Trying to take care of the basic business of your life while leaving enough time to have as many memorable and meaningful emotional moments as you can." He stepped forward and zipped it.

"Want to take some pitches?" I asked.

"You bet," he said, opening his glove to receive the ball. He caught it, and after I'd kneeled down he went from a full windup and delivered a fastball. His pitches had enough heat on them to make me wish I were wearing something thicker than a fielder's glove. Cutting through the warm evening air with a hiss, the ball smacked into the strike zone eight times in a row. Then he added his junk, throwing curves and change-ups.

"This is just like when I was a kid," I said, "taking pitches from my neighbor Matt Wilson in the front driveway before it got dark."

"Yeah," he said, and kept on gunning them. They were almost all on target. If we had imaginary batters, we would have laid down three or four in a row. With darkness looming, I issued my final request.

"Give me something special," I said. What came from his hand was a ball that neither curved nor slid nor tailed up, out, or in. But it sure as hell was fast. As it slapped into the leather for the last time, I rose from my crouch. "What were you working there?" I asked.

"I was throwing you some version of the split-finger," he said as he began laughing, "but one that probably would've been deposited in the bleachers."

Several hours later, I was on Interstate 70, heading back through Missouri to rejoin the back roads at St. Joseph. It was a vacant stretch of highway and I drove along in something of a daze, the white stripes pulsing in my headlights like a metronome.

Whatever I had expected to experience in meeting Bob Costas had evaporated in his last twenty or so pitches in the fading light. We were just two guys, out there searching for the perfect strike. He invited me in for dinner before I hit the road, and as we ate across from one another at the kitchen table he told me a favorite saying of his.

"I don't care about being celebrated, as in a celebrity," he said. "I'd just like to be appreciated."

Just north of Kansas City, I pulled into a Super 8 Motel and got a room. I had driven over seven hundred miles since waking up in Norton. And I could hardly get to sleep.

Checking into a hotel was somewhat of a luxury, and I extended the experience as long as I could, sleeping soundly until 11:00 the next morning when the house-keepers rapped on the door. I took some notes over a hot cup of coffee and some pancakes at a truck stop near Cameron, Missouri, then pushed on around midafternoon into Chillicothe. After spending the rest of the afternoon there, playing catch with people in the city's main park, I pushed up the road through mist and light rain toward Trenton.

The drive was a splendid one, the sky darkening and my headlights laying long columns of light down on the glistening asphalt. The ramen dinner set well in my stomach as I racked up the miles; an Italian aria spilled from the speakers and filled my car.

Later, with a resounding crack, a young man hit a three-run homer in an American Legion ball game under the lights in Trenton. I sat in the stands, pulling my jacket flaps up around my neck to guard against the cold. An hour or so later, I nestled in my sleeping bag at Crow-der State Park, rain droplets popping against my tent and lulling me to sleep.

———————————————

As I crossed through southeast Iowa, the clouds relented. At an old Texaco station in Sigourney where there was no self-service, the attendant ran the chamois through hand-cranked rollers and wiped down my windshield. As I closed in on Kalona, Iowa came alive with sprawling fields of green against the graying paint of old farm buildings. Here wheat, there corn, and everywhere a crystal blue sky and slow-moving traffic.

I spent the afternoon in Kalona interviewing various people, with a particular focus on the Amish. After I tossed the ball with Hannah and Dean Yoder, two kids belonging to the Beachy Mennonite sect, they invited me out to their church youth group's volleyball game that night. Following fried chicken, mashed potatoes, and two cups of coffee for dinner, I navigated country roads out to the court and passed the evening hours playing volleyball.

Girls in flowing blue dresses and boys with short hair and sunburnt faces filled the air with hoots and hollers as the silhouette of the ball danced around against the backdrop of the set-ting sun. We played game after game after game, all the kids getting into the action. After retiring to the church for lemonade following the games, I had time to reflect: Over the course of eight games in two hours, I hadn't heard a single profanity from the more than twenty kids. It was something.

One of the kids at the game invited me back to stay at his apartment and I accepted. The hours before I went to sleep were filled speaking in slow English to him and his mother, both recent immigrants from Russia. He was an auto mechanic, and his mother sorted eggs at a packaging factory. We talked and ate cherry-nut ice cream into the night, his mom smiling widely with a sparkle in her eyes. The apartment was decorated in squeaky-clean detail with plastic flowers and a new stereo. After shaking the mother's hand and thanking her, I stretched out to sleep on their new foldout bed. She left for work at 4:00 the next morning.

———————————————

After breakfast in Kalona, I hooked onto Interstate 80 and pushed east out of Iowa. At Davenport, I merged onto I-88 as the verdant, rolling hills of Iowa gave way to the commanding flatness of Illinois. The interstate miles were as wide as they were straight, and I pushed the accelerator to deliver my car and its contents into something different.

Within a few hours, just as talk radio WLS filled the speakers, Chicago erupted before me. Sticking to I-88, which becomes I-290, I blasted toward Lake Michigan, not changing my direction until I was immersed in the heart of downtown. Making a left on Michigan Avenue, I found myself one Honda among a hundred taxis. As I rolled down my window, the heat of the asphalt, the beeping of horns, and exhaust poured into my car. I hung my head out the window, trying to see the sky.

———————————————

Chicago couldn't be further from the beaches of Southern California. But I headed south from Evanston on the El train the following day to make a California-Chicago connection. As graffiti-covered buildings flashed by the windows and heat waves shimmered from the tracks, I flipped through the pages of my spiral notebook until I found the address under the name Mary. I got off at the Addison stop and, after asking a newspaper vendor for directions, navigated the streets of the Wrigleyville neighborhood to the intersection of Grace and Clark.

I had met Mary Prassa on Newport Beach in California two days before spending time in the squad car with Sergeant Collins. There, in the fresh breezes coming off the Pacific, we had begun to play catch and she invited me to stop by if I made it through Chicago. Now, a month later, I pushed open the door to Uncommon Grounds and ordered up an iced coffee. As I took my first big slug, the door opened and I faintly recognized Mary. I had played catch with over seventy people, and some of the images had begun to fade.

She saw me across the restaurant and radiated a big smile. "Long time no see," she said, crossing to where I sat. "Hold on, I've gotta get something to drink."

Five minutes later, I stood out on the sidewalk thirty feet from her. At our feet stood pints of iced coffee, beads of water forming on the clear glasses and leaking onto the sun-splashed sidewalk. She worked her long, tan fingers over the strings.

"It's Prassa," she said, sounding out each letter. "P-R-A-S-S-A." Rhymes with "boss-uh."

"What do you do, Mary?"

"Well, a few things. First, I work at the front desk for an internist doing billing and such. I work there Tuesdays, Wednesdays, and Thursdays during the day, and then I work at a little neighborhood tavern. I cocktail on Friday nights, which I hate, and I bar tend on Saturday, which I love." Stepping a muscled leg forward, she swept her hand smoothly through the air and sent the ball spinning toward me. "And I'm going to school to be a high school English teacher."

"How far away are you from finishing?"

"Too far. I'll be done with classes a year from this summer and then I'll student-teach a year from this coming fall. So probably in about two years, I'll actually start teaching." Pop. She wrapped her glove around the ball.

"Why high school?"

"Basically because I think high schoolers will be challenging. I mean, I've taught little kids swimming and I love them, but I'd rather have some adult conversation during the day." She ran her hand through her hair, her blond highlights catching the abundant sunlight.

"Tell me about your background."

"You mean growing up?"

"Yeah," I said, holding the ball as I picked up my coffee.

"I grew up in the southwest suburbs here in Chicago in a pretty middle-class neighborhood. My dad was an accountant for Amoco Oil so he worked downtown and my mom was a housewife, homemaker—whatever the politically correct term is—she wouldn't care. Oh yeah—I was adopted, as was my brother, so that's kind of different." The ball again flew between us.

"Did you always know that you were adopted?"

"Yes, ever since I can remember, so that means I knew before I understood the concept. My parents used to read the 'adopted family' storybooks and such, so I knew what was up."

"Are you markedly different than your parents?"

"Yeah, I'm different physically and, basically, in every other way that you could think of. No one in my family is tall, they all have dark hair, they all have dark eyes, they all wear glasses, and they're all much more conservative than I," she said with a laugh. "Much, much more."

"How was growing up in the suburbs of Chicago?" She paused to lift her glass from the cement.

"My parents are very Catholic, especially my mother. Very, very, very Catholic." She chuckled again, tightening her grip on the ball before tossing it. "They raised me Catholic, although at this point, I don't go to church." She threw casually.

"Then I went to school at Indiana, after which I moved to Florida for four and a half years. I started there in retail, then sold medical supplies. Then, about four years ago, I moved back up here."

"Why did you quit the sales job?"

"Well, I was making a lot of money, but I didn't get any fulfillment out of it." She placed her fingers along the strings. "Not that I'm going to be doing the planet some great good by teaching, but I just think that it'll be more personally fulfilling. I don't need a ton of money to live the lifestyle that I like to live. One of the things that I've found I really enjoy doing is traveling, so teaching will give me enough money to travel plus the time to go do it."

"Do you want to have a family?"

"Yeah, I do. Time's ticking away but . . . " She paused and rotated the ball in her grip. "I have the attitude that if you're too worried about getting married, you might settle with the wrong person, but at the same time I think the people who say 'I'm not going to marry until I'm thirty-five' or whatever might let the right person slip by. I mean, I always wanted to be a younger mother than my mom was to me, but that's already passed by so I guess I can't worry about it. The only thing I worry about is that if I hit thirty-five and there's no marriage in sight, I might just have a kid on my own."

"Does that have a strong appeal?"

"I just think it would be great to have kids. I mean, it's a lot of responsibility and definitely, I'd have to settle down some—I couldn't do as much traveling and such as I do now—but it's a possibility."

"Do you travel a lot?" The ball spun from my hand.

"Yeah, with ultimate, I'm on the road quite a bit."

"Tell me about the sport."

"Well, it's unique," she said, tossing the ball. "It's the only sport where you can't score yourself. In basketball, you shoot it yourself; in football, you can run it in; in soccer, you can kick it in. But in ultimate, you have to throw [the disk] to someone else, so it's very much a team sport.

"I started playing when I moved back to Chicago from Florida. . . . A friend of mine had been playing for years and told me about it but I had never even seen it played. When I moved back here, I went to his house for Christmas Eve dinner and met a woman who played on the team, and fortunately, it was at a time when the team was rebuilding. Normally, they wouldn't have taken on someone with no experience, but I got lucky. I mean, I'm still pretty much of a rookie on our team, even though I've played four years."

"And it keeps you on the road a lot?"

"Yeah, it's a long season. The first tournament is usually in Santa Barbara during the spring, then Boulder over the Fourth of July weekend, then it slows down until fall. There's usually an all-women's tournament in Ann Arbor during the autumnal equinox, then we have sectionals, regionals, and nationals—those end a week or two before Thanksgiving. Our season basically runs from May through Thanksgiving, with two to five tournaments in the spring and another three to five in the fall."

"Do you travel outside of that?"

"Yeah, every spring I go to the Jazz and Heritage Fest in New Orleans—this year will be my fifth." Mary stepped forward and put the ball in flight. It crossed six squares of cement and slapped into my pocket.

"What are you the most proud of in your life?"

"Well, that's hard to say. I mean, I haven't had any major accomplishments. I suppose I like my independence and I like the lifestyle I lead, you know. I've done a lot of things and I've had a lot of experiences, lived somewhere else besides here. I mean, some of my friends went from home directly to college, back to home, then to their husbands' houses without ever going out on their own, which I did. But in the big picture, with the teaching, hopefully the best is yet to come." Stepping forward, she threw.

"Mary at forty. What do you see?"

"Well, hopefully I'll be married and have a family who loves to travel."

"And what would you teach your family?"

"That you need to constantly pursue things that make you personally fulfilled and happy, and not put too great a concern on money and material things. I think it's important to be accepting of all others, no matter who they are or what they are." She stepped forward and tossed, her eyes looking through me as she sorted her thoughts. "You know, don't do bad things to other people, and then you'll be okay. I mean, life is really an individual thing, but in the course of doing your own thing don't hurt anyone." She wrapped her glove around my return, her right hand swinging at her side.

I peered down at her feet and noticed Mary's coffee was running low. Mine was too, and my T-shirt had begun to stick to my chest.

"How about we call it a day?" I suggested.

"Yeah," she said, "I've got to get to the office." We went back into the air-conditioned salvation of the coffee shop and deposited our glasses. As I sat down to make some notes, Mary packed up her small bag and extended her hand. "Thanks," she said, her palm meeting mine in a strong handshake.

"You'll make a great teacher," I said. She smiled and turned toward the door.

I watched her through the window as she crossed the intersection and walked down the opposite side of the street. Her figure became smaller and smaller as the heat waves licked up from the sidewalk and distorted her image until finally, as a bus shimmered past, I couldn't see her at all.

Later that afternoon, my Chicago experience became whole. Standing on the vacant expanse of deep right at Wrigley Field, I was playing catch with a young woman who worked in the on-site publication division for the Chicago Cubs. As she told me about her long commute from the suburbs and how successful she had been since finishing junior college, I was in awe of the park. We continued to rotate around an imaginary point so as not to mat down the grass as the ball arced calmly between us.

After exhausting most of my questions, we paced around the circle, throwing the ball without words. It popped cleanly into the gloves, the sound losing its strength before the vine-covered brick of the outfield fence. I circled under the scoreboard then back around so that I was facing the grandstand, the ball dancing between us all the while.

The young woman was comfortable throwing in silence and seemed to understand that just being out here was plenty enough for me. "If I ever get a chance to play catch with God," I said, "this is where I want to bring Him." She smiled and held the ball. I closed my eyes, my feet planted in the perfect sea of grass, and tilted my head back. It felt like a symphony.

The next morning, I left Chicago.

MARK HAXER

I didn't fully appreciate the evening spent playing volleyball back in Iowa until I rolled down my window just west of Kalamazoo, Michigan, on Interstate 94. That's when, as a mass of hot, sticky air crushed through the window, I realized that not since Iowa—four days past—had I felt cool.

The humidity in the Midwest, by its own weight, created a murky sky. Since I passed Davenport, the temperature difference between the dead of night and the apex of day was never great enough for me to stop sweating. By the time I approached Ann Arbor, I decided to try a new tack: early morning catch.

———————————————

Two days later I cornered Mark Haxer, a fellow out on an early morning jog through the trails near Ann Arbor's Pioneer High School. He was an unusually pleasant-looking man, the kind of person who, even at a glance, you'd figure would interrupt a morning workout to talk with a stranger. When I asked him if he'd be interested in playing catch, he suggested he go home to dress for work and meet up with me in half an hour. He did. And, after he returned to the high school, we spoke.

"You are Mark Haxer."

"Yes, I am sir. Ask away." He had fitted the glove to his fingers and took care to plant his feet solidly in the grass, about shoulders' width apart. I took measure of the green grass that separated us on the athletic practice field, raising the ball to my ear.

"Tell me about your life." I threw.

"How nutshell do you want it to be?"

"I don't know. Just start and if you're getting too detailed, I'll let you know." He caught the ball, pulling it from the webbing with his throwing hand.

"Born January 25th, 1953, in Detroit. Grew up in Mount Clemens, which is a little 'burb about twenty miles north of Detroit. Graduated from Mount Clemens High School in June of 1971." Without moving either foot an inch, he wrapped his hand back toward his ear and brought the ball down, sending it in an arc. "Went to Central Michigan University, graduated with a bachelor's in 1975, got my master's in December of 1978 from the same university." He paused for a moment, staring upwards to regain his thoughts. "Got married in 1979, November 9th; had my only son—actually, my ex-wife had my only son—on December 22nd, 1981. Got divorced in December of '86 and that's it." His arm came down, feet motionless. "Worked for the State of Michigan for twelve years before I came to the University of Michigan, and I've been at the U of M since December of 1988, working as a speech pathologist in the department of head and neck surgery at the U of M hospital."

"And that means?"

"Well, a lot of patients that I see are post head and neck surgeries and they're missing various portions of their anatomies and I teach them how to talk and or swallow after surgery is done." The ball found a cadence and moved between us with an exact rhythm.

"What was it like growing up in the suburbs of Detroit?"

"Well, my father died in 1961 of a heart attack so my mom raised us—me and my younger brother. . . . What was it like growing up in the suburbs of Detroit? . . . " He asked himself the question, his deep, clear voice trailing off as though holding the ball gave him an unusual opportunity to reflect on his thoughts. "Everything was cars, you know, cars, cars, cars. I mean, the whole area was wrapped up in the car industry." The ball took flight. "Probably the thing I remember most about growing up was we had a tremendous race riot in . . . '67?" he asked himself, holding the ball. "Yeah, summer of '67, all of Detroit went up in flames, and with Mount Clemens being so close to Detroit, you could see the fires burning and what have you. There was a race riot at my high school my senior year that closed it down for a week. . . . So I mean, race was a big thing growing up." The ball had returned to its normal meter.

"How old are you now?"

"Forty-one."

"How was it crossing into your forties?"

"You know, Nick, it was no big deal. Thirty was terrible, forty was nothing. Had a party over at my mom's house, you know. My ex-wife was there with her husband and my kid and all my ex-in-laws and all my friends from high school. But the best thing was, there's a group of, let me see, five of us that have been together since kindergarten. We've all stayed in touch, and the wife of one of the guys had a party for all of us the September of the year we all turned forty, which was last year. She got all of us together and we pitched in and had a huge dinner and just had a blast. I mean, we go back a long way."

"Do you see them a lot?"

"We don't see each other as much as we'd like because one of them is a dentist in Kalamazoo, on the west side of the state, another is a city planner over in the Detroit area, another is working with Bendix or someone like that, another is in Grand Rapids as a sportscaster, and

I'm here. So we don't see each other too often, but it's one of those friendships where it's like time hasn't passed, if you know what I'm saying. When we get back together, we catch right back up." He brought down his hand, the ball spinning.

"Is it kind of a Midwest thing—where you're born here and you stay here?"

"You know, I don't know, because when I went back to my twentieth high school reunion, for instance, a lot of people had gone out of state, but I'd say the vast majority stayed in Michigan. Maybe moved up north but still stayed in state. I don't know why we all stayed here, to be honest with you. I guess I was lucky enough to find a job in the Detroit area right out of college, and I mean, my friends were here, my family was here, and those things mean a lot to me. Then there's Justin, my son—I wanted to be around to support him. I just opted never to leave."

"What do you do, outside of work?"

"Well, I like to cook a lot, and musicwise I trained as a classical musician before I ever trained to become a speech pathologist." As his mitt closed around the ball, Mark's feet didn't budge.

"What do you play?"

"Viola. I played for about fourteen to sixteen years. In my school district, if you wanted to play an instrument, they started you in the second grade. So I started on viola, which is one size larger than the violin, and was trained classically throughout elementary, junior high, and high school. Played in the Mount Clemens High School Symphony Orchestra, played for all the choral things we did, played in the Mount Clemens Symphony, then was in the Saginaw Symphony for one year. By about my sophomore year in college, I decided that I probably couldn't land a chair in any major orchestra because, I mean, I was good but I just wasn't exceptional, so—you know—I decided to go into something else. But I still retain a lifelong love for classical music. I'm in the choral union here in Ann Arbor and I'll follow the Detroit Symphony wherever they play, so music is a big part of my life." The ball flew from his fingers.

"You throw well. Did you play ball as a kid?"

"No, not at all. When I was a kid, I weighed two hundred sixty-five pounds."

"What?" I froze, holding the ball.

"Well, I wasn't exactly a kid. I weighed two sixty-five when I was a sophomore in high school."

"How much do you weigh now?"

"One fifty-five."

"Man alive!" I threw the ball twice, not knowing what to say. "So you had a bit of a weight problem, as they say."

"A bit of a weight problem?" He laughed as he threw. "You're so diplomatic—I was a fat slob."

"How did you get that big?" The ball slowly regained its meter.

"Well, if you think heredity plays a part in it, certainly my father and his side of the family was big, but I mean basically, it was, you know, shovel a whole lot of food into my mouth and not do a whole lot activitywise."

"When did you start losing weight?"

"Well, there was this girl from Birmingham—have you heard of 'Birmingham on the West Coast'?" I shook my head. "Well, she was very chic—very tony, I think the word would be—and I fell head over heels for her and figured she might like me a little better if there were a little less of me, so I took off a hundred pounds. I went from two sixty-five to one sixty-five in college and fluctuated between one sixty-five and one eighty-five afterwards." Pop. Into my glove.

"Then, about ten months ago, I found out my cholesterol was very high, so I had to go on a low-fat diet and about another fifteen pounds came off. That dropped me down to about one fifty-five."

"What are you the happiest about, Mark?"

"Justin is the best thing I've done in my life. He's a good kid. I think probably after him, coming here to U of M—that's been a major thing. I suppose, too, you know, just appreciating family and friends and staying in touch with them. . . . But Justin is the crowning achievement, he's the best." He threw the ball a few times in silence, then held it. "I have no regrets about my life."

"Tell me about your work." On the street adjacent to the playing field, the morning traffic was picking up.

"What I hope to do for all my patients is—once the doctors have done what they need to do—just rehabilitate them to the best of their ability and bring them back to as normal a life as I can. Sometimes, you can bring them back to a near-normal status, if you want to call it that. Other times, you just can't. . . . " His feet remained still as the ball slapped into his mitt.

"But that's what makes the job worthwhile, when you see someone after surgery who's having a helluva time swallowing—they can't swallow or if they can it's minimal. They're aspirating, they've got stuff running out of their trachea site and, you know, they may be sick because they can't swallow. Over time, you work with them, and then a few months down the road you see them back on a normal diet, eating anything they want to. . . . That's gratifying. That's really gratifying." There was great feeling in his voice.

"And it's not me that does all that. I mean, I have a wonderful bunch of patients. My patients have—I would say, by and large—the largest amount of dignity I've ever seen in anybody. They face an ugly form of cancer, they face cancer that oftentimes has left them disfigured, dysfunctional, and they face it—again, by and large—with a tremendous amount of dignity and courage. I just guide them in what to do. They do the majority of the work."

"There must be incredible strength in your patients."

He took a deep breath and held the ball. "I would say, with the humanity that I see, that their finest quality is probably their ability to look positively at life given the curveball that life has thrown them. See, the people that I see are pushed to the wall, you know what I'm saying? I'm seeing people who are *forced* to deal with what life has handed them. But only very rarely do I have a patient who maintains a long period of depression or what have you. Granted, they may get depressed, and I expect that with a lot of my patients. But once they work through that aspect and find that life does go on, their resilience—I suppose I would call it—is what really impresses me. Because I don't know that I could be that resilient if someone told me I had the 'big C'." He finished the thought and pushed the ball into flight.

"Can you keep from becoming a pessimist in such work?"

"I guess I'm an optimist." The ball popped. "I like to think that our generation will hand our children's generation a better world. You know, that's just me. Not to say there haven't been people through the years who've tested that optimism, but I guess I tend to look at humanity as a whole on the positive side."

"What will people say about Mark Haxer when you die?"

"I think probably that he did for others before he did for himself. I mean, I look out for myself, but I'll never turn down a friend who comes and asks for help. Ever." He threw. "I'm not saying I'm perfect," he added with a chuckle, "but I guess on the overall meter, I'm okay."

As the first earnest amount of sweat began to permeate my shirt, I decided to wrap up and let Mark head off to work. Before I left, I had one last inquiry about his style of playing catch, one in which over the last forty-five minutes, his feet hadn't moved so much as an inch.

"Ever lift your feet?" I asked.

He looked down at his shoes and laughed. "Yeah, I ran this morning—was out the door by ten 'til six."

―――――――――――――

By noon, I had moved on from Ann Arbor, headed south. Outside of Clinton, on Michigan Highway 12, I played catch with a high school French teacher on summer vacation. At her side, she had a massive Newfoundland named Otis, a dog who must've heard from Ed in Almena, Kansas, that I was on the way. The entire time the ball flew back and forth between us, Otis sat at the ready, his eyes tracing its path. Just when I thought his enthusiasm was flagging, a new strand of drool oozed from his jowls onto the grass.

But not once did we drop the ball and not once did Otis budge from his position on the lawn. He, like Mark this morning, the teacher who stood next to him, and the printer I later talked to in Adrian, was a midwesterner.

And whereas in the West they planted crops and buildings and ran their lives around them accordingly, in the Midwest they planted their feet. And around them, the world slowly turned.

OHIO STATE HIGHWAY 127

ROAD RAMEN

1 package ramen noodles with flavor packet
2 whole carrots, sliced
1 broccoli crown
or
1 zucchini, sliced

Place two inches of water in small pan and bring to a boil.
Add sliced vegetables and boil aggressively for five minutes. Add noodles and cover,
boiling an additional five minutes or until noodles are done.
Drain excess water until approximately one inch remains.
Empty contents of flavor packet (Oriental preferred) into mixture and stir.
Eat directly from pot. Serves one.

By the time I took a right on Ohio State Highway 20, I had run out of dinner ideas. What that translated to, as it had at least twenty times since I left Grand Junction, was that I'd be eating Road Ramen by nightfall.

As I headed west for a short distance in the northernmost part of Ohio, I spied my gas gauge nearing E. Pulling into Alvordton, a small outpost in a massive scape of trees and pastures, I filled up and asked the attendant the best way to head south.

"Just passed it," he said, nodding his head back up the road where I had come. "Toodle back up there and make a right at Highway 127, it's nice." I thanked him and turned to hop back in my car, but before opening the door I noticed he was studying my feet. "Them sandals?" he asked, curling his lower lip.

"Yes sir," I answered with a smile. "They keep my feet cool."

"Uh-huh," he said, nodding his head once with finality. "You have a good trip." A long mile back up the road, I hit the blinker and turned right onto Ohio State Highway 127. Within ten miles, it was clear that the old man at the gas station understood what sort of road I was in search of.

Ohio State Highway 127 wasn't just a stretch of asphalt, it was a carefully laid transition from the thick trees and urban development of southeastern Michigan into the rich farmland and straight-shot roads of Ohio. Trees became less and less dense as I headed south through Defiance County, and by the time I pulled through Pauling, agriculture began to take over the majority of the horizon.

Further south, Van Wert's squat brick buildings cast shadows over the spotless sidewalks where I stood and tossed the ball with a waitress on break from a local cafe. After limbering our arms with the ball for a while, she invited me back inside and gave me a large, ice-cold soda. We talked wheat prices for a bit, then I pushed on.

I spent the late afternoon in Celina, playing catch with the associate editor of the local newspaper before hunkering down on the bleachers and taking in a couple of hours of Little League baseball. After two seven-inning games, I got back onto 127. It was then I realized that the road had saved its best for last.

As the sun began its fall to the western horizon, I pulled into the Brotherhood of the Precious Blood, an old monastery near Carthagena. Jutting up magnificently from the surrounding acres of wheat and corn, the brick structure had a gravity all its own.

After getting an okay from a retired Catholic priest at the front desk, I went outside and erected my tent in the shadow of the towering building. At 9:15, as the sun folded and sent pink rays bursting into the clouds, my Road Ramen came to a boil and I pulled it off the camp stove. I sat out on the sprawling lawn, surveying the serene beauty of the surrounding fields and the flicker of fireflies dancing over the grass. That evening, sitting in front of the old monastery, I had the best dinner of the trip.

JANAE MASSEY SCHOOLGIRL – *Hamilton, Ohio*

The farm country from Carthagena south to Greenville was stunning. Tall grain towers and sturdy farmhouses awash in the morning light kept watch over thriving fields. On past Greenville, the pastoral qualities of Highway 127 slowly began to dissipate, the landscape dotted more and more frequently with wooded areas.

As I crossed Interstate 70, the scenery made a final shift, and like a river spreading into a delta, the romance of the road slipped away into the hectic constructs of Hamilton, a suburb that lies twenty-odd miles north of Cincinnati. While it is distinct from Cincinnati for those who live there, Hamilton appears—to the outsider—to be joined with it, one sprawling mass of brick buildings, heavy trucks, and heat waves reflecting off the pavement.

The crisp, clean acres of wheat and corn were replaced by pungent air, exhaust spewed from big American cars, and the shrill squeak of garbage truck brakes. Girls in pink plastic sandals stood at crosswalks waiting to dash across the street. Two men sat on the concrete step in front of a liquor store, brown paper bags hanging from their sinewy fingers.

And in the backseat of my car lay the baseball gloves. That realization set my eyes to looking again, to see past the shimmer of heat waves to the people. The first image that struck me was a porch full of kids hanging out on the wooden steps. I pulled a quick right off the highway onto Central Avenue and stopped in front of the house.

A young boy and three girls—two who weren't quite teens and one who was just past toddlerhood—stopped talking and watched as I approached the house. The mom and grandmother inspected me head to toe, and after I convinced them of the innocence of my intentions, they agreed to let me talk to their kids. The boy was quick to be gone, and while the youngest girl was eager to be included, her incomplete mastery of English—and her short limbs—precluded her from playing catch.

That left the two preteens, who were all white-toothed giggles. They introduced themselves as Janae and Jolanda, then showed me some of their various awards and pictures in the house before we walked to a weedy patch of grass down the street. Both girls nominated the shorter of the two—the smart one, they said—to play catch. She put the glove on her hand as though she'd done it many times before. Straightening out the bright, clean stripes of her shirt with a tug, she looked up at me.

"That's Jan-aye?" I asked.

"Janae," she said and spelled it out. "J-A-N-A-E. Janae Massey." I pulled the ball from the red All-Star bag lying on the ground and readied to toss it.

"And you're twelve now?"

"Yes," she said, the ball slapping softly into her glove.

"So tell me about Hamilton, Ohio." Her elbow jerked a bit—as though rusty—as she flung the ball.

"It's fun and stuff. I've got a lot of friends and it's a lot of nice people down here. I try to stay involved in things so I won't be bored around the house." She lobbed the ball. "When I was in school I was in a group called show choir. We used to dance and sing, but now that it's the summer, I go to the boys club and play around. They got all kinds of activities. And I play basketball—it's my favorite sport." Having spoken with grown-ups over the past several days, I had forgotten that when you're twelve, all topics somehow relate to one another. And mixing them together makes as much sense as peanut butter and jelly.

"Are you pretty good?"

"Yeah, I'm good. And the coach at the school I'm going to this year, the junior high, he wants me to play basketball." Her elbow turned and the ball rainbowed.

"Tell me about some of the awards you showed me earlier from school."

"One I got from Bill Clinton," she said with a large smile. "It was a Presidential Award like, for um, being a real good student. And I got a good citizenship award . . . because my teacher said I had a positive attitude and they like to be around me, *and* I got an award for honors in the fourth quarter for making almost straight As." The ball arced between us. "I got all As and two B-pluses, I think. I didn't think I was going to get the award from Bill Clinton, though. I was real surprised when they called my name for it."

"If you could go to Washington and tell the president anything, what would you say to him?"

"I'd say that I'm glad he's our president and I think he's doing a real good job. I wouldn't have any advice for him, but I'd ask him for advice." She gloved my toss with a soft slap.

"What about?"

"About troublemakers and how to make peace with them 'stead of getting in fights." She cocked her arm at the elbow and her tone changed to a reassuring one. "That's not a big problem right here where I live. My street is very peaceful; it's quiet at night and stuff. But some areas of the town is bad."

"Oh yeah?"

"Yeah, people stand out on the corners and stuff—but now we got a curfew. Weekdays we gotta be in at 10:30 and on weekends—you know, like Fridays, Saturdays, and Sundays—we ain't gotta be in 'til like 11:30. But my mom, she makes us come in earlier." Her words spilled out as the ball moved between us. "If she's on the porch with us, we come in at like 10:00, on the weekends—since it's the summer."

"What do you think of your mom?"

"I think that she's very nice and I'm glad that she's a Christian because some people's moms, they don't know where their mom's at. But my mom's always there for me. She's like my best friend." Jolanda stood to our side, smiling widely at some of her sister's words.

"What does your mom do?"

"She works in a factory."

"What kind?" The ball closed on me.

"A brush factory—the kind that's on street cleaners." I stepped into a toss and lofted it.

"Is she pretty tough with you guys?"

"Oh, she's *tough* with me and my sister, she's real tough, man." She glanced at Jolanda and laughed. "She mean. . . . Like I got a little, like, kind of a boyfriend and she checked him out but she likes the way he is. And it's like one of my first times that she let me have a boyfriend."

"Do you want to be like your mom when you grow up?" The ball arced from my hand.

"Yeah, I want to be a Christian woman like my mom and I want to have kids like my mom but I only want to have two." She thought about that number for a second and then let the ball fly. "But when I grow up, I want to be a doctor."

"What kind?"

"I want to be a children's doctor—a pediatrician." She sounded each syllable with precision.

"Why do you want to be a doctor?"

"Helping children," she said with finality, tossing. "Like, if a family can't pay for their bill, I won't charge 'em. And if I keep practicing, maybe I can use sports and academics to get a scholarship to college—to go and study medicine. I think maybe I'll go to Notre Dame or I might just go to a medical institute." The ball slapped into her mitt. "But I want to move out of this area—maybe to Seattle or a city I've never been in so I can help people." Jolanda watched us with a shy smile. If she caught me looking at her, she'd roll her head sort of sideways to hide her rows of perfect white teeth. Otherwise, her eyes followed the path of the ball in flight. She was content to listen to her sister talk to the stranger.

"What's a typical day like in the summer?" I lofted the ball.

"Well, in the summer, I usually, like, go to the boys club and go swimming and be around my friends or just sit around the house and read a good book."

"What do you like to read?"

"All kinds of books. Sometimes I like mystery books and scary books and, like, books that tell about my past and stuff, my ancestors. I like *Roll of Thunder, Hear My Cry*—that's a very good book—and I checked out a book about famous black Americans, one about women and one about men. I learned a lot more than I used to know."

"Who's your favorite author?" Her elbow jerked and sent the ball arcing.

"R.L. Stein—he's scary—and the 'Baby-sitter Club' series too, and 'Sweet Valley High' and the person that wrote *Roll of Thunder, Hear My Cry*—I forgot her name. It's very good."

"What else do you do for fun, besides reading?" I set my fingers with the strings and threw.

"I play basketball and sometimes in our field—we got a little field down the street there— we play baseball. We do a lot of activities. And then, they got, like, show choir in school and they got 'art in motion' at my school." Her thoughts piled atop one another. "But now that I'm going to George Washington—the junior high—they got a lot more things, like I'm gonna be playing volleyball, basketball, I might play baseball, and they got track." The ball descended into my webbing.

"Is the junior high mostly white, or are there a lot of African Americans? It's 'African Americans', right?"

"Blacks," she said, giving it little thought. "The junior high is mostly white with a couple of buses of blacks, but the elementary school was pretty mixed, I guess. It don't matter to me." She threw without pause.

"When you go to school with a bunch of different kids, what do you think the best things about them are?" I returned the ball in silence. It took a few tosses before her words came.

"I think that you should have a good education to fall back on—like if you get hurt playing basketball or baseball or something like that. I like people's personalities and I think that people should have, like, a good, positive attitude towards life, and I like it when people be nice, and um, those are about the goodest qualities I can think of." The words flowed in a constant string. "Like, when you be good to others as you want to be treated by them—that's how I try to act towards people. Kind of the Golden Rule type of thing." Elbow jerk. The ball flew.

"What do you think of America?"

"It's very fun in America. I mean, I love America. I don't know. I don't think I could make it in another country." She rainbowed the ball. "I want to *visit* other countries but I couldn't live in one. I mean, there's a lot of things you can do in this country—opportunities—tons."

"And what do you think of this book idea?"

"I think this is great. You should let people out there know that, like, everybody out there's not bad. There's a lot of good people in the world, but you just really don't hear about 'em." The ball arced from her fingers. "I want to let the world know that it's not all bad in Hamilton. It's good people here and this is a good place."

"Yeah," said Jolanda. I turned to see her smiling at me. I looked back and Janae was grinning, too, her glove wrapped around the ball.

"Any other comments for the world?" I asked.

Janae walked toward me, stretching out her hand to give me the ball. "Naw," she said. "You be careful."

A short while later, I pulled off the road at a strip mall south of Hamilton and played catch with a fireman who had just finished his shift. His unusual enthusiasm despite having worked through the night became clear through the course of our conversation: He was about to get married.

Highway 127 dumped me into a maze of streets in downtown Cincinnati. After several ill-conceived turns down one-way avenues, I passed the tall buildings of downtown and, within a few miles, crossed into Kentucky. As I exited the metropolis on Highway 27, the road opened to reveal rolling hills and open fields of tobacco.

I stopped in Cynthiana, spending time at the county courthouse, chatting first with a judge, then a single mother about to appear in juvenile court. Further south, in Paris, I turned onto Highway 68 and drove an unimaginably beautiful stretch of road into Lexington.

I stopped several times at the large horse farms that lined the passage, my arms dangling from white fences as I stared at acre upon acre of trimly kept fields dotted with animals. I thought of the road today, of how it had taken me from the calm of Carthagena to the traffic and flashing railroad crossings of Cincinnati and then back out here, to the serene pastures. As I leaned up against the rails, I wished I could have had Janae with me. Because everybody should get to see something this beautiful when they're still a kid.

CLIFF GOLDMACHER

SONGWRITER – *Nashville, Tennessee*

The miles southwest from Lexington were striking; rolling earth and large hilltop farms bordered the asphalt that linked Harrodsburg with Perryville and Lebanon with Raywick. Shortly before Hodgenville, I pulled over and played catch with a woman who farmed tobacco. The entire time the ball flew between us, her two kids sat against a fence near us with constant grins. Before I left, I asked the kids what was so funny and they ran over to whisper in their mom's ear. "Wouldn't you know it," she said as she handed me the ball. "It's your accent."

Past Hodgenville on Highway 31E, the heat of the day rose, with an ever-greater quotient of humidity buffeting my windows. After I merged with Interstate 65 north of Nashville, the traffic knotted and I spent the next thirty minutes crawling along a sweaty river of asphalt lined densely with lush trees. After pulling onto the streets of Nashville, I followed a set of directions to the home of an old friend. We spent the afternoon in an air-conditioned bar chatting up a storm and sipping cold beers.

Later that night, we leaned back against the bleachers at Greer Stadium and watched Nashville's triple-A club take a drubbing at the hands of the Royals' farm team. The night air was filled with the tumbling of children's yelps and the hisses and pops of fireworks over the outfield. My friend and I talked at length about my travels to date, about the people from different walks of life I'd talked to, and what they had to say.

Before I went to sleep that night, he mentioned the name of Cliff Goldmacher, a young songwriter. "You've got to play catch with him," he said. "He's what this town is all about."

"Cliff Goldmacher in ten years," I said, my words enunciated like a TV anchorman's. "Where do you see yourself?" I placed my forefinger and middle fingers against the strings and put the ball in flight.

"I'll be a recording artist in ten years, no doubt about it." The ball slapped cleanly into his glove. "It may be less than that—maybe like five to seven years. I'll be out on the road playing a lot by then, and certainly in ten years I'll be there."

A lot of guys wear baseball caps. Some guys wear hats with major league logos on them. Some guys wear hats from minor league teams. Some guys wear their hats turned to the side and still others wear them completely backwards. Some guys wear hats that advertise Cat Diesel or Mack Trucks or something like that. Some guys wear hats with NFL logos on them, but I've never seen one worn in an actual football game. And some guys, of course, don base-ball caps for the reason that you're supposed to wear one in the first place: because it's Satur-day morning and you haven't showered. Cliff Goldmacher was such a guy.

The two of us stood atop Love Hill, a knoll that juts up from the surrounding residential streets a few miles west of downtown Nashville. You can see the city skyline in the distance. About fifty feet in front of me, where the grass began its break down the steep slope of the hill, stood Cliff. His eyes were shaded by the bill of his cap, but sun fell brightly on his baggy T-shirt and shorts. Standing with both arms hanging loosely, he cradled the ball in one of his hands. His fingers maneuvered until he had a good grip on the dark red strings.

"Why a professional musician?" I asked as he stepped into a toss.

"I think really it was a feeling that music had always been a part of what I was, and I realized that it was much more important to me to be doing something that made me happy every day than in some sort of a theoretical way." The ball returned to Cliff's mitt with a slap; his words flowed with ease. "I had taken the law school entrance exam and was headed down that path but law school just didn't appeal to me at the time. And that's not to say that, you know, it may not in the future, but music was always a very appealing thing. I really felt like I was able to express myself and use all the different parts of my personality—the musical part, the business-minded part—but still do something that was for me and about me, as opposed to something that I think I was supposed to do." He stepped into a toss, kicking up his right heel on the follow-through.

"But you hardly seem like a 'Coal Miner's Daughter'."

"Yeah, I had a fortunate upbringing. My dad worked internationally for Pepsi so we moved around a lot with his job." The ball spun backwards out of my hand. "Then when I was in about the seventh grade, he took his last transfer, to Memphis. I went through school there and then off to college."

"Where to?"

"Stanford. I finished up there in '90." He kneaded the fingers of his glove with his other hand. "After college I went overseas for a year and had a cushy job teaching English in France. Also, I landed a gig in a cafe playing songs six nights a week, so that's sort of where the music started to roll." He closed his mitt around the ball. "By the time the year was over, I had decided to really give music a full-time whirl. So after getting back, I returned to Cali-fornia and spent the next two years pursuing it."

"What did that involve?"

"Well initially, when I returned to California, I wanted to open a small recording studio with a friend but that sort of fell through—he decided to go to law school and do something responsible. But I basically got to the Bay Area and realized that, especially in the Menlo Park–Palo Alto area, there weren't a lot of solo acoustic guitar players. And as a result, it was really easy to find a lot of work. I was playing bars, coffeehouses; I actually played for a while—although it's not a point of pride—at the Hyatt happy hour. It paid well, but in terms of artistic integrity," he laughed, "I didn't reach any sort of pinnacle." The ball moved between us with no great effort on either part. Cliff had been a ballplayer—his motions looked almost lazy but he produced toss after accurate toss.

"So did you live the life of the starving artist?"

"No, I was actually pulling in the equivalent of about twenty-five grand a year just playing bars, which works out to a couple hours a night probably five or six nights a week. It was something I really enjoyed. I got to take care of all sides of the business and learn a lot, which is important because the more you look at the music industry and the people who are really doing well now, they're very savvy." He worked the strings in his fingers. "I mean, the days of the Elvis Presleys of the world who just had this amazing gift and let everybody else take care of everything are basically over. The success stories today really know what they're doing. So working on my own out in California was a great chance for me to learn about all that stuff." He resolved the thought and put the ball in flight.

"And as I was there for a while, I realized playing cover songs was nice but I really wanted to do more of my own material, which led to a gig I had at a great coffeehouse where I played every Thursday and Saturday for about a year. That was where I really started playing my own stuff and writing more. Things went well there but by the end of the two years, I decided I wasn't—in terms of breaking into the industry—really getting anywhere. . . .

"I found myself pretty lacking in my knowledge of what goes on between the guy who's playing songs in a bar and the guy who's touring and playing stadiums. I wanted to sort of look in between there to see what makes all of that stuff possible. Not that I necessarily want to play stadiums—I mean, you wouldn't have to twist my arm, I guess—but I just wanted to get deeper into the industry." Rotating his shoulder, Cliff delivered the ball.

"So I came to Nashville, and it really is remarkable. I mean, you don't have to be here a week before you start meeting people and begin to realize the enormity of the musician and songwriter population. It's alternately completely inspiring and utterly depressing, but I wouldn't trade it because I think it gives you a much more realistic view of what you're up against."

I placed my fingers across the strings. "And what do you think of Nashville, having been here for a while?"

"'This is a city full of small-town heroes,'" he answered. "That's the best expression I ever heard and it pretty much covers it, as far as I'm concerned." The sun was climbing into mid-morning and heating up the sweet, humid air as the ball slapped from glove to glove.

"So I'd guess you're marketing yourself mainly as a songwriter?"

"Probably more as a recording artist but recording my own material. Songwriting's a big part of it, but it's also somewhat of a back door into the industry. For example, record companies like—from what I've learned in my short time here—a sure thing. And if they know that your songs are getting recorded by other people and doing well, that's one more reason for them to consider you for a deal."

"Are you supporting yourself by playing gigs?"

"No, Nashville doesn't work that way—I learned that in about three seconds."

"How's that?"

"Well, when you come to a town where everybody and his brother can do as good if not a better job at playing solo guitar in a bar than you, it becomes apparent you need something on the side. And I got lucky." He threw. "When I was back in Memphis, I had picked up a copy of a magazine called *Performing Songwriter*, looked at the cover, and noticed it was the first issue. Well, I looked into it and found out the editor was from Nashville, so when I got here I met up with her and told her I'd sweep her floor. You know, I just needed some sort of work. Well, she eventually needed help and now I'm the assistant editor to the magazine. Sort of like one of those grandfather stories, you know—'and then I bought the business.' So I've got a job where I'm basically working out of my home and also, through the magazine's subject matter, meeting a lot of people in the industry."

"Have you made many contacts?" The ball smacked into my glove.

"Oh, yeah. As a matter of fact, without even trying, you're bound to meet significant people in the industry, which is great, but you have to be up to the task in terms of your material." He gloved my toss. "In other words, you can know the head of CBS Records but that isn't going to get you a record deal if your material isn't up to par. So I'm in the right town and I'm learning a lot, but as of now I'm not ready to start pushing my end of things yet." With a fluid step forward, he tossed.

"When you do get to pushing your end of things, what do you hope to contribute?" The ball slapped a few times against leather.

"Well, I think more than anything, my music is about trying to reach people." He held the ball. "I think a lot of songwriters'll tell you the same thing: You want to be able to identify with what you write. But there's also the danger, which is something I'm learning, of being too preachy. So you sort of have to walk the line—you write from here, you know." He touched his glove to his chest. "You write from the heart, but I'm learning that there's considerably more craft in it all than you may think." He put the ball in motion. "You can have all the emotion in the world in your songs, but if you don't know how to put the feelings in a palatable way, you tend to lose people."

"Are you playing any clubs right now?"

"I'm playing—as opposed to the twenty-five times a month that I used to play in California—probably three to four times a month now."

"Are the gigs better?" Slap. Into my glove.

"They're better artistically because I'm playing all my own material but I'd like to be playing more often—that's something that comes about as you begin to tour. I mean, I learned from talking to people and just observing that if you come to Nashville and think you're going to kick ass when you come in the door, you're going to be very disappointed"—he froze his hands—"really fast." The ball zipped off his fingers. "Then again, if you come knowing there are a lot of great people here who can teach you a lot of things, then I don't think you can ever be disappointed. If you're open to it, there's a lot here to learn." He gloved my toss.

"What's songwriting about?"

Without pause, he spoke. "It's about taking what's bubbling around inside you and turning it into something that is beautiful and that people can relate to. Something shiny and polished and interesting—'interesting' is the key word and I hate it 'cause it's so bland but if it doesn't keep your interest, you know . . . " His words trailed off as he laid his fingers on the ball. "You've basically got three to four minutes to take someone and shake them up a little bit, and if your stuff isn't really sharp then it's not going to work."

The ball lit out from his hand and connected with a slap in my glove, returning the conversation to me. "So standing up here, looking at all the different neighborhoods of Nashville and knowing you want your music to reach out to them, what do you think the world's about?"

"You know—and this is probably going to sound a bit self-absorbed—but the world's about me. And the way I mean that is not in a self-centered way but rather that what I'm experiencing, other people are experiencing." The ball rolled from his fingers. "Granted, you know, I hap-pen to fall on the more fortunate side—I wouldn't deny that nor say that my experiences are going to be everyone's experiences—but in a lot of cases, in terms of emotion, they are.

"The world to me—or at least the way I'm writing currently—I write from what I've ex-perienced and hope that that's also an experience that's shared by a lot of people." My toss re-turned to the middle of his chest. "I think you can only be convincing when you write from what you know," he said and again touched his heart with the empty glove. "So I think in terms of how I see the world, I write music from inside—music that is true to me—and hope that other people respond." He nodded approval of his answer as the ball slapped a final time, filling his mitt.

_____

Around noon that day, I sat down to lunch elbow to elbow with members from every level of Nashville's working classes at Hap Towne's. Over a lunch of meat and two vegetables, a sta-ple in southern dining, I struggled to hear the music filtering in over the clank of forks and the voices filling the room.

"Who is this?" I asked the waitress as she filled up my sweet tea.

"Who's who?" she asked, raising an eyebrow at my question.

"Never mind," I responded with a smile.

J O H N   L A C H S   UNIVERSITY PROFESSOR – *Nashville, Tennessee*

After I spent a night in downtown Nashville taking in the banjo twang at the Bluegrass Inn, morning hit early. On the recommendation of some friends, I had scheduled to hook up with a philosophy professor over at Vanderbilt University and throw the ball. After putting a fresh tape into my recorder, I tossed it into the All Star bag and headed toward the campus.

Just as the cracked and vacant sidewalks of Inglewood, California, had heightened my anticipation of talking with Pookie and K-Nut, the spotless walkways and immaculate expanses of grass on the grounds at Vanderbilt left my senses piqued. It was as if all the care given to the opulent buildings and majestic trees on campus would by itself elevate the level of thought on the grounds. I pushed open a glass door and jogged up a set of polished steps in Furman Hall.

The man was pure energy. Standing about five foot six and wearing a grin, he shook my hand and gladly took me up on having a chat. Only I was foolish enough to think that we'd be playing a lot of catch.

As we walked outside to an empty patch of grass, he exclaimed at the beauty of the morning. His voice had the slightest tinge of an accent, just enough that I could occasionally tell that he was from somewhere overseas.

"Professor John Lachs," I said as I stepped backwards until about twenty feet separated us.

"Yup." He issued the response rocking from heels to toes and swinging his gloved hand at his side.

"Do you have a middle name?"

"No, I didn't have much say in the matter," he said and smiled. He stood under the flickering shade of a thick-trunked tree, and his clean-shaven head shined when the light fell upon it. The leaves created dancing shadows on the grass under our feet, and his eyes, particularly when the sunlight struck them, irradiated light blue.

As I fingered my grip on the strings, he began swinging both hands, nearly touching them in front of his waist before passing them by his hips. Tenseness crept into his frame as I stepped forward to throw the ball; his eyes widened as it took flight. Both hands were abuzz with motion as the sphere closed on him. It was slow motion: The ball, a gloved hand, and a bare hand collided like a traffic accident in front of his sternum. There was something like a muffled pop and his bare hand emerged victorious, stuffing the ball deep into the webbing as he grinned. I wouldn't see it again for five minutes.

"Tell me about your years growing up."

Separating his hands, he used the glove, its webbing rounded by the ball, to direct the flow of words. "I was born in July 1934 and grew up in Budapest, Hungary, during the years just before the Second World War. In my formative years, I went through it. They weren't exactly what you'd describe as exciting times—more times to basically just try to survive. Hungary is a small country, as you know, and was dragged into the war in a way that many people in the country didn't want." He lifted his bare hand, drawing my attention to the words that followed. "The war—particularly to the intelligentsia in the country—didn't seem to be one that Hungary could do well at, yet there wasn't much choice in the matter." The ball stayed in the mitt, in motion only as a pointer to a blackboard that was nowhere to be seen.

"So I grew up under those circumstances—was raised an incredible Hungarian nationalist," he said with a chuckle. "Everybody in the schools was. You know, it was the kind of attitude where to be a Hungarian was the height of creation, the very best thing that any human could be. See, all great inventions were by Hungarians, all great composers were Hungarians, the Hungarian language was by far the best language there was, that God clearly spoke Hungarian—that was the attitude. It was kind of a difficult thing to realize that those things may not be true." Chuckling again, he held his glove up to emphasize the point.

"My father was a businessman—he ran a small lumber operation—and my mother was, as were many women in those days, a housewife. As I was growing up, everyone around me who was of age was being drafted and going off to war, including my father, and then the next thing you know, everything was collapsing as the Germans were being beaten and the Russians were overrunning Hungary." His hands found a moment's rest at his sides, then joined in motion as the story continued. "They—the Russians—spent six weeks outside of Budapest shooting up the city, which we spent in the cellars—all of the big houses had cellars. And then there was the Russian takeover, which basically boiled down to the Russians coming in, robbing everybody, and raping all the women." He shook his head, his eyes closed. "And so that's kind of the history. I was about ten or eleven through all of that." The story reached a break and John pulled the ball from his mitt. After turning it over a time or two with his fingers, he placed it back in the pocket and brought the glove to rest on his hip while his free hand rose to take over the next segment.

"After that, things seemed like they were stabilizing—until the Communist takeover around 1948. They had an organization called the Economic Police—a Communist Party creation—the function of which was essentially to shake down businessmen, take away their enterprises, nationalize them, and then accuse the owners of secreting away money in Switzerland or wherever. And if you denied it, they'd beat you until you died, essentially. So my father, who was basically an independent businessman, having seen several people treated that way, picked up and left. He went to Austria, and my mother and I followed him."

On a walkway behind him, three girls toting leather backpacks made their way from one cluster of university buildings to another. As they crossed behind John, his free hand opened, palm upward, and regained my attention.

"We spent a few years there—I was around fifteen years old or so at the time—but we basically wanted to leave Europe and start a new life at a time in which very few countries welcomed refugees. One of them was Canada and they had a Hungarian quota so we eventually landed there, in Montreal, where I enrolled in high school. I completed one year of high school and then went on to McGill University, where I got both a B.A. and a master's in philosophy and then went on to get my Ph.D. at Yale. After that, I looked for employment and for warmer weather." The three girls had walked out of view.

"How did you manage to land at Yale?"

"Well, I learned English relatively fast, or at least fast enough to fool people. And Nick, I had the sense—early on—that I'd found a field that I was really interested in and that I wanted to devote my life to. I remember asking a professor, when I was a senior. I said, 'Geez, I really like this philosophy stuff, but how do I make a living with it?' and he said, 'Well, you teach,' and I said, 'Oh, okay.' And I proceeded to get myself ready to do that." Shifting his weight from one foot to the other, he continued.

"I spent two years at Yale—'57 to '59—before running out of money. Or better said, I ran out of agencies that were willing to pay for me to go to school. So I had to get a job in '59 teaching at William and Mary and then finished the dissertation two years later. After receiving my Ph.D., I stayed on at William and Mary until September 1967, when I came here, and I've been here ever since." His free hand reached into the glove and extracted the ball.

"Did you marry?" I raised my glove, hoping for the ball. I don't think he noticed.

"Yeah, in '67, just before I came down here. My wife is a Greek and Latin specialist—got her master's from University of Michigan. We met, strangely enough, in Europe. I was in Vienna at the time on my way to a philosophy conference in Yugoslavia; she had just finished her master's and was on her way to Rome and Athens. We happened to go to the English-speaking theater; she sat in the front row and I sat in the second. It was a funny play—*The*

Owl and the Pussycat—I don't know if you know it." He paused long enough for me to shake my head. "It was very funny. Anyway, we started talking and the rest is history, as they say." He let out a warm laugh and smiled, still holding onto the ball. "I also have a son and a daughter, since you seem to be in the middle of getting the facts. My daughter is a second-year law student and my son is waiting to go to law school himself."

"How about throwing that thing?" I asked, bringing his hand to a pause.

"Oh, sure," he answered quickly. "Here you go." With that, he stepped forward and swept his arm at an angle just above horizontal. The ball went wide left and I stabbed my glove in its direction. It came to a halt in my mitt and I righted myself, several feet from where I'd begun. I looked up and he was grinning, arms swinging at his sides. I decided to hold off the return toss.

"What was your draw to philosophy?"

"Well, I suppose I was influenced to some degree by the wartime years, and I've always been interested in what I call the big questions. The real issues, the big issues: The meaning of life. Is there a God? How do you relate to God? What's happiness all about? Those sorts of questions. So when I went to college, I basically sought out the people who dealt with questions like that."

I cut in. "But when you say 'philosophy,' the first thing that comes to my mind is a deep thinker sitting in a quiet room wondering about trees falling in forests and the noises they make. Does that ring true?"

"Well, it does and it doesn't. The first thing I'd say is that you've got to be sure that not only do you get philosophy out into the world but that you get the world into the philosophy class. I think one of the saddest things that happens in the academic world is the kind of abstractness that occurs. I mean by 'abstractness' the way in which so many of us in the academic world—and so many of us who are not in the academic world—separate the intellect from the rest of what we do. If you do that, the intellect is going to stay dry and your life, for the most part, will stay unintelligent. And that's very sad.

"So I would say what philosophy has to offer is ways in which people can think—methods in which people can think—about those issues that are of relevance to all of us. All of us worry about human relations, all of us worry about what life all amounts to, all of us have concerns about what there is on the 'other side,' if anything." His glove rolled over at the mention of each topic. "Philosophy deals with those issues." Pointing his glove conclusively, he added, "And if you deal with them effectively you won't necessarily get answers, but you'll be able to show people—and yourself—how to think about these issues more constructively, more creatively, more critically, and more satisfactorily."

As he finished, I placed the ball in my throwing hand. His arms quieted and his eyes became riveted as I moved my hand from behind my ear and threw. As it closed on him, his hands somehow tamed the ball into the leather pocket. "I'm not very good at this," he said with a grin. "It interrupts my thoughts, more than anything." Removing the ball from his glove, he placed it in his palm. I took his subtle invitation toward words and away from catch.

"So as far as being a professor at a university, are you optimistic about philosophical 'progress' fitting into the world?"

"Well, in looking at progress, I think it is very unfortunate that we have this contrast between technology—which is usually restricted to high tech—on the one hand, and on the other hand, the rest of life. Because I view just about everything we do as involving a technology." His glove turned over, setting up the explanation. "For instance, right now you and I have not just the technology of your tape recorder, but the technology of communicating. I'm trying to convey ideas to you, I'm using words to do that. But words function as tools, designed to bring certain ideas to the fore in your mind. And your questions are technological means—low ones, to be sure—to bring out certain responses."

His glove punched in my direction. "Now, if you think about it that way, you realize that it makes very little difference whether you use the human voice, a clarinet, an orchestra, a synthesizer, or a record player—it doesn't make any difference which of those you use—to sing. Any of them will work, but all of them are technologies. Now, in that same sense, philosophy is a technology. It is a technology because ideas are themselves tools to bring about certain results. So if I can think the right kind of ideas—if I have the right angle—I can deal with the human situation better. If I don't have the right angle and don't use the right ideas, I muck up." He rose to his toes for an instant.

"For example, here's a technology, perhaps the most important of all for human beings: how to try things and how to decide when you've tried enough and when to move on to the next thing. You experiment and then you pull back. That's exactly how we decide concerning our purposes." He raised his hands and continued, "You hatch some idea. I don't know where in the hell it comes from—it just comes, like your whiskers.

"In fact, that's an example: You've got your whiskers." Picking up speed, his words were kinetic. "So you wake up with them in the morning; now what are going to do? You look at them in the mirror maybe, or you see this pretty girl and see if she notices if you've got whiskers and comes over when you whistle. You try it. If it doesn't work, you pull back and you try something else." He brought both hands together below his chin, the ball resting in his first three fingers.

"That's a technology—the technology of individual judgment, of trial and error, of intelligently choosing your purposes. So in that sense, I think philosophy enables you to focus on the most important technology of all, namely focusing on your purposes, understanding what your purposes are, and knowing how to get them and when to abandon them." He finished the sentence and without warning sent his shoulder into rotation, the ball zipping from his sidearm delivery. His fingers whispered as they slid off the seams. Reaching—not as far this time—to the left, I brought the ball to rest in my pocket with a slap.

"What do you think of the American dream?"

"It's there. Only people without energy don't see it. Imagine where else you could do what you're doing. No other place in the world. There's no other place in the world that rewards initiative the way this country does. It doesn't mean that the American dream is something that's gonna come to you and they're gonna deliver to your door UPS and say, you know, 'You're in this country, here it is, here's your dream.' It doesn't work that way. You've got to work your ass off for it. But it's possible. Other places in the world, you can work your ass off and it's not possible. It just doesn't happen." Unsolicited, he raised his glove, inviting a throw. I stepped gently onto the grass and sent the ball into the air that separated us. The MacGregor on his hand rose in one motion and stopped as the ball sounded in the leather with a crisp pop. "Hey-hey," he said and smiled.

"What do you think of the book idea?"

"I think it's a great idea," he said, using the glove again to direct his thoughts. "There's so much alienation in our country because the institutions in which we live—while they are wonderful for us—are so momentously huge, so gigantic, that the individual disappears in them. And we're all hungry for that one-on-one which is not even there as it should be in education and which is part of the reason why, I think, you're getting people to talk with you. Because they, too, face an impersonal world in which you really don't get through to anybody. Now, if you play catch with somebody and maybe talk about something that really matters, that's really important. Important and rare. That's what we need." He brought his hands together, transferring the ball from glove to bare hand.

"What do you hope to contribute to the world?"

"Well, on a personal level, I want to resist the question because one can overemphasize this idea of 'what do you want to be remembered for' and 'isn't it wonderful.' Actually, if you're really dead"—the empty glove rolled over—"I mean, if there's no afterlife, it doesn't make the least bit of difference to *you*. The really important thing is not what will people remember you for, but what contribution have you made to their lives—such that they may not even remember that you made it. That's what's really important." He pointed the ball toward me. "Now *there*, that speaks to me because I really hope that I'm making a contribution to the lives of many people—my students. I don't care a hoot in hell whether they remember me, so long as they carry something away that will benefit them. That's really what I want to do."

"And if a student asked you the meaning of life, what would you tell them?" He turned his head askew and squinted, fingering the ball. His hand cocked to throw as he loaded up a thought.

"Well," he said as his hand swept around parallel to his waist and he threw, "there are many meanings of life." The ball slapped into my webbing. "I think the meaning of life is the totality of life, so that now it is the catch and this conversation, but an hour from now it will be something else. So the meaning of life?" Sunlight spilled in and brought his eyes to life. "Why not focus on every one of those things that we do, and perform them with vigor."

A couple of hours later, after interviewing two students in summer school and a groundskeeper who operated a gas-powered leaf blower, I left the campus. As I walked down the sidewalk of West End Avenue, what had started as a faint drizzle soon turned into a raging downpour and I ducked into the Ham 'N Goodys restaurant to dry off. I ended up staying there for a long while, fighting off the chill of the air conditioning with hot tea and iced lemon cookies. As I reviewed the tape and wrote down notes, I had time to reflect on Professor Lachs' words.

Over forty-five minutes, they had taken me from Nashville to wartime Hungary to Canada and back. They had addressed technologies, the role of universities, and the outlook for humanity. They had imparted education, inspiration, and humor. And he had thrown the ball but three times.

T O M   B E A N   Candidate for Sheriff – *Hot Rock, Tennessee*

The following morning, after hanging around a car wash off Granny White Pike and tossing the ball with an older couple, I left Nashville headed south. Picking up a milkshake for lunch as I passed through Eagleville, I continued down Tennessee Highway 41, passing through towns like Rover, Unionville, and Elbethel at about 25 mph. In Shelbyville, I stopped for gas and to replenish the ice supply in my cooler. Turning right in the middle of town, I got on Tennessee 231 headed dead south and rolled down the windows. The humid air charged through the car as I began to sweat my silhouette into the driver's seat.

The rolling hills and tiny towns that dotted the route south were similar to those of Kentucky but more overgrown and somehow not quite as striking. Nothing much caught my eye as I piled up the rural miles until I emerged from a series of tight curves about ten miles outside of Shelbyville. There, pounded into a lawn, was a bright white sign with black letters that read: ELECT TOM BEAN. SHERIFF. At the edge of the lawn stood a cluster of small white houses. Gearing down and hitting the blinker, I pulled up in front of a home with a few folks sitting out on the porch.

I approached the first, an older gentleman wearing faded blue coveralls and an equally weathered red baseball cap. With the light striking his glasses, I couldn't see his eyes. As he and the other two seniors on the porch studied me head to toe, I asked if any of them were Tom Bean.

"Noooo . . . " the fellow drawled, "he's out back." After making sure that the dog—who looked to be lurking for a recreational attack—was chained up, I ventured behind the house. There, crossing the lawn, I encountered a gentleman whose picture I would expect to see if I looked in a dictionary under "Candidate for Sheriff in Rural Tennessee." He had thick, leathery hands and a sternly set jaw. Short-cropped hair offset his bright eyes, their lids a bit sleepy as he studied me.

I asked him if he wanted to play catch and he responded, "You bet," as though it were something that happened on a regular basis along Highway 231. After I handed him the MacGregor, we split a good forty feet apart on the expanse of grass between two of the white homes and I raised the ball to throw. In a neighboring backyard, a lawn mower whined as it made neat swaths in the grass.

"Tell me about yourself." I stepped forward and arced the ball his way.

"Well, I's born 1941, March 25th. Took place over in Petersburg—I's born at home. Grew up, graduated from high school in the county, then went to the military for three years." The ball nestled in his weathered hand. "Got out of the military in 1962, went to work as a policeman in Huntsville, Alabama. Stayed there for eleven years. Left down there, came up here, and ran for sheriff in 1976. Got beat. Ran again in '78 and was elected—and stayed sheriff for twelve years." The ball remained cradled on his fingers. "Ran in 1990. Got beat. And I'm running again this year."

Tom Bean spoke in simple sentences, his words honeyed with a soft drawl. Instead of saying "Nashville" tight-lipped, as if every enunciation were of equal importance, his mouth relaxed to produce "Naishvull"—a slower, smoother version. Those of the Tennessee old guard speak with a lulling softness and brevity about the state of affairs.

"You're 53 now?"

"Yes," he answered, the word flowing like milk. His hand raised the ball in a similar smoothness and, in one motion, lifted it into flight just past his brow. It arced gently against the backdrop of lush trees and into my waiting mitt. Pop. The humid breeze ceased for a moment and the thick, sweet air sagged between us. The lawn mower crescendoed momentarily as I raised the ball to toss.

"Tell me about being the sheriff in—is it Belleville?"

"It was in Fayetteville, th' seat of Lincoln County. We're about ten–twelve miles outside of it, here—this is Belleville."

"How was being sheriff?" He fingered the ball from his glove and bent both knees as he softly rocked the ball into flight.

"Well, you know, it's a rural area here and while I's in Huntsville—a bigger city—I got a good education and got a lot of good experience in law enforcement. So with that experience behind me, I'd say it was good."

"What have you done since losing in '90?"

"I've been an investigator for the public defender's office in Fayetteville. See, I live on the other side of the county, but we cover three counties other than Lincoln. We cover Bedford County, which is Shelbyville; Marshall County, which is Lewisburg; and Moore County, which is Lynchburg." He listed off the county seats as the ball arced from his hand. "And what we do is when a person commits a crime, if they can't afford an attorney, then our office—the public defender's office—is appointed to represent them."

"So you don't live here in Belleville?"

"No, I's just here visiting. I live in a little place they call Hot Rock. It's a little village on the other side of the county, not even as large as Belleville here." His mitt closed around the ball.

"What do you think of living in rural Tennessee?"

"Well, Tennessee—course I's raised here." He pulled the ball out and let it hang again at his side. "I lived in Huntsville, which is a large city, for about fifteen years. But as far as being here in Belleville, people here still look at things probably like they did in bigger cities twenty years ago. It's more of a slow pace, people are still considerate of their neighbors and try to help each other out, and it's just a good ole country lifestyle—old-time lifestyle." He brought the ball from rest and arced it toward the canopy of leaves. "Like it used to be."

"Did you raise a family?"

"I've got a son that's twenty-five years old, and I have a wife." The words were smooth as butter.

"What does your wife do?"

"Oh, she stays at home."

"And your son?"

"He works in Fayetteville in a garment factory as a mechanic on the machines." He laid the mitt on his right hip. "He went to the public schools here."

"So you were in the military for three years, then law enforcement for twenty-six?"

"Yessir."

"What do you think of America these days, coming from that perspective?"

As I finished the question, he paused in thought. After a moment, he let the mitt fall from his hip, retrieving the ball from its webbing and rocking his knees into a toss. "I think we've lost a lot of discipline. You know, you lose discipline in school where we discipline our children, discipline at home where we discipline our children, and in turn you lose self-discipline, which, you know, used to be there." He reached out his hand to make a catch. "When I went into the military, it still had a lot of discipline and now, to me, it doesn't.

"You see, when I was a police officer in Huntsville, I was a sergeant. And when you selected people for your squad—when I first went down there—you looked for people with military experience. When I left, it didn't make any difference because the veterans weren't as disciplined as when I started out."

"And that's a problem?" The ball descended from its apex with a slap in my mitt.

"Sure," he said with a slow drawl. "Sure. You know, it has to do with the order of everything—the drug problems and whatnot—it has to do with all that."

"What would you create in your life to help that out?"

"I would create more pride in people, to where in communities they'd stand together. See, when I was raised up around here—and most people my age or older—you were taught that as long as you thought you were right and you stood up for what was right, you know, everything'd be taken care of." He shook the ball in his thick fingers. "And we've got to get back to that.

"If we don't want drugs in our schools and on our streets, we as a community have to stand up and let the drug dealers know that they're not welcome there. If we want prayers back in our schools, we're gonna have to stand up at a football game or whatnot and say 'em. And if they say that we can't have a prayer to open our football game, why not stand up and say, 'Yeah, we're gonna have a prayer—and to stop us you're going to have to walk over us.'" He raised the ball again to carry the point. "And I guarantee you, the majority of people want it that way. It's the minority of the people that're controlling these things, you know, through the pressure on the Supreme Court and so on and so forth." Loosely rocking at the knees, Tom sent the ball into the air.

"And if the majority had their wish, how would the world look different than it does now?" The sphere slapped in my webbing and I held it there, allowing his smoothly drawled words to proceed.

"It would be more like it was, say, at the end of World War II and on up through the '50s. To me, you had more of a sense of community and of closeness than you do now, and that's what we've got to get back to. I mean, people've just gotta have a little common horse sense; that's all it boils down to." The breeze rustled anew through the trees, shaking the overhead canopy.

I fingered a grip across the strings and stepped forward onto the soft grass, rotating my shoulder and flinging the ball. "So what should people do to change things?"

"Well, it depends on what age. If I'm givin' advice to a young person, I'd tell 'em you gotta have education and good communication with people. And then, I'd tell the ones that are my age, hey, we have a few years left and let's get off the stick and make it a better world, because we have screwed it up." Stepping, he arced the ball. "The generations before us left us in pretty good shape. Then we set back and discussed political things on the front porch or around the store or whatever and haven't done anything. We set back and allowed—*allowed* the things that are going on today to happen. Things like drugs. Things like the discipline problems with our children. Things like prayer in schools and public places. You know, our country is the most blessed country by God that's ever been. I mean, you look at it and look at history and what other country do you have like we've got? God has given us democracy, where a man can be free, and what're we doin' with it? We're spittin' right back in His face." He shook his head slowly and stepped into the next throw.

"You know, it's not a Godlike world where you're afraid to walk down the streets at any hour of the day or night, where you're not secure in your home. And people my age have allowed that to go on by settin' back and lettin' what I like to call educated fools make all the decisions, you know, the ones that spent their whole lives in schools and colleges and then they get a big degree and they're hired to advise on education or what have you." His mitt slapped closed around the sphere.

"'Fact, my idea of why the educational system is in such shape in this country is the people that're tellin' us what to do with education have never lived out here in the real world. They started school when they's six years old and went all the way through college with their different degrees and graduate work and all that, and then they go into all these jobs with education, but they've never lived in the real world to know what it's like and to know what a person needs to survive. You know, what you actually need to get through this world is not written down in books."

"What is it that you need to get through this world?" The ball descended from its arc into my glove.

"What we're doing right here—talking and understanding people and being considerate of other people. That's what it takes to make it. I can go out here anywhere and if I can get along with people, I can get a job. I mean, if you can get along and talk with people, and have true concern for people, you know, when you leave here, if you go down the highway and find somebody with a flat tire or out of gas and you stop and help 'em and you're concerned, that's becoming something unusual now." The air sagged again as the breeze fell off.

"So what do you think it's all about?"

"Life?" he asked slowly, drawing out the word.

"Yeah, life." The ball slapped into his glove.

"I think we're all put here for a purpose. And I think what'll be a successful life is how you have treated your fellow man and what you have done for your fellow man. And to make it a better place for everyone." He separated the ball from his mitt. "What this is all about—and life's not worth livin', to me, if you don't realize—is that we're all livin' for the next generation." He motioned with the ball near his cheek and spoke. "What my life's been all about is to make it better for people like you, you and my son. And what I hope y'all's lives'll be about to make it better for your children. So in the end, what else is there, if it's not to carry on?" He raised his shoulders while asking the question, then relaxed them and let the ball fly.

I gloved it and looked him in the eyes. "And how do you plan to carry on?" I sent the ball through the air.

"Well, you know, I got a lot of good experience in law enforcement so there's a lot I feel I can do to upgrade law enforcement in this county as sheriff." Tom gripped the ball in his leathery fingers. "If I'm elected."

"How's the campaign going?"

"Oh, pretty good—'lections are August 4th; we been in the campaign about two months now." I fingered a final toss and as it popped into his webbing, he continued, "Right now I'm ahead—I been ahead the last coupla months—and I feel like I'll win. So I guess I'm the front-runner right now. Least that's what people tell me." He separated the ball from his mitt.

"Best of luck with the election," I said as he traversed the distance between us.

"Appreciate it," he answered. He reached out his hand to grasp mine and shook it firmly, the thickness of his palm and fingers dwarfing my own. "And if you're ever through here," he added, his drawl calm and sincere, "stop on by."

───────────────────

Half an hour later, I entered Alabama. Passing through Huntsville, I stopped at a hardware store and threw the ball with the owner. I mentioned Tom Bean and he said he thought he may have heard the name once. As I walked back to the car, I passed a bike shop and thought about the cyclist back in Washington, wondering if he might pass this way on his ride to Atlanta.

I tossed the gloves into the backseat and continued south along Highway 231, which turned into Highway 79 somewhere south of Blountsville. The road was flatter than I thought it would be and the landscape thick with trees. There was a radio program on about crickets and I listened to it intently, driving through the sprawl of Birmingham in a distracted frame of mind.

South of the city, as the radio segment drew to a close, I realized it was much later than I thought and pulled into Jim & Nick's, a barbecue house, for dinner. After a brisket sandwich and a few mugs of sweet tea, I continued south to Pelham, where I staked out a patch of grass to set up my tent. As darkness crept into the sky, the thick forests around me came alive with the undulating chorus of crickets.

I sat on a camp stool as darkness rose in the east and thought about Tom Bean, how his firm, calm words matched the life he lived. It was exactly as the man had said at the car wash that morning: "Give a New Yorker a minute and he'll tell you all the news in the world," the man said with a nod, "but give a southerner an hour and he'll slow you down."

By the time I went to sleep, the crickets were so loud I couldn't hear myself breathe.

KATIE HUNG Law Student – *Columbus, Georgia*

By 8:30 AM, I had folded up my tent, packed it into the car, and pulled back onto I-65 headed south. At Caldera, I got off the interstate and stayed on two-lane roads through Talladega National Forest toward Selma. The landscape shined bright green with acres of leafy kudzu growing up tree trunks and telephone poles as far as I could see.

South of Selma, I pulled off Highway 80 at a palm-reading establishment. With eyes that wandered about the room, Sister Jackson held my hand in hers and, in a light Romanian accent, uttered the following words: "You will live a long life."

I asked her if she wanted to play catch and she just stared at the wall behind me, shaking her head as though my words were interrupting the flow of valuable information. "Turn east," she added, her head nodding from side to side, "as soon as possible." Two miles down the road, I headed toward Montgomery.

South of White Hall, I played catch with some men at Carne's Service Station before sitting in the shade of the garage and downing a couple of sixteen-cent frozen Jolly Pops, orange and purple. After passing through Montgomery, I stacked up miles under the hanging sun and thick air on Interstate 85.

Past Tuskegee, I got back onto State Highway 80 and, as the afternoon waned, stopped in front of an old home near Society Hill. Constructed of wood, the weathered structure stood on squat brick stilts, keeping watch over the cotton fields across the road. On the porch, I spoke with a young mother and her two young boys, one of whom scurried around astride various fallen branches, frothing at the lips while making his "motor" noise. Their uncle, who sat on the porch with us, had a worn stub of cigar that danced in the corner of his mouth as he detailed his truck-driving career. I bid a good-bye after tossing the ball for a while with the mother and pressed on another half hour into Columbus, where I stayed the night with the parents of an old school friend.

With a kindness that was almost overwhelming, they sat me down at their dining room table and fed me a feast of southern proportions: chicken pie, squash casserole, "buttuh" beans, and fresh-baked rolls, with sweet tea and fudge pie for dessert. After the meal, we piled into their car and toured around Columbus, chatting up a storm about everything while glancing out the window at downtown's Mill Row and the row of strip joints that line Victory Boulevard leading to Fort Benning. My day in the South came to a close with the three of us seated on the hood of the car, staring at the Army jump towers in silence as the sun retired over the military base.

The following morning, I stood in their backyard, not more than fifteen feet from a young woman whose dark hair framed a round, smiling face. The folks I stayed with had her come over first thing in the morning. "I haven't had a glove in my hand since, probably—when we had to play softball in school," she said with a tumbling laugh, "so let me toss underhand, to begin with." The ball lobbed between us several times and she began to get the hang of it. "There we go."

"So it's Katie Hong?"

"Hung, as in past tense of 'hang'."

"Tell me about the life and times of Katie."

"Well, let's see, I was born in Plymouth, Massachusetts—" A burst of laughter interrupted her words as she tried to catch the ball. "I don't know if I like to catch in front of my face. I fell on my face when I was really little so I'm paranoid about face things." Her fingers returned to the strings and she tossed. "But I'll try." The ball resumed its soft lobs between us.

"So, let's see, I lived in Plymouth and the Massachusetts area, then moved to Charleston. My dad was in the Navy so we lived in Charleston for a couple of years, and my brother was born there. Then, in 1976—right before I turned six—we moved to Columbus. So I've been here most of my life, and basically I consider Columbus my home." Katie had a bright and engaging voice, some of her words carrying a southern tinge while others had none at all.

"What about your parents?"

"My parents have sort of an interesting story. My dad was born in Hong Kong and grew up in China. Actually, he escaped China and returned to Hong Kong, where his mom was, then took off to the States. He came directly to the Northeast, met my mom, got married, and then moved down here."

"What do they do?" I backed up two steps and threw.

"My dad's a pathologist and my mom was a nurse, then went back to school and got a master's in counseling—eating disorders is her big thing. She works part-time now."

"So your dad's experience was the immigrant success story?"

"Completely. My dad lived the American dream. I mean, he came here with two hundred dollars in '66 and worked his tail off to make it—and obviously I'm grateful for that. But for me personally, it doesn't seem like being Chinese has been a big struggle. I mean granted, at certain times I do identify with exploitation of the Chinese, when I see it in films and such. But only on rare occasions—only on grad school applications—do I describe myself as an Asian-American woman." She smiled and put the ball in flight, adding thoughtfully, "I mean, really, in the big scheme of things, as the daughter of an immigrant or not, I've had a damn good life for the past twenty-four years. I have wanted, basically, for nothing."

"How was growing up in Columbus?"

"Well, if you look at what you'd call society, I'm first generation here so I don't really fit into that. I wasn't a debutante, I didn't do a lot of the things that other girls did. I'm still friends with all those people, it's just something I didn't do."

"Did that bother you?" The ball lifted into the air.

"I'm okay with it, because I know it put a lot of pressure on the girls sometimes, just because you always have to know who so-and-so is and you always have to chat and be nice, you know? You still have to be sugary sweet to the people you hate, whereas it's not that offensive for me." She rolled out laughter. "But it was okay. I mean, during deb season with all the parties, I thought it'd be fun if I got to buy a white dress, too, but—you know—most of the girls weren't that wild about it anyway. I mean, I got invited to all the things my friends did, I just didn't go through it myself."

"When does that happen—the debutante parties?"

"After your freshman year in college. I mean, don't get me wrong. It's fun. Those parties are lots of fun; it's a good time." The ball traveled back and forth between us after I conceded two more steps.

"So you went to school here?"

"Yes, I went to Brookstone. It's a private school. Actually, I went there from grade school through graduation. After high school, I went to Boston College for four years and studied psychology." She fingered the ball from the webbing. "Actually, I had started out with pre-med but switched to psychology. Then after graduating, I went straight to UGA—University of Georgia—and got a master's in social work. And there's sort of a long history behind that. I had a serious boyfriend and thought we were on the marriage track and all, but we broke up about five months ago. Suffice to say that I ended up back at UGA, got my master's, and I'll be entering law school there this coming fall."

"Were you a good student?"

"At Brookstone I was; I was one of the top two girls in the class. At BC I was middle of the road, mainly because of my first semester with the premed stuff, it just set me back so far. But I was very involved with a lot of extracurricular stuff, there was a leadership program I was in, and I worked with a lot of student programs." For the first time, and with no fanfare, Katie lifted the ball to her ear and flung it overhand. "Then I had a mild foray into the political thing; I ended up being the campaign manager for someone who was running for student government president. It was a funny story because his main competition actually wanted me to be his vice-president and I never knew, because I'd already committed to this other guy. And neither one of them won; they divided the vote. It was an interesting experience because even in the tiny microcosm of college, it was amazing how dirty politics was."

"Oh yeah?"

"Oh man, major mudslinging, and it just divided people, you know? For some reason, it just really got ugly." She wrapped her fingers around the ball and let it fly. It arced with accuracy from her hand.

"Why are you going into law?"

"I know, no one needs me," she answered with a rolling laugh. "But I think that with my background in social work, there'll be some really interesting opportunities when I get my degree. For instance, one of the things I did in one of my social work internships was working with the legal counsel on certain cases, particularly those involving children's advocacy. I mean, I like to think of everything I've done, in some fashion, as something that helps people. And I know people don't think of lawyers being helpful, more just sort of money-mongers or whatever, but the kind of law that I want to practice will, I think, help people. I mean, we'll see what I end up doing, but what I envision right now is something that's going to benefit people, perhaps children."

"Where do you see yourself in ten years?" Without thinking, I launched an overhand toss. It popped softly into her mitt.

"I will have a law degree and hopefully I'll be married by that time—at least I would like to be. And if possible, I would have liked to have had a child, but I don't know. You know, I'll be twenty-seven when I finish law school, and I don't know what kind of job I'll have." She threw the ball a few times.

"I don't know. I mean, I know what I see for myself in the next ten to fifteen years and I think that basically, I'm a good person and I have a lot to offer. And that's sort of, like, what I'm struggling with right now, you know. I'm like, I could just be content and work hard enough to live the way I want to live, but can I really push myself and do something spectacular? I vacillate between this comfort zone and then this zone where I'm like, 'You're so lame, get off your butt.' You know?" She caught the ball and held it in her hand.

"Do you hope to move back to the area?"

"Not necessarily to Columbus, but I definitely want to stay in the Southeast."

"What do you like about the Southeast?" From a neighboring lawn, a mower started up.

"Oh boy. . . . I don't know if it's what I like so much as it's just what I know." The ball resumed its travel. "It's just so comfortable, even though it's hotter than hell right now." Her laughter tumbled out. "I mean, I've lived in the Northeast. It's expensive up there and it's real fast-paced. And as beautiful as it is and as many friends as I have up there, I just can't do that. You know, I've visited friends in New York City and I'm not into it. I think what's important to me is being close to home—at least within a day's drive, that's as far away as I'd want to be. Because, after growing up so far away from my grandparents and having my Chinese relatives on another continent—I mean, I never met my grandmother—staying close to family is a very important thing."

I fell silent and we threw the ball several times, the lawn mower from next door filling the sweet, humid morning air with its whine. "Your baseball's coming right along," I said. She smiled, fingering the strings before releasing an overhand toss.

"So how does a woman who grew up in a neighborhood like this in Columbus, Georgia, relate with children in a big city?" The ball continued its flight. After several throws, Katie spoke.

"Well, I'm trying to think of how I connect all of my experiences—my world—with some of the worlds I've come in contact with. Because like, when I did my social work internships in Athens, I had a lot of clients who lived in the projects. I worked for the Department of Family and Children's Services and came in contact with all sorts of different people. I don't know, it's a tough question." She took a long pause as the ball arced between us, gradually collecting her thoughts. "I guess, on the very basic level, we all want the same things, you know. I think we all want to feel safe and be happy and be loved and be able to love someone, you know?"

"What would help out the types of places where you did your internships?"

"Well, I think there have to be changes, and I hope they will come from either the baby boomers or our generation. I think we're just self-centered right now and eventually, we're going to have to hit rock bottom, in some way, before people start to say, 'Wait a minute, I'm not the only person in this country.' I think we're still a little bit in the 'me generation.' I mean, I think capitalism's great and it makes the world go around and that's fine, but selfishness is taking its toll. . . . "

"How so?" Pop. Into the mitt.

"For example, I just wish you could make people not have babies unless they could prove that they could really take care of them. I wish you could make people take a test, or at least some sort of mandatory parenting class, for all mothers in the hospitals before they can take their babies home. 'Cause that's what breaks my heart in my work—I'd see these infants who were clear cases of a failure to thrive and it just . . . it just killed me. 'Cause I was like, 'Gosh, there's some family out there that wants this baby and could give this baby everything she needs.' It's just frustrating." She shook her head once and threw.

"And that's where the social work was frustrating. I mean, I went in with such a positive attitude thinking, you know, I'm going to help at least one family. And I don't think I hurt anyone, but I don't know that I made any marked improvements in anybody's life."

"What will people say about Katie Hung?" The ball rolled off my fingers.

"Well, I want to be a good parent, I want to be a good companion to somebody, and I want to be, obviously, good in my career. I want to be able to say that I'm happy to go to work and that I'm happy to come home to the people I come home to at the end of the day." She transferred the ball to her throwing hand and held it near her waist. "I don't know. I guess when I think about it, I just want to be remembered for being a good person." She smiled and tossed the ball. "Yeah," she added, "that'll do."

––––––––––––––––

Several hours later, I was making progress across Georgia on State Highway 96. Clouds that had been gathering in Columbus began to reach a critical mass, and as I pulled into Fort Valley to throw the ball with a candy store owner, the first of the rains started to fall.

Further down the road, I stopped at the Evans Peach Packing Plant as the brooding clouds let loose a fierce downpour. In the ten seconds it took me to run across the parking lot, I was soaked down to my socks, which squished warmly in my shoes. After talking with a young woman working at the gift shop cash register, I went into the factory, where the workers sorted tens of thousands of peaches, their hands moving in a disciplined frenzy over the bustling conveyor belts.

The rain relented to some degree in Perry, and I drove a stunning stretch of road reminiscent of New Mexico's Pecan Highway through orderly peach and nut orchards toward McRae, my tires hissing on the freshly soaked asphalt. I pulled off in Chauncey and talked with a mother of seven, mostly about the weather, before heading off.

The respite from the storm was temporary, however, and as I neared Vidalia, rains let loose like I'd never seen. My wipers couldn't begin to keep up, and after trying in vain to make sense of the road I pulled in under the awning of a repair garage to wait out the worst of it.

With the weather, it occurred to me that not only did I have no idea where to stay for the night, but that camping out anywhere in the area would be like sleeping on a well-soaked sponge. As small reservoirs of rainwater leaked slowly from the sunroof onto my right shoulder, I longed to be back on the porch with the young mom and her two kids in Society Hill, soaking up the lazy sun as a crop duster made his passes over the cotton fields.

Until the Carolina coast, the highways that had captivated my spirit were ones that delivered me into a new segment of the trip. Invariably, they had been recommended by a local who knew a certain stretch of road to possess qualities that separated it from surrounding corridors of travel. South Carolina Highway 17, however, gained an identity because of the stretch of luck I'd had in getting there.

Back in Georgia, as I pulled out of Vidalia, the rains had mellowed to cyclical outbursts as I drove down Highway 280 toward Reidsville. A gray evening turned slowly into a dark night, and after learning that I'd shown up too late to camp out at local Gordonia Alatamaha State Park, I took to aimlessly driving the local streets.

A pair of Georgia State Patrol officers, keeping the streets of Reidsville safe, mistook my slow search through the town for inebriated driving and, after stopping to check me out, suggested that I head over to The Huddle House restaurant and try my luck. There, an officer offered to let me sleep at the police department. Within ten minutes, I was stretched out on the chief of police's office floor, drifting to sleep amidst the blurts of noise from the dispatch radio, the cops coming in and out of the small station, and a blaring TV. I couldn't afford to check into a motel.

I awoke with a snap at 6:00 the next morning when the female dispatcher said, "Git up, sleepyheeead!" She chuckled while taking a healthy pull on her morning Marlboro. "You best be gone before the chief shows up." Lordy. I rolled up my bedding, tossed it into the car, and drove seven miles outside of town to a dirt road in the middle of a cornfield. There, I leaned forward and slept two hours more, my forehead planted on the crest of the steering wheel.

By noon, I made it into Savannah, and after taking in the scenery of Factor's Walk, I headed down by the river and talked with a retired schoolteacher baiting his hook for mudhead catfish. He landed a couple, and after showing me his old, brown Cadillac, gave me directions up over the suspension bridge and into South Carolina. I got on Highway 17 headed into Charleston and did little more than watch the clouds massing for attack, which they did as soon as I hit downtown. It was midafternoon and I'd had a day full.

As I pulled out of town, however, the rain ceased, and by Awendaw the grassy marshlands were being caressed by sun and the first cool breeze I'd felt in weeks. In McClellanville, an old shrimping town, I got camping tips from a dentist out raking her lawn and then got back on 17, the sight of marsh and fir trees easing the crick in my neck from last night's sleep.

I pulled into Huntington Beach State Park toward sunset and set up my tent on site 109. After watching alligators lurking in the inland tidal pools, I returned to my picnic table and cooked up some Road Ramen. As the tide of the Atlantic sprayed and hissed in the background, I felt a million miles from the hard floor of the Reidsville police station. Sometimes it isn't so much the trees that line the road or the stripes that mark it but where it drops you off that is the salvation.

After a solid night's sleep, I pulled back onto Highway 17 and drove to a cafe in Garden City Beach for breakfast. I worked on some notes for a while and then struck up a conversation with an older woman. We swapped tales. After I related the story of my night in Georgia, she nodded her head conclusively. "Well it's gonna be a different world now, son," she said, pulling her lips off the porcelain mug to reveal a freshly made bright red lipstick mark. "You on the coast. And the Carolinas deliver a man from the South back into the world."

TERRI HAMILTON FORMER DeMARCO SISTER — *Washington, North Carolina*

Main Street in Washington, North Carolina, runs more or less parallel to the Pamlico River, whose calm waters undulate through the middle of town, dividing its east and west sides. If you take one of the first rights after crossing the bridge, you exit from North Carolina Highway 17 onto East Main Street, a residential passage lined with prim and proper lawns, bushes, and trees that frame home after immaculate home, all coated flawlessly in white paint.

I had originally canvassed West Main Street but the best I did was find a doctor who sent me to the other side of the two-lane highway. He promised that if I knocked on a certain door, I'd find Terri Hamilton, who, he'd said in a buttery drawl, "is probably round about what you are lookin' for." Moments later, I pulled up parallel to the curb in front of a building divided into split-level apartments. I climbed a couple of steps and knocked.

A long wait later, I heard a deadbolt tumbling and fingers fumbling with the security chain. Slowly, the door conceded a four-inch gap through which a pair of eyes studied me.

"Terri Hamilton?" I asked.

"Yes," she replied in a puzzled tone.

"My name's Nick Hartshorn; I was wondering if I could talk with you for a while."

"With me?" The security chain remained taut in front of her startled brow.

"Yeah, a gentleman down the street told me you'd be worth talking to for a book I'm working on."

"A book?"

"Yes," I said, "I'm traveling around the country playing baseball catch with people."

"What kind of stuff are you looking for? Just everyday Americana stuff?"

"Yeah, I just ask people about their lives and such and take a few pictures of them."

"Take pictures of me? I don't know about that. You know, I'm a professional. I don't know whether you know that. I mean, I'm part of a singing group and my son's an actor and I'm writing a book myself now so I just 'soon not have any pictures, okay?" The Brooklyn-flavored words flowed in a constant string.

"Oh really?"

"Yeah, because I never know what I might do with my book and—I don't know—it just might conflict. I mean, I don't know what you want because I don't think this is the interview

I think that you're looking for. You're looking for something that's indigenous to this town, right? And I'm not. I'm a New Yorker. I mean—" I interrupted her.

"Well, if I were to use this interview in a book, would that be okay?"

"Well, I guess." She adjusted her hold on the door, relaxing her arm. "So you're inter-viewing small-town America?"

"Well, small and big. I'm headed to New York in a couple of weeks."

She lowered her head and spoke under her breath, "God, that's my town." She raised her eyes to mine, and a muted smile crossed her lips. "Where're you from?"

"Grand Junction, Colorado."

"Wow, Colorado." Her eyes widened at the mention of it and the chain slacked for the first time.

"Do you mind if I come in?"

As her hand reached to unfasten the brass slide, she shook her head and smiled. "No, come in for a while."

She opened the door and I stepped inside, the red duffel in my right hand. The room rushed at me: knickknacks placed squarely in the middle of shelves, understated furniture arranged in neat formation around a coffee table—and pictures. Pictures of movie sets, of fa-mous people who'd autographed glossy black-and-whites right in the middle, of casts of actors with bubbly smiles and flashbulb eyes. Pictures of years gone by.

She motioned for me to take a seat on the couch. In front of me, she lifted the lid off a glass bowl filled with pistachios. "Want some?" she offered. I nodded and took a small handful.

"How about you?" I asked.

"No thanks," she said as she shook her head. "I hate them. I mean, I don't hate them, they're just too annoying to eat. I like french fries."

I pulled the tape recorder from my bag and set it on the table. "So it's Terri Hamilton? Give me a nutshell biography."

"Well, oh . . . I don't know, I mean, uh . . . "

"You were born . . . " I led her.

"I was born in Rome, New York, and we moved to Brooklyn when I was about five years old. My father taught us how to sing. I was part of a singing group called The Five DeMarco

Sisters. We were on the 'Fred Allen Radio Show' for many years and after that, we just did—you know—the Copacabana, the 'Ed Sullivan Show,' all those places."

"Really?" I cracked open a shell.

"Oh yeah, we played the Copa with Frank Sinatra once and with Martin and Lewis once—Dean Martin and Jerry Lewis, you've heard of them?" I nodded. "And we did all the TV shows at the time: Ed Sullivan, the 'Colgate Comedy Hour.' Jack Lemmon had his own bit comedy show and we did them all—just sang, my four sisters and myself." Her words emerged quickly and without pauses, their speed and tenor like a Brooklyn bus. "Then, I met my husband—Murray Hamilton—he's the actor who was in *Jaws*—you know, the mayor in *Jaws*—and *The Graduate* and all that."

"What did he play in *The Graduate?*"

"He was Mr. Robinson, Anne Bancroft's husband—and *Anatomy of a Murder*, and anyway, he did a lot of movies and plays." She hardly drew a breath. "Anyways, to make a long story short, when I married Murray, I couldn't travel anymore with my sisters so I left the act—my last show was in Las Vegas, 1955—I was twenty-three. Then I left, to be with Murray, you know." I rustled my hand into the pistachio bowl and drew out another round.

"What sort of stuff did The DeMarco Sisters sing?"

"Just, uh, regular pop stuff, I mean—the songs of the day, show tunes and such. I have a tape of us doing 'Somewhere over the Rainbow' on the 'Ed Sullivan Show'—you know, things like that." She looked over at a picture-covered wall and grinned. "We were five young Italian gals singing five-part harmonies; we made a pretty good name around the East Coast. Then we went to California and did one movie—*Skirts Ahoy* with Esther Williams—God, it was awful with those costumes."

"Were you around show business from a young age?" I popped a nut into my mouth.

"Oh yeah, we started when I was about five on the 'Paul Whiteman Show.' My father taught us how to sing 'cause he wanted us to be able to make a living somehow."

"Tell me about him."

"Well, he had come over from Italy, but he was an invalid from the time I was about this high." She held her hand out about three feet above the carpet. "So we made the living for the family from club dates; sometimes we'd sing and they'd just pass the hat around or something, you know."

"Where did you fit in among the sisters?"

"I'm the second youngest. I've got a picture if you want to see it." Before I could nod, she stood up and walked me across the room to a wall under the staircase. There, her finger directed my eyes to a black-and-white photograph of five young women, all svelte and with shiny black hair sculpted around their heads. She pointed to each of the sisters and told me their names.

"What are your other sisters doing?"

"They're all living in New Jersey, more or less retired. They're married and with children, you know."

As we turned, I reached down and tossed the unfinished nuts back into the bowl. "How about going out and tossing the ball for a bit?" I asked.

"Well I'm not much of a ballplayer," she responded. "I mean, I love my sports, but I don't know about throwing."

"Trust me," I said, grabbing the bag.

"So how did you end up in Washington, North Carolina?" I fingered the strings and tossed the ball across the twenty feet that separated us. With nervous hands, she cradled the first delivery in the palm of the glove.

"This is Murray's home, where he's from. He left here when he was eighteen, hitchhiked to Hollywood to try and make a career for himself. I lost Murray, of course, seven years ago." She palmed the ball and with a jerk of her arm sent it in my direction.

"How did he die?"

"He had cancer. That was tough. We'd been married thirty-three years. He was sixty-three." I stepped into a return toss. "But his family's still here—I've got nieces and nephews, my sister-in-law's still here. But anyway, I've got my son who's coming tomorrow from New York. I can't wait."

"And he's an actor as well?"

"Yeah, he is. He's a singer and an actor and we wrote a play together. I mean, I wrote a children's story—that's what I'm doing now—and David adapted it as a musical and we're going to put it on. That's what we're into now, David and I." The words continued to rush as her arm jerked the ball into flight.

"But my greatest ambition right now is to get back to my city." The ball slapped. "I love New York more than anything else. It's the greatest city in the whole world. I mean, there's everything for everybody there. Nice little town, this is, but there really isn't much here." A throw slowed her words, but only for an instant.

"Why have you stayed here for four years?" I asked.

"Well, I left New York because David went his way and it was just too much to keep up the apartment. It started to get a little bit lonely and my sisters were all in New Jersey and David was out on his own, so I came down here for a little while and I sort of got in a rut and just never went back." She gloved the ball. "And that's about it. I'm here and I'm writing books and stories. But anyway, the play is the thing that David and I are working on and it's the thing that we're the most excited about."

"For now?"

"Come again?" she said, looking puzzled.

"I mean, the play is the thing you're most excited about for now?"

"Yeah," she answered, holding up an empty glove.

"What are you the most excited at having done in your life?"

"Well, I haven't really done anything on my own. My success was with my sisters. Vaudeville"—she almost groaned the word in delight, rolling her eyes—"that's what I loved the best." Wrapping her slender fingers around the strings, she jerked the ball into motion.

"But the happiest I've ever been in my life was when I went to California with Murray after we were married and we were waiting and waiting for this job to come through—*The Spirit of St. Louis* with Jimmy Stewart. It finally happened, and little by little we got an apartment. We had a little shack right on the beach in Malibu—two airline stewardesses lived on top and we lived on the bottom—that was the happiest." The ball arced between us. "He drove from there into Hollywood and did the second 'Twilight Zone' they ever filmed. It was just great living, you know, until he ran out of work and we were broke again, but that was a happy time."

Terri had a brilliant smile, exposing bright white teeth against her olive skin. She smiled more and more often as we went on, the ball dancing lazily between us as I asked questions and she let flow torrents of words to answer them. After several tosses, we returned to talking.

"What do you think of the world today?" The ball closed in on her mitt.

"Boy, we've got a mixed-up one, haven't we?" She shook her head. "I mean it sounds corny, but I wish people would be honest, mainly, and less greedy. Greed is taking in every area—even in my sports, which I love so much. I mean, it's ruining everybody." She held the ball in a clenched fist.

"There's so much money—now a million a year isn't enough for the players. . . . It's just greed in every aspect of the world. You know, if there was just a little less greed, if people would be a little happier with what they got and would maybe share a bit more, you know? I know that sounds corny, but I really think that's at the root of so many things.

"Whatever you're greedy for—whether it's for money or for power or for relationships. . . . And kindness—gosh, if people would just be kind. Even as a country, you know—I don't want to get into politics but—this hating thing, I mean, we're making the refugees and so many poor people suffer. I don't know, it's just horrible. . . . " She shook her head and put the ball in the air. It traveled back and forth as she collected her thoughts. "I mean, let's face it— everybody doesn't have to think the way we think and they can still be nice people." Her speech had slowed and the feeling she once put into her songs now moved through her spoken words.

"What gives you optimism about people?" The ball arced.

"As a whole? Gosh, I guess sensitivity would be it. I think deep down we're all fair-minded and sensitive, you know, if it gets right down to it. Like, people make fun of all the cab drivers in New York all the time, but I remember back in the first blackout in New York—about 28 years ago—the whole city was dark." Her words came alive. "Anyway, David was in our apartment with a baby-sitter and I just had to get home to him and I see this cab crawling by and I asked him, 'Please, could you take me?' and he drove through the streets and took me all the way home and didn't charge me a penny. So there's compassion—you know—deep down in everybody."

"Even in Brooklyn?"

"Even in Brooklyn," she said with a smile. "If we didn't have that at a fundamental level, we might as well give it up."

"With all of the showbiz days behind you, what would you like to be remembered for?"

"I don't. I always think people say, 'Well you know, I'd like to be remembered' and 'I'd like to leave my mark by doing this . . . ' and I say to myself, 'You don't have to go out of your way.'" The ball descended into my mitt.

"Every person who was ever born leaves a mark of some sort on the world. Because your life affects other people, doesn't it? You grow up—when you're a little boy or girl—you're making somebody happy, for a while, anyway—your mother. Or you could just be walking along the street and say a hello to an old person sometime and that person will remember you, so that's a mark, you know what I'm saying?" Soft slap into the leather. "You don't have to do anything famous. Course it would be *great* if you could find a cure for cancer; I don't mean there's anything wrong with that. I just mean that everybody has a mark to leave. Some leave a bad mark and some people leave good marks but everybody leaves something, just by being." She jerked the ball into the air.

"What's it all about?"

"What, life?"

"Yeah," I said as the ball arced from her hand.

"I think it's about sports—no." She laughed for a moment. "No, I think it's all about just, you know, not expecting too much and being happy in the moment. I really do. Always wish for what you want but not so much so that you're missing the moment. To live every moment, no matter what it is." She finished just as the ball slapped loudly into the palm of her glove. Wincing, she pulled her hand out of the mitt and looked at her fingers.

I ran to her and asked if she was okay. She thrust out her index finger, a blood blister in the first joint already filling up. "It's just a blood clot," she said, her hand across her brow. "I'll be dead in an hour." I didn't know whether to smile or not. Then a wide smile broke her lips and she spilled into laughter.

I asked Terri if she had any last thoughts for America and she said she didn't. Then I asked if she would sing something for me. "What do you want to hear?" she asked.

"Oh, anything," I responded. She cleared her throat and began.

"*I'll be seeing you*," she crooned, her clear voice filling the air, "*in all the old familiar places, that this heart of mine embraces, all day through . . .* " She finished the verse on a high, sweet note and again smiled widely.

After returning to my car and driving north, I rewound the tape three times to listen to her sing. It was beautiful.

I passed by a wedding at a country church south of Williamston with a toilet-papered Chevy pickup in the parking lot then drove on through the tobacco fields and grain elevators of northern North Carolina. After some quiet time down by the water in Edenton, I pushed on through Hertford, whose billboards advertised it as the hometown of hurler Jim "Catfish" Hunter.

With the slow-moving main streets of Maple, Currituck, and Sligo behind me, I crossed into Virginia. I was in my sleeping bag by 9 PM, Terri's melody still singing in my ears.

CARL ANDERSON

C.F.O. & Wheelchair Athlete – *Virgina Beach, Virginia*

With crowds of humanity massing for the Fourth of July and stifling heat everywhere, I was glad I hadn't planned to stay in Virginia Beach. However, wanting to get a feel for the place, I headed down to the waterfront, where I spent fifteen minutes playing catch with a T-shirt vendor. Then I threw the ball with a nurse vacationing from Bethlehem, Pennsylvania, after which I drove south through Sand Bridge to the Back Bay National Wildlife Refuge, where I hiked around for a few hours. All of which put me so late into the day that I scrapped plans to drive to D.C. and decided to stay in Virginia Beach after all. Heading away from the Atlantic, I pulled off Virginia Beach Boulevard, thinking that I could find an area among the trees to set up my tent and still have some time before nightfall to catch up on notes.

What appeared to be a forest, however, turned out to be a mass of trees concealing street after street lined with homes. I drove through them in vain, searching for a plot of open space that didn't exist. Within a few aimless turns, I had become so entangled in the web of streets that I couldn't even find my way back to the main thoroughfare. Just as my disgust was beginning to carry the moment, I spotted a license plate on a Bronco parked in the driveway of an anonymous house. WP SKIER, it read.

Since I'm from Colorado, it seemed almost my duty to inquire at the residence as to the meaning of the plates. I closed the door of my car and approached the single-level house, having left my gloves in the backseat.

I rang the doorbell, and waited for a healthy couple of minutes before trying it again. It figures, I thought, no one's home. With the sun inching toward twilight, I turned back toward the car, cursing myself for not having bypassed the area altogether. As I reached the end of the driveway, I heard a voice coming from the house: "Can I help you?"

I doubled back and looked at the door, where someone appeared to be sitting. I began to speak as I passed back by the Bronco. "I was just wondering," I asked, "what your plates mean—I'm from Colorado." As I got closer to the door, I saw that the man in the doorway was sitting in a wheelchair.

"They're for Winter Park. I ski in the disabled program there," he said.

The next five minutes were filled with an exchange of cursory information: He was learning to ski on his vacations to Colorado; I was from Colorado and had taught in a disabled program; he lived here in this house; I was traveling the United States playing catch with people; this area wasn't a campground. The important stuff.

Ten minutes after I'd killed my engine, I stood fifteen feet in front of the man on the wooden slats of his poolside deck. One of his hands was stuffed fully into the fingers of the Mizuno; the other hovered over the left wheel of his chair, prepared to make any needed adjustments in position.

Taking more time than usual to focus on my target, I gripped the ball and readied it for flight. I had the feeling that accuracy was, more than any time before, a must. The air was thick with chlorine wafting from the pool.

"Here," he said, raising his mitt.

"So it's Carl Anderson?"

"Carlton Bruce Anderson, actually." The ball popped squarely into his pocket.

"Tell me about a typical day of yours, Carl."

"A typical day? Well, get up at about 6 AM and the first thing I do is iron my shirts on the floor." I raised my eyebrows. "I know," he continued, "I'm the chief financial officer of a very successful company and I still wake up and iron my own shirts on the carpet. Anyway, then I have some coffee—I don't eat breakfast—and then commute to work, which is hellish." He laughed quickly in the pause, one of those laughs that sounds a little like machine-gun fire. "Come home, swim about fifty laps in my pool, eat dinner, maybe read a little or watch TV, then go to bed." As the chair stood still, he brought his right arm down and released the ball, the strings spinning slowly. It arced evenly and fell with a pop into my waiting mitt. The motion gave me a momentary reprieve from his words, which came softly yet with great speed, as if he were one of those guys who works for a classical music station but is forced to read the news in as short a time as possible.

"What's your biography?"

"Oh, boy." I tossed with dead aim as he spoke. "Born in 1954, California, traveled in about seven states with my father, who was a colonel in the Marine Corps, ended up in Virginia Beach in 1968 as a thirteen-year-old. Did junior high and high school here, then went to William and Mary for undergrad—'75 through '77. Actually, I did two years at Junior Wesleyan College first—it's a local Methodist college here—then transferred up there." He grouped his words in compact clusters. "And after graduating from William and Mary in '77, I looked for work." He transferred the ball from the glove to his hand and, moving to throw, positioned the mitt over the left wheel.

"Tell me about your disability, if you don't mind." The ball slapped into the pocket.

"Well, it's very unique and it doesn't bother me a bit when people ask me about it. When I was thirteen, I'll say April 22nd, you know, I was the star of the baseball and the football teams. I was very good at both. I was headin' toward, I thought, some type of pro baseball career. And then April 23rd I woke up and I was stricken with this disease they call transverse myelitis, which is some type of debilitating nervous system problem which—well, how can I explain? You know how the right side of your brain controls the left side of your body and vice versa? There's a transversing mechanism in your spinal cord that sends electrical impulses from your brain to your extremities, and it gets blocked somehow." He held up his glove again to remind me. I tossed the ball.

"So that resulted in me having weak limbs, you know, basically from my chest down. They were worried at one time that if it crept up above my chest that my heart'd stop beating and I'd die." He fingered the ball from the webbing with a spurt of laughter. "And that didn't happen, which was good." Lowering his glove to secure the wheel, he brought the ball into a smooth arc. "I'm thirty-nine years old now so I've spent the last twenty-six years on crutches, basically. I was in the eighth grade when it happened, so I finished eighth grade in the hospital and then I was home-taught in the ninth and tenth grade."

"Tell me about that." The ball flew.

"My ninth-grade teacher was an elementary schoolteacher who was beautiful. She was about twenty-two years old and I was about thirteen or fourteen. So she would come over and I would just be dazzled by her." He fingered a grip across the strings and held the ball at rest. "I was paid back in the tenth grade by this very mean, strict older woman who just, you know, grilled me and gave me work left and right.

"Course, looking back, that was probably the best thing that could've happened. She set me on the right path. Then in the eleventh grade, I was mainstreamed back in, I guess the word is now. I was scared to death but I was accepted right away—I had a lot of friends. I had to be driven to school by my mother every single day in the eleventh grade; finally in the twelfth grade I got a car that had specially equipped hand controls so I could drive to school and all." His mitt didn't move as the ball slapped into the pocket.

"What was it like to have that strike you at thirteen?"

"Well—you know—it was night and day—a whole different life the next day. Like that." He raised his hand and snapped his fingers. "And then you don't see the people you've been hanging out with—you know, your whole life—other than your true friends. All the people you go to school with, they're just vanished—completely. You never see them again." He pulled the ball from his glove and tossed it, the chair dead still. "But basically, I wasn't sick. I didn't feel bad or anything, I just couldn't move my legs.

"So I spent seventy-seven days in the Portsmouth Naval Hospital, them trying to figure out what was wrong with me, and I was just bored to death." He gloved a toss. "And this was back in 1967 and '68, the height of the Vietnam War, so I was running into all these young kids that had actually been shot and stuff like that—serious injuries, you know—and they weren't much older than I at the time."

"Did you still have feeling in your legs?"

"Well, I got to the point where I could get around on crutches, but you know, it's hard to describe after twenty-six years because I can't remember what it was like *to* walk, you know? Basically, I have some movement, and the ability to walk on crutches has been fortunate—a lot of people are wheelchair-bound entirely." Bringing the ball down from his ear, he threw. "I use the wheelchair more for convenience—and laziness—to get around and go shopping and stuff like that. During the week, I don't use a chair too much. I use the crutches to get to work and such—they're good exercise for me. When I come home at night though, I get in my wheelchair—it's a lot safer around the house."

"What was the most threatening time for you, in terms of your disability?"

"The move to college scared me to death. It was a tough school to get into and I really had to study my butt off."

"And after college?" Pop. Into my mitt.

"Well, I graduated with a degree in accounting and took my C.P.A. exam in November of 1977. Finally in January of 1978, I got my C.P.A. and after three months of looking, I found a job working for a C.P.A. firm in Williamsburg. It paid four bucks an hour." He shook his head and spoke in disbelief: "College degree, four dollars an hour."

"Really?"

"Yeah, it was kind of shocking. And they paid you once a month. So you'd get paid $560 once a month, and it was feast or famine, you know. You'd be great for a couple days and then all the sudden you'd run out of money." His chair shifted slightly as he threw.

"I worked there for about nine months and then moved back home and worked for Virginia National Bank and then took a job in government up in northern Virginia workin' as a contract auditor for the Defense Department."

"And since then?"

"Well, I've worked for a few different companies as a chief financial officer, and in '92 I finally found an offer where there was a stake in the company—a lot less pay and a lot more travel but the opportunity was there, and so I took that and it has worked out well so far." The ball lobbed upward.

"Do you think your injury has helped you get jobs?"

"Well see, you've got to remember that I didn't think I was handicapped. I wanted to be seen just as normal as possible. And in those days, with the way I walked, it just looked like I had a broken leg or a busted ankle so people thought I was just—you know—temporarily injured. I mean, if people'd ask and I didn't want to go into it, I'd just tell them I had a broken knee or whatever." Bringing his hand down, he tossed. "So it was a different stereotype for me. My disability was less than a person who's in a wheelchair so it was easy to mainstream back in. But then, I've been very lucky in my life, too, as far as being in the right place at the right time, and yeah, I guess some companies would hire you because they were getting a person who knew what they were doing and they'd also get the quota that they needed." He touched his wheel lightly and moved the chair to make a catch.

"But I've been employed at a high level most of my life so I've been exposed to a lot of different people, and in today's society I don't think it's a problem for anybody. See, the people I know—they see my personality and see Carl on crutches, not 'here's the crutches with Carl.' So it's a part of me and it doesn't even click with them anymore. And that's what's nice about the friends I have; they accept me for what I am, not for what I once was or could have been—you know, for what I am."

"Were you ever married?" The ball arced.

"Yeah, I got married once. In 1988, I married a girl I met at the first company I was working for; she was a contract manager. We were together for four years and then, back in '92, she just up and left, out of the blue." The ball lit out from Carl's fingers. "It was strange. Everybody called us the perfect couple but I guess she just got bored with the married routine." I fingered a grip on the ball. "So she moved out and left me with this place." His words had slowed somewhat and while they still came in clusters, I was struck more by their soft-spoken tone than their speed. The sun, thankfully, seemed to be hanging eternally in the twilight sky.

"What are you happiest about in your life?"

"Well, that'd be tough." He caught my toss and stared at the ball as he placed his fingers across the strings, speaking again as the ball took flight. "I guess I'd have to say the way I've been able to overcome this disability and be successful—not in a materialistic way necessarily, but more how I've been accepted. I have a lot of great friendships and an excellent professional reputation." He paused a moment. "I also looked at when I got married as coming full circle—you know, overcoming all the disabilities and all the stereotypes. That wasn't the reason I got married, but I thought it was an accomplishment at the time." We tossed the ball a few times before I spoke.

"What words do you live by?"

"Oh, I don't know—" Carl caught the ball and secured the wheel with his free hand. "Do the best you can and accept people for what they are, not for what they do or their lot in life. And again, I had a different perspective, but I accept a person as a human being first—no matter what walk of life they are or what they do for a living—and then I go from there." The ball remained tucked in his mitt. "Like, if I get in the elevator and the janitor's in the elevator or something like that, it's 'Good morning, sir.' It's not, 'I look at this guy as a janitor, he hasn't accomplished anything in his life.' And a lot of people see it that way." He tossed the ball as water lapped against the edge of the pool.

"What would you like to be remembered for?"

"Somebody once said life is in the struggle, not the victory. And I've had a lot of struggles. I'll still have a lot more. You know, being physically challenged doesn't exempt you from all the other problems—loss and diseases and emotional ups and downs and everything else. I still have those. So I guess I accepted the challenge, basically. And I'm very happy with that. And I've been very lucky. I really feel that way." He raised his mitt.

"And probably the greatest luck I had was my upbringing. I had wonderful parents and three older brothers who gave, and continue to give, a lot of support. And the friends that I have, as I say, are true friends, and, more importantly, what God gave me inside—the necessary strength to carry on. You know, a lot of people say I'm an inspiration to them and all but you know, I don't wanna be; it's just that I'm doing my thing. I want to be accepted for what I've done, not for what I can't do." Scooping the ball out from my pocket, I tossed it straight for his mitt.

"You pretty much figure you're just an average guy." Pop.

"Oh, yeah," he said, fingering the ball from his webbing. "An average guy who wants to be accepted as an average guy."

An hour later, I was sitting with Carl and his fiancee having a dinner of barbecued shrimp and scallops. Between succulent bites of seafood and slugs of ice-cold American beer, we talked about skiing and Virginia Beach and the Fourth of July until the late hours of the night. As our eyelids became progressively heavier, Carl decided to turn in. "You're welcome to stay as long as you want," he said, shaking my hand firmly before wheeling off to his room to sleep.

Moments later, I curled up on his couch and fell quickly into slumber, my ten-minute detour into Virginia Beach complete.

I don't think I'd call Washington, D.C., the land of mortgages. Of the six people I played catch with during my stay there, not one of them owned a home. They all rented apartments: a woman who worked at the Smithsonian Institution's National Museum of Natural History, a guy who had finished in the top twenty at the most recent Ironman Triathlon in Hawaii, and a woman who cleaned the pool where Katie Couric went to high school. Then there was the guy who operated one of the novelty vending carts out on the Mall. I never did quite understand where it was he lived.

But of all the apartments I heard about, I visited only one: the western Arlington dwelling of David Burgdorff and Alex Jimenez. Their names were given to me by a friend of a sister of David's co-worker, I think it was. "You should interview them," she told me. "They're both HIV-positive."

Like many people I know, I like to consider myself open-minded. But upon hearing the letters HIV, part of that open mind raced wildly with images of men in hospital wards, other men coming to talk with them, stare at them, and offer saltines to thin, blue lips. Trying hard to squelch such pictures, I pulled up outside David and Alex's place.

As I walked across the lawn, a crowd of fat-chested little birds tucked into the trees surrounding the lawn filled the air with chirps. Behind the shrill noise of the birds, thousands of crickets—probably hidden in the dense thickets creaked rhythmically under the late-afternoon sun.

I nervously approached the door and knocked. The crickets' call ebbed as the door opened. "You must be Nick," he said, shaking my hand firmly. "I'm David." I was introduced to Alex, and within a few minutes we stood out on the pale-green grass of their lawn.

David slipped the glove on his left hand and stood squinting in the sunlight. Moving his solid body, he stepped into his tosses with familiarity, the ball arcing smoothly from his fair-skinned arm into the muggy air. He stood about five foot eight and carried himself with ease. The baseball seemed to fit comfortably in his hand as he'd scoop it from the webbing, rolling it onto his fingers as he moved into a toss.

Alex, on the other hand, wasn't a natural. While his torso was constructed from plates of muscle and his tight clothes stretched over firm flesh, he struggled with the glove. When he had finally stuffed the left-handed glove onto his fingers, the heel of his hand sagged out of the leather.

Standing a few inches taller than David, he looked like the kind of guy who could've thrown a baseball across the Potomac. However, when it came time for throwing, it was apparent that he couldn't. He tossed the ball ineptly at the end of a labored motion. It flopped into my mitt, and my return toss—which I took care to throw softly—brought a look of terror to his eyes.

Against a chorus of crickets waxing and waning, David spoke in a soft voice. "I was born in Indiana in a little town called Evansville. My parents both came from farming backgrounds, and we had what I considered the Norman Rockwell life." David stepped forward about six inches and lofted the ball through the air. "Both my grandparents were farmers so I got to spend—you know—the weekends and summers on the farm. Went through the public schools and high school back in Indiana and did one year of college in Evansville." Pop. "And then moved out here to D.C. when I was twenty-one, looking for 'the great job.'" He used his gloved hand and free fingers to bracket the last words in quotes.

"How was it growing up gay in small-town Indiana?"

"Um, it wasn't bad, but there were some trying times." As the ball moved between us with an unhurried meter, David's words followed suit. "I mean, for the most part, I feel very fortunate. My parents were very supportive of the fact. And it wasn't like they said, 'Oh, this is a wonderful situation, we're just so glad you're gay.' I mean, it was more like, they realized there was something going on and they both came to me separately and said, 'If there's something you can't talk to us about or talk to the preacher about or if you need a psychiatrist, we'll get you one.' But I was like, no, it's not that bad, it's fine." The ball slapped into his glove.

"But—you know—as things happened, there was an incident at a high school party once where they were going to 'throw the fag in the river.' We had two different crowds—you had your A-B student crowd and you had your parking lot crowd. And it was the parking lot crowd that was going to throw me into the river. But some people stood up for me and so nothing happened, but it scared me. It was the first time I had to face it like that. I also didn't know how they found out." He moved the ball into flight.

"Were you part of the A-B crowd?"

"No, I was the middle of the road, one of the ones who kind of floated back and forth between the two. But I was well accepted; people liked me."

"Was it something you kept pretty quiet?"

"Oh yeah. I had a girlfriend all through high school, went to prom and the whole bit. But the charming part of that story, I guess, was that while we were dating, she had a curfew of eleven and mine was midnight, so I'd drop her off and then go downtown and cruise what they called 'sissies corner' before going home—just to see, you know? It was like 'What do they do? What's out there?'" The ball spun backwards as it left his fingers.

"How old were you when you clued into the fact that you were not like the other boys?"

"I was seventeen. It was like a week before my seventeenth birthday."

"How did that occur for you?" About twenty fat-chested birds flew off a nearby power line and over our heads.

"Mine was such that I think for years I had seen different body parts, and like if I saw a handsome chest, I would think, 'Boy, I hope my chest grows in hairy like that.' It was like I kept seeing things and thinking, 'Isn't that attractive?'" Slap. Into his mitt.

"And then one day I realized, 'Oh my, it's not that you want it on you so much, it's like you want to put your face in it, you want to be embraced by it.' So, that was sort of an awakening but, you know, I never had to make a decision until somebody gave me their phone number at a job. I was working at a grocery store. I got this piece of paper and it only had their first name and their address and I knew what it was for. I had already dreamed that this was how it was going to happen and it did."

"This was in Indiana?" The ball arced skyward.

"Yeah. And sure enough, I went over to his house and I was like a wide-eyed puppy—like, 'Well, what do you call yourself and how do we do this?' It's like, all these questions I had that were all pent up. And I happened to lock onto someone really special that—you know— played mentor. He just kind of held my hand and said, 'You don't have to change anything, you don't have to carry a purse, you're just yourself. The sex part is just an extension.' You know, you're either into it or you're not." He gloved my throw.

Starting from his left hip, Alex rocked the ball back a few inches and then brought it through, the underhand delivery sending the ball in a high parabola. I stood not ten feet away and cradled the incoming ball in my glove, though it would have been just as easy to bare-hand it. My return toss was painstakingly soft and Alex caught it squarely in the palm of his glove.

"Try catching it in the pocket—" I ventured, "the deep part."

"Okay," he said, his low, smooth voice filling the space between us.

"So you're Alex Jimenez." His arm came from the hip and whispered the ball into the air.

He nodded. "Born in Cuba, 1958. Came here in '61 when I was three years old. I was raised in New Jersey in a town right across the river from Manhattan—Union City." Although I had expected a Cuban accent, there wasn't a trace—just words couched in a baritone voice. "It was a Hispanic ghetto. A lot of Cubans in 1961 either went to Miami or went up north, and my parents headed north. It was fun, it was warm—my childhood was good." I held the ball. "Dad is an electrical engineer. Mom was a social worker. They're both rocket scientists—very bright, very literate and very cultured, so I was exposed to a lot of that." He froze as my toss crested, his glove palm side up. After a light pop, his body relaxed.

"What brought them to the states?"

"Communism."

"And your schooling?"

"I went to a private Catholic school, like all good Cuban boys—I'm a recovering Catholic now." He held the ball and laughed deeply. "I graduated in '76 and I went to Rutgers University, was in a premed program for two trimesters and basically, it didn't work out. So I did some night courses for a while, some business management courses, but school just wasn't where my head was at. I wanted to party." His hand came forth with greater ease and arced the ball.

"So basically, I got into the insurance business at eighteen and I've been in the field ever since. I currently sell a policy for the students of Johns Hopkins University. We write their entire undergraduate and graduate students. It's a lot of fun."

"Tell me about growing up gay in your family."

"Well, actually, we didn't talk about it. I think that I came out to my parents in '85—right before I moved down here—and it didn't go over well at all. And basically, at that time, it was like I stated it and it was never brought up again." Without struggling, he gloved my throw. "And then the next time I brought it up was in 1988 when I went into detox for alcohol and drug abuse."

Sunlight glistened off the blond hair covering David's arm as he swept it through the sky. "After the one year at college a lot of things happened at once. I got bored with the job I had managing two record stores, felt like there wasn't room to grow, my relationship at the time ceased—we decided to split up, and my best friend—the man who was like my mentor—committed suicide so I was in a real depressed kind of funk." I lifted the ball from my mitt and tossed. "So all of that, combined with the fact that there weren't any jobs in Indiana at that time, led me to think of moving. I came to Washington to visit a friend on New Year's and decided it was, you know, a big city that I would actually enjoy living in and I moved out here the following May."

"Did you find 'the great job?'" I spun the ball sideways.

"I started work in retail for Conrad's. I worked in several of their departments and then from there, got on with the showroom at the design center here in Washington." The ball continued its casual arcs. "Then I was a consultant for the wool bureau for a few years. Following that job, I lived in New York for six months. I had a boyfriend up there, but the relationship didn't work out. Now I'm working as the office manager for a residential interior design firm—I've been there since last December. And I have to work part-time—at least fifteen hours a week—at an outdoor sporting store because that's where my health insurance is." His right foot began to mat the grass where he stepped forward to throw.

"After growing up in rural Indiana, how do you like the city?"

"Washington? It took me three years to get used to it. You know, first, you don't have all the support mechanisms that you're used to—even simple things like getting to use all of Dad's tools when my car broke down." The ball popped into my MacGregor. "And also just the friendships. People here were much more political than I was used to and it took a while to find a group that I enjoyed hanging around."

With each toss, the motions were coming with greater ease to Alex's limbs. It was like watching one of those people who figure out how to water-ski on one ski their first morning out. Strong. Balanced. Athletic. While he still held the glove with the palm facing up, he moved it around more and more like an extension of his own muscled arm. "I moved down to Washington in 1985 after living up in Boston for a while—New York, Boston, then here— and I started seeing David in 1988."

"Tell me about the detox."

"There's a lot I can tell you about that. For starters, I also found out, at the time I entered the program, that I was HIV-positive. And I think that as a crisis and a catharsis for change, detox was the most wonderful thing that ever happened to me. I mean, not that my life before that was horrible and meaningless or I wasn't having a good time, but it really opened my eyes to a lot of things; made me grow as a person." His glove closed around the descending ball.

"Let me put it to you this way. I'm not a big 'program person' so I won't sit here and throw the book at you like some of my friends do, 'cause I think there's more to life than following twelve steps, but nonetheless, it was good." Without fanfare, he turned his glove over in the middle of the sentence and caught the ball normally. Then, placing his fingers against the red strings, he put it into a soft flight with a jerky overhand toss. While my eyes followed his athletic transformation, he continued his line of thought.

"Prior to detox, the extent of conversations with my family was, 'How's the weather? How's your job?' And all of a sudden, it was like, 'Hey folks, we're not gonna talk about the weather anymore.' And the last five and a half years have been the best of my life. I mean, we talk; we have very good, intimate conversations now."

"What led you to drinking and drugs?" His glove popped.

"I don't know, it just happened. You know, I could sit here and give you a bunch of reasons and say, 'It made me somebody else' but the bottom line is—you know—hey, it was fun." He smiled as a deep laugh erupted from his chest. "Let's get real, you know.

"I went into detox in October of '88 and I found out I was HIV-positive that same day—October 22nd, 1988. I had gone in for one of those blind tests 'cause my allergies were really bad that year and my primary-care doctor said, 'I know your story, I know what's going on here, but my trying to treat you when you have these symptoms is like trying to perform brain surgery with a pair of blindfolds on.' So she recommended that I go get an antibody test." Soft pop into the pocket.

"And to make a long story short, I had this little old lady and this guy and they said, 'Well, you know, your results have come back and you're positive.' They said, 'Are you upset?' and I said, 'No.' And they said, 'Are you surprised?' and I said, 'No,' and then I walked out and there were all these hugs—you know, touchy-feely shit, which I know they have to do." The ball picked up speed between us. "So I went home—I had this brand new bottle of Stoly in the freezer—and proceeded to drink myself into a stupor. And that night, part of me said, 'You're a mess; you're thirty years old; look what you've done to yourself; your life is coming to an end,' and I tried to do myself in. The next morning, I woke up—I had blacked out—called a friend of mine, and I said, 'I need help.' So I went to a local clinic and booked myself in for outpatient. I was in detox for four months." Wrapping it in two fingers, Alex tossed the ball.

"Was your sexuality an issue that you confronted in detox?"

"No, you see, that was never a really big issue for me 'cause I had a lot of fun. I mean, there are a lot of people out there in their midthirties, and they'll say, 'I didn't know what it meant' and 'I had a lot of dilemmas,' but for me, no. I knew what was on and I had a ball. Or two." Gripping the ball, he smiled.

As the sun sank behind the bank of trees, the birds lowered the volume a notch. The crickets upped their chirping and filled the air with a calm noise. "And you're HIV-positive now?"

"Yeah," David said, his rounded left shoulder rocking his upper body into a toss.

"Tell me about that." Pop.

"Well, you know, by '82 or '83—a year or two after I moved here, there were people I knew that were getting sick and I already knew people who were dying. And I guess in '84, Johns Hopkins started a thing called Project Share, to see if they could find any answers as to what the similarities were, why people were getting sick." The ball lobbed from my hand. "I decided—you know—that I wasn't making a lot of money to donate to causes but I could donate my body. So I'd go up every three months for tests and it was supposed to be like a three-year thing and it was through them that I found out my status. So I've known since '85 but the blood work can go back as far as '84."

"But you seem healthy."

"I'm atypical—my T-cells haven't dropped. I've stayed right at a thousand ever since the beginning of the study." Strings spinning, the ball slapped into my mitt.

"So, how's living with it, if you don't mind me asking?"

"Well, the HIV—it wakes you up. You know, some people get really angry and others'll say, 'Well, maybe I should get my life together.' At first I thought maybe I needed to deal with grieving but in truth, I hadn't lost anybody, you know. I had gotten a disease." David stepped onto the matted circle of grass. "And when I went to seek help with that—through a psychiatrist—then all of a sudden I unearthed a lot of other things, too. You know, I call it my recovery. I kind of got my act together." The ball traveled between us.

"And part of that was, you know, for a long time, especially with relationships, I was getting in and out of new ones every year. So it woke me up to that and what I was doing wrong and I was finally able to uncover my feelings. I mean, ask me what I thought and I always had an opinion but I had no idea what I felt. So by getting in touch with those feelings, it allowed me to have a relationship with Alex."

"How long have you been together?" I tried a knuckleball but sent it spinning.

"Five years. We celebrated it this past spring."

"Were you both HIV-positive when you entered the relationship?"

"Uh-huh." Pop. Back into my mitt.

"Does it change your intimate life?"

"Well, of course it changes it because it limits you in some sexual ways but it was also a bonding element for us because we had something that we shared in common. We had been dating for a while, and when I finally broached the subject with him to let him know I was positive, it was such a relief to find out we both were because it was like, 'Oh, thank God.' And, I mean, it's pretty weird to say, 'Thank God we both have AIDS' but it was reassuring. Because with someone who is HIV-negative, the relationship just has different dynamics." As he stepped forward, his right foot found the matted circle of grass.

"How long do you figure you'll live?" Slap.

"In '85, I thought I'd probably have three years. And at that time—you know—it was like, well, run up the charge cards—who cares? You're not going to be around anyway. So I did that, but in hindsight, it's just a form of denial. After a while, you realize that you still need to be account-able so you swing back around to being responsible again." Another row of the round-chested birds peeled off a power line and darted behind the trees, their wings beating against the wind.

"But also somewhere in that period I had a dream—and I really believe in my dreams if they reoccur like three times. Anyway, in this dream, I was like forty years old and I was consoling this kid who was about eighteen who had apparently just found out he was HIV-positive. I kept saying to him, 'Look, I'm forty years old. I've been living fifteen years with this. I mean—it can be done, it'll be okay.' And I really believe I'll live to be at least forty."

"Does death scare you?"

"No, no, the death doesn't. I mean, I have my religion, so I'm not scared of the death as-pect." Pop. Into the MacGregor.

"Which religion?"

"Evangelical Reformed Church of Christ." He put a sideways spin to the ball.

"What does having your religion mean to you?"

"Oh, that's what my spirituality is based on—on my teachings as a child. And when I go, I'm still very much comforted just by my church and the way that they talk. They were never one to say, you know, 'All gay people are gonna go to hell.' Granted, I don't know that they knew I was gay. I mean, the people who went to my high school and went to my church knew, but I was only there for another couple of years after the river incident. Then I moved to Washington." The ball ascended.

"But I was still living with my parents for a year after they found out, and I think that that was good, too, because they could see that David hadn't changed, you know—that he hadn't become some kind of subversive character, but they just knew the pieces that I'd been hiding." I rocked my shoulders and sent the ball in motion.

"Do you have brothers and sisters?" Slap.

"Uh-huh, I have a brother who's three years older and a sister that's five years younger."

"How has it been for the family as far as you testing positive?" His foot pressed on the grass.

"It's funny because I think only recently have I realized that they went through more angst than I thought. I mean, they've always been very giving of unconditional love. For instance, when my brother had his first child and I went home, there was no hesitation about me holding the child, you know, so I thought everything was great." I placed my fingers across the strings.

"But recently, I was talking with my mom and she was saying how they had talked about it a lot before I came back because they didn't want to do the wrong thing. But of course they were nervous about putting the child in my arms—they weren't sure. Because of our openness, it allowed that to be okay." The chirping from the branches crescendoed and David looked over his shoulder at the huddled masses of birds.

"How many people do you know that have died?"

"Hundreds." Turning back my way, he tossed. "Maybe even a thousand. And partly because I've been very politically active in the community, I've known a lot of people. But I stopped counting around a hundred 'cause it just got too depressing."

"So since then, you've been working in insurance and surviving your disease?" I brought my hand down smoothly, delivering the ball into a soft arc that terminated in Alex's mitt.

"Yeah, I just got some news last week. I've been taking AZT for the last five years. And I just found out that it's time to switch therapies and go on DDI, which is another one of the FDA-approved drugs, but it's not the drug of choice because it has some side effects."

"Does the change in program mean that your condition is worsening?" The questions felt frozen against the backdrop of other sounds: the birds, the crickets, the whispery pops of the ball into the leather.

"Yeah. There's a marker that's used. It's a ratio of white blood cells to another type of white blood cells and in a healthy person that ratio is one to one. My ratio is now below point-two-oh, which is not good, 'cause that's when things start to happen." He made an overhand catch, following it with an overhand throw.

"Healthwise, tell me about the progression of HIV."

"Well, I've had the disease for six years and these markers—these white cell ratios—start to decrease, and as they decrease, you find yourself—like, for example, I get really fatigued, tired. Emotionally it takes its toll because you'll go through stages—not like depression, but you just don't want to think and you almost feel like you're in a vacuum."

"Did you have symptoms before you tested positive?" Pop. Into his mitt.

"No, I didn't have symptoms but I definitely knew that I had probably been infected. I mean, I had had a lot of fun and lived a pretty wild lifestyle." Alex pulled the ball from the mitt and cradled it in his left hand.

"But then, when I learned I was infected, I became like a walking library about the disease: I couldn't read enough, I couldn't find enough material, I subscribed to every newsletter known to man. I mean, part of maintaining my sanity and my wellness—physically—is reading, having a real good interactive relationship with my doctor and trying alternative therapies like herbal stuff." He stepped forward for the first time, and his left foot rocked his body into a toss.

"I mean, yeah, I still love donuts and junk food, but I take better care of myself. I just ran a 10K race in April and I want to run the Army ten-miler in October. So I feel fine, but let's just say if you had a cold or were sneezing right now, I'd probably stay away from you 'cause my susceptibility is high." I gripped the ball and moved into a throw.

"How are your parents dealing with your disease?"

"I think fundamentally, it's not dealt with at all. I just told them Saturday about the change in my treatment and my mother didn't say a word. All I heard were these uncontrollable sobs on the phone. And my feeling was, hey, we just have to deal with this one day at a time, you know?" He caught the ball and gestured with his glove. "I mean, let's get real. I'm probably not going to be around in five years. And I'm not being fatalistic; I'm just being realistic.

"I think occasionally Mom thinks that maybe someday she's gonna wake up and if she waves this magic wand over me, it's gonna go away. And I think that there's almost this little death wish that they go before I do 'cause I know that they won't be able to handle it. And there's almost an underlying feeling that—I don't know how to say this—you leave a country when your child is three years old so that you won't have to subject him to Communism and a horrible life and then you get here and guess what? Thirty-five years later, he kicks." He unwrapped the ball from the pocket and rainbowed it my way. "You know, there's some irony in that."

"What do you think of death?" I fingered the strings.

"You know what? There are times when I really welcome it. I don't know. I'm not afraid of it. I guess my big fear is dying a slow death." The ball landed in his pocket. "My brother-in-law died of AIDS in December—my sister's husband. And it was really ugly 'cause he was this really vibrant thirty-year-old guy. He was a Marine, he contracted it in the Philippines—you know, a real all-American boy. And he just sort of held on forever and ever, and—I don't know. I don't want to go like that."

"What are you the happiest about in your thirty-five years?" David reached over his left shoulder and snared the ball.

"My relationship with Alex."

"Do you consider yourself married in any sense? Did you go through a ceremony?"

"We exchanged vows; I guess we're as married as we could be. We think of ourselves as married you know—in a committed relationship." He turned his shoulders in line and threw.

"What's important to you, David?" I gloved his toss.

"I still believe, as my grandfather taught me, that honesty is the first. 'Cause if you're honest with everyone you deal with—no matter how poor or rich—you'll get by."

"What do you want to be remembered for?"

"I'm not sure." Pop. "I think what my friends will say—which I don't actually like—is, 'Oh David, he's such a nice person.' You know, I want to be known for something more out of the ordinary, for being a character, you know? My extended family is full of characters and I guess that's how I'd like to be seen." I floated the ball into his glove.

"I don't think I have the type of job or career that I'm going to leave this great mark on the planet." He held the ball and laughed. "Sometimes I think my claim to fame will be that when I watch the evening news every night and they show the stenographer in the House of Representatives, I'll know I had a hand picking out the fabric that covers her ergonomic chair." A broad smile remained on his lips as David tossed the sphere.

I pointed over to the black motorcycle parked at the lawn's edge, asking if he got out on it much.

"That's not my motorcycle," he said, raising his mitt. "That's my psychiatrist. . . . It gets me out into the country, out into the open."

"Are you content?" I asked.

"I'm a whole person," Alex said, gloving the ball more comfortably now. "I used to be really splintered. You know, there was like an Alex to Nick and there was an Alex at work and there was an Alex to my parents. The best thing that's ever happened to me is that since detox, I've been able to pull all those pieces together and be a whole person. I wouldn't give up the last five and a half years for the thirty that went before it." A string of birds ascended from the ground and took cover in a tree behind Alex.

"What's it all about?"

"It's about waking up in the morning and knowing that it's not just you—that you're part of something that's much bigger than yourself. And I think that's something that's really crucial to me. One of the problems we're having right now, as we speak, is that we have lost, as a global society, a sense of what it all means." Alex gloved a toss and kept the ball tucked in the glove. "And it has to do with looking at you and not seeing you as a separate entity, but basically seeing that you and I are the same thing. Just like a guy down the street—that your experiences and his experiences are all the same thing. That's what it's all about. And how I perceive you is eventually how I will perceive myself." Removing the ball, he placed his fingers on the taut leather and threw.

"What do you think the best traits of humanity are?"

"We have a wonderful ability to regenerate ourselves. But I think that with our basic rape of the planet and rape of each other's minds and bodies and stuff like that, that trait is beginning to lessen, as it were. Fortunately, I think there's an amazing movement of people that are saying we need to stop and nurture and support one another more. We need to realize that if we don't start taking care of each other, we might not be around in another millennium or so." The ball popped in his pocket. "I think that ultimately, we're still waiting for one great crisis that'll turn it around."

"What sort of crisis?"

"AIDS is a crisis." He held the ball and motioned with it. "Because it has forced us—not just as Americans but as a global society—to look at this epidemic and say, 'Oh gee, this is happening to a lot of people. It's happening to those poor black people in Africa, and in the

Philippines.' And it's not just a gay thing, you know. It's the lady next door, who maybe had a boyfriend who was an IV drug user. And who's going to pass judgment on all those kids who are left homeless because their mothers died of AIDS? It's impossible." He raised his hands. "So no longer is it something that I can sit here and say, 'Hey, it's only those fags—look at what they do.' I don't think things are sent by the universe randomly. I think that things happen to consciously wake us up and I think that AIDS is just a wake-up call." He finished and my waiting glove slapped around the ball.

"What do you hope to be remembered by—and forgive me for the question; most folks I talk with don't think that they'll be dead in a couple of years."

"No," he said, his deep laugh filling the air. "I know what you're saying." Pop. Into his webbing. "You know, it's funny—I work for this large corporate entity with the politics and the good ole boys and it's very stressful, and there was this guy that I was sharing an office with for a while and one day, jokingly, he says, 'You know, if you got hit by a Mack truck when you walked out of the office, what would you want people to say about you?' And I said to him, 'That Alex was an okay kind of guy.' That's all." Putting his weight on his rear foot, Alex held the ball in his free hand.

"I don't want to be Mother Teresa. I don't want to be regarded as the sinner of all time. Just that I was all right."

The following afternoon, I escaped the beltway surrounding D.C. and sped up Interstate 95 on a detour to Baltimore. In a swampy ninety-eight-degree heat, I sat in the third deck above the first-base line at Camden Yards, watching the Mariners and the Orioles taking turns swatting home runs into the outfield bleachers and beyond.

After the game, I went down near Baltimore's Inner Harbor with about fifty thousand others and watched fireworks explode against a black sky filled with stars. I looked all around at a million faces, smiling and laughing, whooping and hollering. When there is wonderment enough to distract people from their own concerns, they unite in the glee of life. And somehow, more than in their sorrow, people appear uniform in their joy.

Interrupting my thoughts, a charge exploded, its globular center expanding in brilliant red while blue rings exploded around it like the rings of Saturn. I wondered if Alex would be alive to see the fireworks next year. On the Fourth of July.

VALERIE BITTNER   FERRYBOAT CAPTAIN – *Bellevue, Maryland*

After another night in Washington, D.C., I left the area by circling the beltway until I hit Interstate 595, a mass of concrete that steers traffic east toward Chesapeake Bay. As I pulled off in Annapolis to gas up, the heat and humidity were almost otherworldly. I handed my card to the man behind the counter, and he smiled. "Sure has been a hot one," he said. I nodded in silence as the rattling from the air conditioner filled the small store, cool air rushing down on his half-bald head.

Having signed my name on the piece of paper, I stuffed the yellow copy into my sweaty right pocket and went back outside. The man didn't know how right he was: The drive had been hot as hell, a constant sweat from Chicago on down through Georgia, then equally infernal and sticky up through Virginia and the District of Columbia—save for the one cool afternoon on the South Carolina coast.

Rising to the apex of the Chesapeake Bay Bridge, I opened my window. The air added another fine layer to the ever-more-permanent film of sweat and salt on my skin that hadn't thoroughly evaporated at any one time since well north of Nashville.

As I drove down onto the East Bay and maneuvered the small highways toward Easton, however, the heat pressed with less force. West on State Highway 33 toward St. Michaels, where I was planning to stay for the night, the air revealed hints of freshness behind its muggy cloak.

By the following morning, I awoke in the countryside outside of St. Michaels to a feeling that I hadn't had in several weeks: It was 8:30 AM and I wasn't sweating. Hopping behind the wheel of my car, I drove to Tilghman Island, taking pictures of sleepy sunflower fields near Sherwood before turning back and stopping to play catch with a retired ad-man-turned-photographer south of St. Michaels. After I celebrated the cool morning by drinking a hot cup of coffee out on his pier, he walked me back to my car and wished me luck. He had the kind of handshake that made me wish I could stay forever.

Passing back through St. Michaels and then Newcomb, I turned right on Highway 329 toward Bellevue, a place he told me I ought to visit. "Try to find the woman who runs the ferryboat," he said, a radiant twinkle in his eye. "She's a peach."

A short half hour later, I pulled up to the lot of the Bellevue-to-Oxford ferry, the sun's rays slowly warming the air again. After talking with the deckhand, Christine, I boarded the stout white craft and was introduced to Valerie, the ship's pilot. I took my place on the rear of the deck while Christine attended to the three cars slowly making their way across the adjoining bridge.

After agreeing to play catch—under the condition that it would be interrupted by the piloting of the ferry—Valerie paced off a distance on the deck and held out her glove. Layered over the deep, quiet idle of the diesel engine, her voice cut through the air in concise syllables.

"It's Bittner," she said, fingering a grip on the ball. "B-I-T-T-N-E-R."

"How many years have you been in this business?"

"Well, it goes back a long way. I'm the sixth generation in my family to be involved with ferryboating." She brought her tanned arm down and sent the ball spinning true into my glove. "Originally, my family had an operation up on the eastern end of Long Island—ran to Shelter Island—and my father came down here in 1974 with an old wooden ferryboat called the *Southside*. She was built in 1923 in Greenport, New York. So he brought that—it was a six-car ferry—to replace the three-car ferryboat that was here with the old operation. Then we came the following year to join him." I threw, threading the ball between the cars parking to my left and the white pilot's tower to my right.

"Then, in 1980, we picked up this all-steel ferryboat. On busy weekends we had both the *Southside* and the tall boat crossing, but we had to retire her in 1991."

"Which?"

"The *Southside*. We sunk her out in the Chesapeake Bay, in the state fishing reef site."

"Was that hard for you?" Pop. Into my glove.

"Well, it was a sad day, but also a fitting end to a long career. So at any rate, we just have the one boat now and operate full-time with her." She had a voice capable of carrying over the sounds of the cars pulling onto the craft, the massive engine, and the passengers chatting on the deck.

"How many cars can you put on this rig?"

"All right," she said, loading up an answer that she had no doubt repeated a thousand times. "This ferryboat accommodates nine cars, eighty passengers, and two crew. It's maxed out in the summer quite a bit, loaded up all the way. In fact, we had a full load yesterday. Our weekends are our busiest time, you know. We generally have a line."

"How long is the crossing?"

"We can make the round-trip in around twenty minutes." As the words cleared her lips, Valerie tucked the glove under her arm, asked me to hold on, and went up into the pilot's tower. Revving up the engine, she called in a message on the radio and slowly urged the ferry into motion. As fresh breezes pushed across the deck and through the open window in the tower, her auburn hair tossed and her sunglasses reflected images of the shimmering water.

After docking the ferry on the Oxford side of the Tred Avon River several minutes later, Valerie surveyed the loading area—no cars. She climbed back down the metal ladder and onto the slowly rocking deck, returning to our game of catch.

"So you were born and raised on Long Island?" The ball arced between us.

"Yes, and my husband, David, is also from Shelter Island—he and I own the business now. We'd both been around water and boats all our lives, and when we first moved here David was already licensed and ready to go. I never got too involved with the operation on Shelter Island—had two young children, you know—until we moved here." The ball spun backwards out of her fingers.

"I decided that one day, if either my father or my husband ever got sick, maybe I could fill in part-time, you know, that it'd be nice to have my license. And as it turned out, my father ultimately did get sick and could no longer operate the ferry. So anyway, I got my license. And as the children have gotten older, I've come to operate the ferry full-time, basically splitting the chore with my husband."

"What do your kids do?" The engine's idle rumbled softly in the background.

"I have one son. He's majoring in accounting at the University of South Carolina and has one semester to go. He's licensed, so when he's back here in the summer, he pulls a shift. And then on the weekends, my daughter, who works with an accounting firm in Easton during the week, works out here."

"Tell me about your life before the Bellevue-to-Oxford Ferry."

"I graduated from high school in 1965 and then went to college in Boston." Her words filled in directly after I'd asked the question, as though she were speaking into the radio. "After graduating, I got married and worked various jobs. Moved out to the Cleveland, Ohio, area for a while—David had a job out there. And then, he decided to go into the Air Force, where he ultimately flew jets—T-38s. He was an instructor pilot in the Air Force and then after that time frame, we came down here—we've been down here ever since."

"How long has that been?" The deck remained vacant of cars.

"Nineteen years."

"Had to get back to the water?"

"Well, we were raised on an island—Long Island—and after you've lived near the water for so long, it's hard to get away. I mean, we fished up there and clammed and scalloped, and it was just a treat to be able to grow up like we did. After that experience, you're always attracted to the water in some way, you know, even if it's just a man-made lake." She threw. "Actually, there are a lot of similarities right here in this general area with Long Island. It's a small, quaint village, there's a lot of history, and we have lots of activities we do around the water. There are over six hundred miles of waterfront in this county alone, which is tremendous. It's fun to explore some of the creeks and we love to fish and crab, too—it just becomes part of your life."

"What's your favorite part of this job?" Behind Valerie, two cars pulled into the ferry lane and readied to drive on board.

"Well again, being on a ferryboat sort of takes you back in history, I believe, and it's real unique to this area because there aren't a lot of systems—particularly privately owned—for some distance. I mean, there aren't that many systems left in the United States on the whole and we have our claim to fame—this operation was started in 1683 and is the oldest privately owned ferry system still in operation in the United States." Christine helped the cars park on board and collected their fees.

"So that's kind of unique in its own way. And I just love—I can't tell you enough—how much I just love to be outdoors. I mean, you see the change of weather, you meet interesting people, and some days it's more challenging than others, depending on the winds and the tides. It really is very enjoyable."

"Where does your business come from?" I worked the knuckler. She gloved it like any other throw.

"I'd say our business is about 85 percent tourism and 15 percent local." As she finished the answer, Valerie turned her head to see a third and fourth car pulling onto the boat. She turned to me but didn't have to speak.

"Go ahead," I said. "We'll pick up later." The next ten minutes were filled with another calm crossing of the Tred Avon, the powerful diesel rumbling its progress through the metallic blue water to the port at Bellevue. After docking, Valerie saw to it that all the cars disembarked safely and then returned to pick up her glove. "Just a couple more questions," I said. "I know you're busy."

"No problem," she said, the ball slapping in her glove.

"As you talk with people from all over—tourists and such—do you find that they have things in common?"

"This doesn't have to do with boating?"

"No, just about your thoughts in general." Pop. Into the leather.

"Well, this isn't going to be my forte."

"Don't worry, that's what everybody says."

"But you don't want to stay in the same vein as the ferryboat business—I mean, you want to get away from that?"

"A bit, yeah."

"I'm going to have to think about that." For the first time during our segmented conversation, Valerie threw the ball in silence, sifting her thoughts. Just when she seemed about to speak, she shook her head, not yet ready. After another few tosses, she began. "Basically, there are so many good people in the world and we see so many nice people out here; it really does a heart good to find out that there are still good, solid people around. Even though you pick up the newspaper and read about all the horrendous things happening in the world, we really do see that 99 percent of the people that come across this stretch of water are genuinely wonderful, wonderful people. And, you know, you can see good values in people; I find that of the people I meet, most all of them really look for the wholesome things in life." She tossed the ball, nodding her head with assurance.

"What are you the happiest about having accomplished?"

"Where do I begin?" she laughed, holding up her glove. After a couple of catches, she spoke. "Well, we're very fortunate, first of all, to live in an area such as Talbot County. It's so unique and we just love having a job that takes us outdoors. We don't have to be behind a desk all day and we both have done that—plenty. And really, it's fascinating to meet people from all over the country, even though we're usually up in the pilot house operating the boat. We do go down on deck and get a chance to talk with people quite frequently. Really, just with living in the area and with two children who've gone off to college, we're very fortunate. We live in a great home, we're on the water all day, so it's great."

Four cars had pulled onto the deck and Valerie's deckhand closed the gate, readying the boat for another passage.

"One last question," I said.

"Can you ask me up there?" she asked, walking toward me with the ball in her glove. I nodded and we ascended the steel rungs to the pilot house, where Valerie radioed in and engaged the throttle. As the ship gained speed and Bellevue slipped away slowly behind us, I set my recorder near the control panel.

"What's it all about?"

"It's about hard work," Valerie said, adjusting her grip on the wheel, "being dedicated." The engine groaned powerfully as we crossed into the channel. "You know, that this business is ours. We've seen it build up through the years, you know, we have good and bad times, but people look forward to coming back every year to see us. And it's rewarding to know that I think we do a fairly good job at it. I think people realize that the service is good and that we try to be helpful and friendly." We cruised along quietly for a few moments before Valerie turned to me a last time. "We spend a lot of hours down here, but there's a lot of satisfaction in it. There really is."

Within several minutes, we docked and unloaded in Oxford and a new string of cars pulled onto the deck. The cycle continued as the engine rumbled, pushing the craft out into the waters toward Bellevue. When we docked there, I shook hands with Valerie and her deckhand, Christine. Both of them returned to loading up the deck as I headed back to solid ground and my car.

I spent a short while in Bellevue, walking vacant streets before poking around a crab-processing plant. There, men toted wooden baskets of soft-shell crabs, their claws clicking together as they were dumped on sorting tables. After he had unloaded a full basket of crabs, I asked one of the men if he cared to play catch. He looked at me as if I were crazy.

Cool breezes along Maryland State Highway 213 filled the rest of the day, a gorgeous stretch of road with small produce stands dotting the terrain at infrequent intervals between Centreville and Galena. South of Chesapeake City, a man touted the sweetest corn in the world. Like Ohio Highway 127, this area of the world was work incarnate, with rows of sunflowers, barley, and corn clinging mightily to the earth.

After tossing the ball with a sportswriter for the *Cecil Whig* in Elkton, I crossed into Delaware and traversed interstate miles into Wilmington. There, I found the key that a vacationing uncle had hidden for me outside his home and let myself in. After watching Bob Costas call a major league ball game on the tube, I filled in some notes and went to sleep.

The following day, with Wilmington as my hub, I headed to Pennsylvania. After tossing the ball with a mushroom farmer in Oxford and a high school phys ed teacher in Morgantown, I drove highways 23 and 340 through Lancaster County. At a restaurant near Intercourse, I had a massive bowl of hand-churned peach ice cream.

Standing among a collection of antique gas pumps, I threw the ball with a carpenter in Kennett Square, Pennsylvania, before exhausting the last of the sunlight watching a Little League ballgame a short distance from his home. "Quite an adventure you're up to," he'd said, "but you mind yourself in the city."

By late evening, I was lying alone in silence, drifting to sleep in Wilmington. Tomorrow, I would leave the napping cows and Amish country pastures and drive up east. To New York City.

N E W   J E R S E Y   T U R N P I K E

I slept later than intended and, after eating a burger, fries, and some lemonade in Wilmington, caught Interstate 95 to Philadelphia. It was amazing how yesterday, forty-five minutes of driving had landed me in mushroom country, Pennsylvania, whereas today the same amount of time behind the wheel deposited me into the southern fray of Philadelphia, where the cars jockeyed for position on four lanes of concrete.

At 2:50 PM I pulled onto the New Jersey Turnpike just outside of Trenton, three lanes of cars drawn rapidly toward the gravitational attraction of New York City some fifty miles away. As a patch of sweat fused my back to the driver's seat, I began to munch on a big sprig of warm grapes sitting in my lap. They didn't taste that great, but I realized that in New Jersey in a car with no air-conditioning at 3:00 in the afternoon, everything is served warm.

The heat persisted as I closed in on the city, the tollway growing wider with lanes that became more congested with every passing mile. I had my windows rolled down to keep some air circulating through the car, and as I neared the southern Jersey suburbs of Linden and Elizabeth I was assaulted by the sounds of passing traffic. Seeing the exit to Union City, I thought of the Hispanic ghetto where Alex had grown up in the '60s. The thoughtscape was interrupted by a particularly loud burst of noise from a passing semi, whose blue exhaust belched into the sky.

I spent the remaining miles leading up to the George Washington Bridge looking to my right at the New York City skyline as I crept along at 10 to 20 mph in a constant grind of traffic. The noise, a mixture of rumbling eighteen-wheelers and shrill horns, reminded me of the nights back in Grand Junction when, as a teen, I'd lie at the end of the airport runway as the jets blasted in takeoff overhead.

Traffic loosened through the Bronx and I stayed on I-95 up through Larchmont, where I had made arrangements to leave my car. After unpacking the gloves and a couple of changes of clothes into a backpack, I caught a commuter train into the city. Three hours after locking the door to the Honda, I opened the door to an apartment in Manhattan. The friends I had planned to stay with were still away on vacation but had left a note: "Make yourself at home."

Exhausted from the drive, I flopped down on their couch to a dinner of salami and mozzarella on crackers. As the television screen sizzled in front of me with the volume off, I decided to call home and check in. There was big news.

Turns out that while I was on the New Jersey Turnpike, probably somewhere in Middlesex County, my sister back in Colorado had given birth to a son. And while I'll always remember how the road had been a transition from the East Coast agriculture of Maryland and Pennsylvania to the crush of New York City, I'll never forget the turnpike for the change I underwent on it: I became an uncle to young Wyatt Cole.

"By the time I'm thirty-five, I'd like to take it kind of easy, you know? I'd like to have a family . . . you know, a little home or whatever, a little car, a little family. My childhood days—my adolescent days—is over with now, you know. Now I'm a man, I've gotta take responsibilities." Shpop! The ball traveled on a line and slapped into my glove.

New York City. One edge of Carl Schurz Park near the mayor's Gracie Mansion rests against the flow of the East River; the other, against streets piled high with luxuriant apartments of the Upper East Side. Across the river, the bulky project buildings jut out on the cusp of Queens.

Against this backdrop sat a man on a park bench, taking in the water and the trickle of evening passersby on the walkway. His new pair of black low-cuts rested on clumps of grass that grew over onto the concrete pathway. I asked him the time and he told me while inviting me to sit down. He was finishing up a sandwich and a soda. Suddenly, three scrawny teens wearing baggy blue jeans, muscle shirts, and black baseball caps zipped in front of us on shiny BMX bikes. Words from passing conversations filtered by on the breezes coming off the water. We began talking.

Phillip Riley is twenty-eight years old, a security guard in a grocery store in the Crown Heights section of Brooklyn. He frequently visits the park for much the same reason as I had: to escape the frenetic pace after a day in the city.

"Yeah, I hustled everywhere. You know, everywhere you go, the almighty dollar . . . "

It was late evening and the shadows cast from the endless rows of apartment buildings behind us had long eclipsed the bench where we sat. Phillip and I stood and walked together down the promenade to its termination at 81st Street. He had a noticeable handicap, the result of being hit by a car at the age of five. His right arm lacked muscle tone and lay asleep across his body; his right foot angled inward to ten o'clock and caused him to limp with every step. We crossed through two lights to York and 81st, where he told me he was going to head downtown. After agreeing to meet the next day, we bid one another farewell.

The next morning, I hopped on a near-empty subway train headed to the Utica Avenue station in Brooklyn. Rising from underground, I found the streets filled with throngs of Crown

Heights' populace in Sunday finery. Polished-clean kids with moms and dads in old American sedans unloaded and marched onto the sidewalks outside the churches that hugged Eastern Parkway. I waited near a bank of pay phones until I saw the familiar limp of Phillip Riley. We shook hands, his left with my right, and crossed over to the sidewalk headed east. A patrol car inched past, the radio crackling out strings of information. Dust flew in our eyes from the broom of a shopkeeper sweeping under a cart of produce. After heading up the street, we descended the shaded walkways of Lincoln Terrace Park to a large patch of overgrown, unkempt grass.

Phillip stuffed the mitt onto his limp right hand and backed up a good fifty feet. He skidded his right foot through the grass as his left arm whipped down and sent the ball sailing. He had a relaxed way of talking, his words coming in clusters after he threw the ball. The refrain 'Do you know what I am saying?' had accelerated to a Crown Heights pace. He caught my delivery, placed the ball in his left hand and after whistling it at me, began to speak.

"I had a stepfather, but he wasn't no real stepfather—knowhutisayin? He was just a mirage, I guess—you know—a image or whatever. I basically grew up with my mom. I was the fourth oldest of six kids. Born in '65. I went to public schools here in Brooklyn and New York." Phillip had a hard time catching the ball with his atrophied arm and compensated by throwing doubly hard with his left. He raised the ball to his ear and sent it hissing through the air.

"My life is very interesting. . . . I made it my first year of high school—you know—and after the first year, then from there it was strictly the streets. . . . I grew up a life of crime, you know."

"Like a hustler or something?"

"Yeah, that's what we call it—you know—hustlin'. I was a street thug, as you would say. I used to stick up, I used to rob. . . . " Phillip paused and hurled the ball a few times in silence.

"Yeah, but it caught up with me. . . . See, this is a long story, man. . . . " He took a deep breath and heaved the ball. It popped into his glove four more times with no accompanying words. He removed it from the webbing, worked his fingers around the laces, and after another deep breath, continued. "It's a long story, man. . . . I grew up in group homes, you know? I was like the bad sheep of my family—knowhutisayin? I was out, you know?" He whipped the ball my way. "At a young age I was hustlin'—you know—so I grew up in and out of facilities and shit—gettin' locked up as a juvenile. I was at detention centers, you know. The first one was up in the Bronx. Then you get transferred from there to DFY, that's upstate. If you got a long bill when you turn twenty-one, you get transferred to corrections."

A patrol car pulled up on the opposite side of the park, under the shade of a row of trees. I tossed the ball in an easy arc. "Tell me about hustling." His foot skidded over a clump of grass as he threw.

"There were about eight of us in our crew. We used to go to school and rob like a m___f___er. We used to meet before school and talk about the day. I was the ringleader— 'standwhutisayin? We'd sit down and make plots. Everyone would always want to go with me." The ball cracked into my glove. "We'd break off in crews and then meet up later in the day, talk about who got locked up if whoever got locked up, maybe smoke some weed, and talk about how much money we made that day."

"And you ended up in prison?"

"Yeah, I went to prison. I went to Riker's, then went upstate—for robbery and assault. The robbery was just somethin' that happened, you know. We was out hustlin'—you know—tryin' to make fast money, and we had got paid that day and we was on our way home and we just stumbled upon this robbery, you know. Then somebody got roughed up and that's where the assault come in. I got sentenced February 4th, 1986, and got sent upstate February 13th."

"What was that like?"

"Pure hell, man. Life in prison is like a question of survival. I stayed six years upstate, then Riker's Island for ten or eleven months. It'll be three years out on September 27th." Phillip lined his fingers on the strings and threw. "Bein' in there is like a city within a city because they got so many opportunities there to better yourself. But it's rough, you know? It's like if there's someone in there and they want to extort you or whatever, then you got to hurt him first or be hurt, you know? It's survival."

"So after growing up on the streets, did being in prison change you?"

"Did I turn my life around? Hell yeah. Because if you met me years ago, you'da thought I was a different person." Screeching tires and a shrill siren erupted in the background; the squad car flashed away from under the shade. Phillip didn't turn his head. Cocking his hand back and raising the ball to his ear, he readied to fire.

"Having seen what I've seen and been through what I been through, this is straight up," he continued. "Words to live by today, man, is like try to understand each other. Because, man, when you grow up rough, in the streets, not knowin' that there's another side of the street—knowhutisayin?—you gonna grow up hard." My toss cut back and slapped into his webbing. "You never been into the streets. But if you ever was into it you be seein' that the money be so good that you don't wanna cross over—knowhutisayin? You may snatch a pocket in midtown and run and get away, right? Then you have a couple hundred dollars in your hand for the day, you know? So it's like that—I didn't grow up knowin' there was another side of the street. But as I got older, I realized that there's another side of the street, so I crossed that street. I crossed over and this is where I want to be."

"What about the people you robbed?" I held the ball.

"When I was out here, when I was out here doin' my thing, you know that it's negative, you know that it's bad—you know—but you continue to do it because you like the fast money that's involved—you know—but you don't think about the consequences." The ball closed on him and popped into his glove. "When you get locked up, you get the chance to sit down and think about it." He rolled the ball on his fingers until they came to rest perpendicular to the strings.

"I always enjoyed doin' nice things—knowhutisayin?—in spite of what I did for a living. I'd go to Central Park with my girl and nobody would never knew I was a thug, you know? But when I got locked up, I used to sit around in my cell and think about doin' everything except what I been doin' to pass time, you know? Go to the movies, go to a show—change my schedule around. When I sit up there by the river like last night, just sittin' there thinkin', it keeps me in memory of where I came from, you know? It keeps me in remembrance that nothin' in your life is free, you know. It reminds me of my freedom.

"'Cause when you in prison, you got to realize you sittin' in this m___f___er, you know, so you f__ed up all the way 'round the board. So when it's time to get paroled, you got to keep in mind that whatever you did to get yourself there, you gotta be doin' the opposite form."

"And what path do you see yourself taking?" I held the ball as Phillip focused on the twisted grass at his feet.

"I wanna own my own business one day as far as maintenance work—you know—because I love cleaning." The ball slapped into his mitt. "When I was in prison, I got certificates in that field because I like doin' that: waxing, polishing, stripping floors—you know. That's what I like."

"How do you shift from the street mentality to wanting to have your own cleaning business? I mean 'taking it easy' by the age of thirty-five won't be easy—and you've gotta miss the almighty dollar, as you said." I lobbed the ball through the air.

"Of course you miss the money, but now I look at it like this: Is the odds greater than the risk? Is they? Not for me no more—'standwhutisayin? The money that's bein' made now, f___ that—you can keep that shit." Phillip's voice raised passionately as he threw the ball. "I can't take another incarceration. . . . Hell no. I feel that that shit—you know, fast money, hustlin'—is for the birds. It ain't for me, you know?" He gloved my throw and fingered a grip.

"I mean it's cool growin' up in the hood—you know—but I want better, I want to do something, I want a change of pace. A person want better, you know? To continue to move on in life—that's what I was taught. Always strive for better, always strive for better." Phillip held onto the ball, moving it to and fro as he spoke. "You know, I feel when you come to these streets every morning—whether you're getting up every morning to go to work or whatever the f___ you do to come up out here—you do it for a reason, for a cause. So I feel like if you're not comin' out here to strive for better when you get on these streets, then there ain't no need in even f___in' bein' out here." His left hand thrust forward, still clutching the ball. "I mean, if you livin' in low-budget homes or whatever and just barely makin' it, then you come out every day to go to work or whatever—knowhutisayin—to better yourself, to improve your sit-uation. So if you just want to hang on the street and drink beers and do drugs and you just layin' on a park bench, then there ain't even no reason for you even bein' on this f___in' earth, if you ain't even tryin' to do nothin' for yourself—knowhutisayin?" He whipped his arm like a snake and the ball hissed into my glove. "That's just the way I feel, you know?" I re-turned the toss.

"If you have kids around you and they just lookin' like any old thing—you know—then you have to instill knowledge in them, man, to remember that no matter how rough it gets, there's always a brighter side. I mean, I told my mom that I spent all my money last night and she bustin' on me for that but I feel just as content bein' out here dead-ass broke—knowhuti-sayin—as havin' to go out there and get that money back. I don't feel the urge to go out there hustlin', but I do feel the urge to strive for better. I know what I want in life, and I want bet-ter." He finished the thought, whistling the ball into my MacGregor.

"Toss me a fly," he said. I lofted it into the sun, and after hanging in the sky, the ball cut through the muggy Brooklyn air.

———————————

Phillip invited me back to check out his apartment, and with the mounting swelter of the day, it seemed a good time to go. After packing up the gloves, we crisscrossed the avenues leading to his apartment building on Union Street. The deadbolt clicked open at the turn of the key and we passed down a gray corridor to the elevator, which stood open. Its yellow over-head light reflected dimly off the hallway floor. As we clanged upward in the close heat, Phillip pointed out the urine stains on the walls and floor, though he wasn't sure if they were from cats or kids.

The apartment was protected by a bank of locks fixed to the door. We entered: the turquoise-flecked linoleum kitchen floor, a couch covered in a yellowed plastic protector, pic-tures of kids and adults in their Sunday finest at picnics, graduations, and weddings. The place smelled of cleaning solvent and trapped sunlight. Phillip emerged from the kitchen holding two glasses of ice water and introduced me to his mother, who was watching a movie on tele-vision. We went to his room and Phillip showed me some of his things—several baseball caps that hung from his wall along with a few pictures of his days in prison.

"So what do you think about it all, if you look back on your life?"

"I guess—you know—when I think on it, I was lucky that I went to jail—you know—'cause somebody coulda killed *me*." He sat back on his bed and stared out the window. "I just buried a friend who got killed a little over a month ago—about a month and a half ago—right down by the park there, right over there where we was playin' catch."

He pulled open a drawer and showed me a picture of his "set"—the group of friends he hangs out with. One kid was flashing a wad of bills, the mark of a good day of hustling. An-other kid stood about six feet tall, dressed sharply. "He's the one who was shot. Honestly to say, man—God bless him—he didn't deserve that. Not sayin' that he wasn't the type of per-son that wasn't out there—you know—but God bless that brother, man. He didn't deserve that, you know? He didn't need to go that way," he added, shaking his head slowly.

We finished the glasses of water, said good-bye to his mother, and then rode back down the elevator. After exiting the building, we hoofed along the quiet Sunday streets through the Jewish neighborhoods of Crown Heights and eventually onto Utica Avenue. As we passed by, Phillip said hello to a woman looking at clothes on a sidewalk rack.

He escorted me to the Utica Avenue station and down the stairs to the turnstiles. One dollar and twenty-five cents later, I was headed north through the screeching tunnels of the New York subway. Just before shaking my hand, Phillip had asked me what I'd tell the folks back home about him. "I don't know," I answered, my hand falling from his. "I don't know what I'll tell them."

Perhaps I'd just watch him in my mind as I had the night of our first meeting: as he disappeared down York Avenue into the canyons of black buildings towering on both sides, his right foot cocked in at ten o'clock, his right arm pinned to his body. The image faded, the deep green and white stripes of his shirt becoming indistinct as the grainy night overtook him.

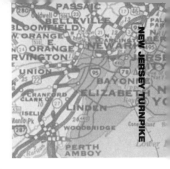

I spent the next two days in New York City throwing the baseball with pretty much anyone who was interested: a high school cheerleader in Brooklyn, a sound engineer from Queens, a retired lawyer reading a *Mad* magazine at a deli, and a Canadian illegal immigrant—who claimed to be a semiprofessional photographer—lurking in front of the Guggenheim Museum. As in L.A., I was overwhelmed by the idea of sampling a metropolis of ten million people by throwing the ball with a handful of individuals. Unlike L.A., however, the sheer enormity of New York stunned my senses.

Seen from above, the place is an immeasurable forest of buildings: mile after mile of pile upon pile in brick, slippery glass, and girded steel. Chasms of architecture are interrupted by the delicate pencil lines of streets and avenues that cut small, vital arteries from one neighborhood to the next. From ground level, however, the streets aren't delicate at all—they are massive rivers of traffic, horns, heaps of trash, quaint bistros, exhaust fumes, and humanity. Humanity pulsing down them six lanes wide three hundred miles an hour toward God knows where, but always away.

The morning I decided to tackle Manhattan started on the hundred-and-fourth floor of the World Trade Center. After spending some time taking in the frenzied scribbles and slamming phones at a currency futures trading desk, I headed down to the sidewalk and began a walk uptown. Six hours later, as the clouds that had been gathering all day began to mist, I stopped at a pay phone and fished for a phone number in my duffel.

After sifting through my things for a few minutes, I found it: There, on a small square of paper written in grade-school-teacher script, was the number of Anne Sadler. The handwriting belonged to Helen Bullock, the woman back in Norton, Kansas, who had hooked me up with Ada Arford. As I was leaving Norton, she had scratched down the name of her daughter. "Look her up if you're in New York. She'd probably be willing."

Anne needed no convincing, and after filling up a spare half hour with a cup of coffee in a small cafe, I headed to Central Park.

By the time I squared up thirty feet in front of Anne, the faint mist had turned into a light drizzle. Pulling the ball from my glove, I fingered a grip across the strings and arced it to her. "Where are we?" I asked.

She tossed her auburn hair over her shoulder with a flick of her head and pointed to the street behind me. "That's Central Park West, and down there a ways is 86th. It cuts through the park." She caught the ball with a soft pop and adjusted her sleeve. The droplets came from the sky faintly, enshrouding the space around us in a calm.

Fingering the ball, whose strings already felt moist, I began. "What's your biography?"

"The rundown? I was born in Norton, Kansas, in 1961 and I grew up there—you know, went to grade school, junior high, and high school. It's a small town—about 3,500 people—and growing up there was great." Anne's voice was clear. However powerful New York City may be, it had done little to change her plainspoken Kansas syllables.

"I mean, I didn't know any different, but it was fun. I came from a very loving family and have really fond memories. The thing that was probably the most important about the way I grew up was the support that my folks gave me. This is probably getting too in-depth for you, but without really saying explicitly, my parents somehow made me believe that, you know, I wasn't any different than boys in what I could achieve, and somehow I got the idea that I could do anything that I set my mind to." She flicked her wrist and threw the ball with a light arc.

"I was involved in a lot of things—sports, music, cheerleading—and my parents used to come to all my events and were very supportive of every single thing. And looking back now, I just realize how awesome that was. It was a great way to grow up: total support and love, small town, no fear of weird things or strange people or anything like that." The rain continued in a lazy drizzle.

"Also—and I hate to say this, because it may sound elitist—but I think in Norton, my father was considered rather well-to-do, and so whether I grew up wealthy or not, I always had the impression that I did. So even though now I'm here in New York and there are people who have twenty thousand times more money than we ever had, I'm not intimidated by them because I grew up thinking that, you know, that's who I fit in with. Which is not terribly important here nor there, but I'm just not intimidated—nor impressed, for that matter—by all the society types around here. So that must've all come just from growing up in Norton, Kansas." Anne laughed fondly and threw.

"And after Norton?"

"I went to Kansas State University and majored in marketing."

"Did you enjoy school?"

"Well, looking back, that's the only time of my life that I have regrets about. I try not to regret much, because I don't think it's very fruitful, but if I had to do something over again, I would choose that period of my life."

"Why's that?" The ball was becoming slick.

"Because I didn't try that hard, I didn't study that hard. It's like I don't really remember the details from school—kind of like I was on what I call 'the conveyor belt of life.'" She finished with a short laugh and wiped the ball in her glove. "I have all these theories."

"Then?"

"Then I went to grad school in business at SMU, after which I went to work for a bank in Houston. Once I started working, things improved. I mean, I had a great job, a great little car, a really neat apartment. I was out on my own for the first time, you know, having fun. And it was there that I met Chris Sadler, the man I eventually married."

"How did you end up out here?" Though the rain hadn't increased, the light was weakening. Against a cloudy twilight, the steady stream of cars on Central Park West ignited their headlights.

"Well, Chris and I got engaged and he had been transferred to New York City, so I moved out here to join him—sight unseen, never been here before in my life, scared to death." She flicked her wrist again, punctuating the ball into flight. "I came into the Port Authority and cried for two days. I wouldn't leave the apartment."

"Did you work?" I caught the ball with a slap.

"Right when I moved here, I did a brief stint in the garment district—worked for an uncle who had a sweater company—and it turned out to be one of the most eye-opening, disgusting experiences of my life."

"Yeah?"

"That's a rough place," she said, blowing air through her lips. "Whew." Moving her hand forward, Anne tossed. "So my first experience here was having moved in with this guy, planning to get married, everything about New York City hitting me, and then working in this really horrible job—just this sleazebag, menacing environment."

"Didn't have you singing 'New York, New York?'" Anne shook her head with a smile.

"So I worked in the garment district for a few months, then I went to work for Pru-Bache down on Wall Street. I was there for two years. Then in '89 I started with an Australian bank and stayed with them for five years. "

"And currently?"

"I work for a bond guarantee company. We guarantee securities in the capital markets." A horn erupted in the traffic and two blasted to answer it. "I particularly do mortgage-backed securities."

"And you're thirty-two now?" I tested my mental math skills.

"Thirty-three," she said, smiling. "Just turned thirty-three." Wrapping her fingers along the wet seams, Anne snapped the ball into flight.

"How long did your marriage last?"

"Four years, but the whole relationship was probably five or six years."

"Why did you divorce?"

"Oh, boy." The ball moved between us a few times. "You know, Nick, I don't know if I could explain it to you even if I had thirty hours." I nodded and left it at that.

"What are you the happiest about having done?" Anne fell silent and the ball moved between us. Tires hissed on the wet street behind us as the ball made rhythmic pops in the webbing. After focusing my ears on the horns and squeaking brakes, Anne's words brought me back to attention.

"You know, I don't think there's a singular moment. I guess the thing I'm glad I've developed is I've come to think that the important thing is making other people happy and feel good about themselves. It's not like an achievement, I guess, but I just feel good, in general, about where I am in life. But not because of any things that I could measure. I mean, it's great to have been successful but it's more on an incremental basis, just every day—you know—being nice to the cab driver or a person in a store or a guy on the street. I mean, I think I have more left to achieve." I closed my mitt around the ball.

"Having grown up in Kansas, then lived in Texas and now New York, what would you say people have in common?"

"Well, I feel like anything I say is going to be kind of trite, but I think that people are basically good inside." The ball slapped cleanly. "There's a lot of things that lay on top of individuals that may keep you from seeing their good side, but deep down inside, I mean—I'd be hard-pressed to pick out people I know who are really bad or evil. Granted, people sometimes get confused and unfocused and totally on the conveyor belt of life or off on some tangent, but I think it's easier to look the other way and point out what's negative. Deep down inside, people are good. . . . "

"Looking at your background—your upbringing, your work history, and now living the upper-class life in New York City—it seems to me like that *is* the conveyor belt of the archetypical American success story. And pardon the broad stereotype, but what does 'the conveyor belt' mean to you?"

She let the ball fly and I returned it as she spoke.

"Really, you're very close to what it means to me. I think there's a definite—and I only know my own life and my own background—but from my background, there's a definite 'should' path." She raised her hands and framed her words in finger quotes. "'You should do this,' 'you should do that.' And I imagine pretty much everybody has that sort of imprint, no matter where they fit in the world. And I just think it's very easy to get on that 'conveyor belt,' which is the path that's been chosen for you by your environment, and just sit on it, letting life happen to you." She held the ball and swept it across a plane, making a grinding assembly-line noise.

"But the danger of that, or at least what I found in myself, is that you don't have to pay very close attention. You can pretty much just get through life by going through the motions." The ball spun backwards from her fingers. "The problem is that you may wake up at some point down the road and find out that you're all the way over here and you don't remember how you got there." She held the return toss, using the ball to direct her ideas.

"It's like that song by the Talking Heads where he says, *'This is not my beautiful house, this is not my beautiful wife'*—I could relate to that so much. It's like, all of a sudden, I woke up and I was in New York City and I was married to this investment banker guy and he was great and we came from the same background and I was making money on Wall Street and I was like, *'Where does this highway lead to?'* as the song goes." She rolled the ball over and over in her hand, the pace of the words matching the dense flow of hissing tires in the background.

"So in my little analogy, if you get off the belt, you have to walk. . . . And walking's a helluva lot harder, because you have to make your own choices. But if you miss out on those choices, I think, you miss out on the whole essence of life."

"Which is?"

"Well, I don't know. I'm still trying to figure it out. It's being aware and knowing that you can't know everything. It's knowing that things are difficult and trying to figure them out anyway. It's being true to yourself and following what you really want to do." Finishing the thought, she rocked her left shoulder into motion and followed with a sharp throw. It popped into my webbing, water droplets flying at my face.

"What'll people say about Anne Sadler?"

"I hope people'll say that I made a difference in their lives, that would be enough. That somehow I impacted the people I know in a positive way, and to me I hope that somehow I make people feel good about themselves and make them believe that they have the power to do anything. . . . I came across a quote in a book about Buddhism recently, and I'm paraphrasing, but it went something like: 'In the end, these things are important—how well did you love, how fully did you live, and how deeply did you learn to let go?'" The ball spun from her fingers.

"Let go of what?"

"To let go of expectations of others, to let go of regrets from the past, to let go of worrying about the future, to let go of loved ones when they die." She spoke the last words slowly, bringing our conversation to a pause as the ball moved from hand to glove and back again.

"Then what's it all about?"

She repeated the question to herself and threw the ball twice. "Damned if I know," she said with a grin. "I mean . . . how well did you love? I don't know what it's *all* about but I think for me, that's the best place I know to start. And I think if I never learned anything else, that would suffice." She nodded and looked at me for another question.

"Any final thoughts?"

"Well, I thought at some point you were going to ask me what I thought about America." She raised her shoulders quickly and then threw.

"I forgot. What do you think about America?" She smiled broadly.

"I think it's the greatest country in the world," she said, her words full of life, "and the more I learn and see things that happen in the world, the more I have an appreciation for our founding fathers and how brilliant they were." She caught the ball and pulled it from the glove, using it to stress an idea. "The most prominent thing that sticks out in my mind is the separation of church and state and how *wise* that is. Because any time you combine your spirituality into your national pride, that gives you the right to cause atrocities to humans." She shook the ball conclusively. "And I think that alone splits it.

"I don't know—" she added, nodding her head to the side. "Maybe everybody knows that, but for some reason, it just came to me over the past few years. I am continually amazed by how brilliant they were, setting up the principles that the country was founded on. The thought that you can be anything and do anything you want—that's huge." She readied to toss with a nod. "You can have that in this country, you can have the American dream." The ball lit out from her fingers. It arced slightly into my glove, the mist spraying me again in the face.

"Well thank you for finishing," I concluded, walking toward my duffel. She nodded with a smile. After peeling the glove from her fingers, Anne handed it to me and gave a firm handshake. After a last exchange of words, she turned to go, walking across the grass toward the streets and clamor of the Upper West Side.

———————————————

I stood on the corner of 86th and Central Park West, watching her figure until it melted away into the crowded sidewalk. In a rush of diesel air and screeching brakes, a bus pulled up, sending small pools of rainwater splashing onto the curb. As I stepped aboard, the fluorescent lights of the cabin shone on the people inside, giving their skin a blue hue. It had been a long walk from the World Trade Center to West 86th, and it felt good to sit down.

SPIKE LEE FILM DIRECTOR – *Brooklyn, New York*

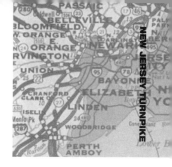

9:27 AM

The editing room at 40 Acres and a Mule Filmworks has a window overlooking Dekalb Avenue. The sidewalks below are packed with schoolkids in baggy jeans and T-shirts, walking in small groups and congregating in larger clusters on street corners.

"So who's paying for all this?" he asked. My attention shifted quickly from the scene outside to the man behind me. As he leaned over a large table, his left hand steadied a two-inch stack of black-and-white photos while his right swiftly scribbled his name near the lower border of the one on top.

"Well, I've got different donations and I—"

"And this is a book?" He interrupted me as his fingers lifted a signed photo and moved on to the next.

"Yeah, this is a book project. I'll compile it one essay per person, and I thought it'd be interesting to get a couple of celebrities involved."

"Why playing catch?"

"Well, because it's a common thread. When I'm playing catch with a gang member in L.A. and a grandmother in Kansas and a celebrity in New York, it puts everyone on the same playing field." His hand continued to scribble his signature over the glossy images of black and white actors from various film scenes.

"So when's this book coming out?"

"Well, hopefully by the opening of the bigs next year."

"Major league baseball?"

"Yeah, if things go well."

"What's the name of the book?"

"*Catch.*"

9:42 AM

After stacking the pictures neatly, he set them next to a stack of film reels on a neighboring desk. I seized the opportunity. "So we can go out and have a catch if you want to."

"I gotta get my glove," he said, swinging the door open.

I was on his heels as we zipped down the stairs and out to a white Range Rover waiting in the street. Throngs of kids on the corner started yelling, "Yo, Spike" as we hopped in. After I slammed the door closed, the noise of the street was replaced by a smooth bass beat from the stereo. Rap music pumping, we cruised the streets around the west, north, and east sides of Fort Greene Park toward Spike's place. He sat in the front seat, scrutinizing his portrait on a Ben & Jerry's poster that was soon to grace New York's bus shelters and subway stations.

9:57 AM

I stood in shadows on a sidewalk that borders the west side of Cumberland Street, opposite the row of brownstone homes. To my right was Fort Greene Park: a green knoll rising from street level, criss-crossed with walkways and graced with old shade trees. Some kids tossed a Frisbee around and several old folks sat on benches, reading papers and watching the morning rise. A constant humming drifted from the laundry room turbines over at the L.I. University Hospital off Dekalb Avenue, about a quarter mile away. I heard a door close and the man walked across the street to the sidewalk, his left hand stuffed into a black Rawlings fielder's glove, his right cradling the ball. Thirty minutes after having arrived in the editing room, I brought my glove up, ready to catch.

Fifteen yards in front of me, he cocked back his arm and—moving one spotless Air Jordan forward—sent the ball sailing on a line as his right arm whipped downward across his body. It spun oddly, as if it were a curveball that didn't quite have the nerve to break. Or to approach the strike zone. Or to succumb to gravity. It whistled past a good two feet above the empty webbing of my outstretched glove and I turned to take up pursuit. The ball jumped playfully as it hit seams in the sidewalk. After hopping over the curb and disappearing first under a Ford, then an Audi, then an old Dodge van, the ball finally rested against the rear tire of a Toyota. I reached down to snatch it up and from somewhere behind heard the voice register a word: "Sorry."

"No problem." I turned and jogged back casually, rainbowing the ball into his glove. "So how much time have we got?" I ventured.

"You've got five minutes."

Five minutes? *Five minutes?* He cocked back the ball to toss. Oh, not again—I wasted twenty percent of the goddam interview chasing down the first one. Without remorse, his hand snapped from behind his ear and delivered the ball into flight with the same wild sideways spin. I felt a moment of panic as the ball soared into the sky. Then, thankfully, after twisting to an apex, it bore down on my general vicinity. Raising my mitt over my right shoulder, I pulled the ball from its path with a soft slap. Thank God.

9:59 AM

Four minutes left. He stood waiting for my toss, his eyes studying me from behind his trademark black framed glasses. Short whiskers surrounded his neatly trimmed goatee.

"Why don't you move back some . . . " he said. I hesitantly conceded two squares of the sidewalk.

"Tell me about making movies."

"I'm proud of the work I've been able to do." He caught the ball with a slap and cocked to throw. "The seven films we've done so far . . . " He tossed the ball twice more. The second time it glanced off my glove. "Oops! Sorry." He was silent as I scampered down the sidewalk and snatched up the ball, then started again as I walked toward him. "I'm also proud of the opportunities I've been able to give to people, you know. There are a lot of talented people out there, but unless you get a shot—" he gloved my toss and stepped forward to return it— "or vehicle, then you just stay undiscovered talent." The ball traveled twice between us. "Like Rosie Perez and Robin Harris and Zelda Harris, the young girl that played Troy in *Crooklyn*— that was her first film." The ball slapped into his glove. "So I just want to continue to do that stuff."

Spike spoke in broken chunks, often tossing the ball twice in midsentence. Such a pace stretched his statements over time and gave them a certain emphasis. Being out in the old neighborhood. In the morning. Talking to people passing by.

"How's being married?" The ball popped into his Rawlings.

"Bein' married is good. My wife is pregnant." He stepped slowly into a toss.

"Oh yeah? Congratulations." It slapped back into his glove.

"Thanks. We're going to have a child in December . . . but we're not going to find out the sex"—he threw—"of the child 'til after"—he caught and threw the ball twice "—'til it pops out. So I'm lookin' forward to that."

"You gonna have a lot of kids?" I held my glove as he fingered the strings.

"I thought I wanted to have a lot of kids—'til I did *Crooklyn*." The ball closed on me with a sideways spin. "I wanted five, but hopefully three is gonna do." Pop. The sound echoed off the sidewalk.

"How's living in Brooklyn now, compared to your childhood?"

"Well I grew up on that block right there." He gloved the ball and motioned down the street with it bulging in his mitt. "My father still lives there."

"What did he do when you were growing up?"

"He was a musician." The ball arced from his fingers. "Jazz."

"How's his jazz going?"

"His jazz is goin'—you know, he's not Kenny G."—he laughed as the ball popped into his Rawlings "—as far as record sales." The ball jumped from his fingers with a spin and flew well past me. "Sorry."

After hustling down the ball again, I returned to my square of the sidewalk. "Did you play ball as a kid?"

"Used to play ball in this park here." He placed a grip on the strings. "We never really played that much hardball. It was always softball."

"Did you have leagues and stuff?"

"Naw, we just had pickup games—all the kids in the block, you know—we'd play other blocks.

"Is this a major league ball?" he asked, pulling it out and looking it over.

Before I could answer, however, an Indian woman in a long, rust-colored trench coat stopped her progress down the sidewalk at Spike's side. "Hi," she said.

"How you doin'?" he asked, lowering the ball to his side.

"Spike Lee?" she asked, her accent thick.

"Yeah."

"I'm a social worker in a shelter. . . . Do you talk to little kids?"

"Yeah, you have to write the office." He rattled out the address and asked her to send any requests there.

She nodded enthusiastically and then lit into another subject. "Those people talking against you about the Knicks thing," she said, her voice hitting a crescendo, "they are very stu-peed. I know you love the Knicks and we gonna get 'em, okay?"

"Okay," he said, as she began to step away.

"So just write it to Spike Lee, right?"

"Right."

"Are you sure you gonna get it?"

"I'm gonna get it," he answered, squaring his shoulders toward me.

"All right, I'll write it on stationery."

"Yeah, write it on letterhead."

"Okay, thank you very much. Have a nice day—and say hello to your beautiful wife." The woman smiled and walked on.

"Awright." Spike focused on me and tossed the ball, which flew in a smooth arc from his hand.

As it popped into my mitt, I shot out a question. "What do you want your movies to do?"

Before he could answer, his shoulder was tapped from behind by a man in a faded knit cap, his white teeth glimmering as a smile parted his graying beard. As he tugged at the bottom of his sweatshirt—one of the old blue hooded ones, with the metal zipper half undone—he looked Spike in the eye. "The Knicks gonna do it, man?" he asked.

"Yeah. . . . Why, you gave up? You gave up?" Spike grilled him, raising his glove and empty hand upwards.

The old guy shook his head slowly. "I don't know, man. We lost the other day," he said with the same smile. "Think we gonna win the next two?"

"Next two, then we'll win game seven," Spike announced. "Bet the house on it." They both laughed as the man stepped off the curb and crossed the empty street.

"So what do you think?" I brought him back to my question.

"I'm thinkin'," he answered, raising his empty mitt. I crunched my fingers onto the taut hide of the ball and sent it wobbling through the air.

"You need no rotation," he said, preparing to wing a knuckler. It lifted from his hand, spinning over the top.

On my next delivery, the seams didn't move. "There you go," he said. He returned his fingers to the threads. "I just think that people . . . everybody just—you know—is in the pursuit of happiness." As his hand blurred across his body, the baseball arced. "And unfortunately—you know—there are people around who try to deny other people's pursuit of happiness." He raised his empty glove. "And that's where we're at."

"So what difference do you want to make with that?" Bringing my hand down, I tossed.

"Well, it's just gonna be stuff I leave behind—which is the films." He caught the ball with a pop. Then came two tosses without words.

"Do you love what you do?"

"Yeah," he said, holding the ball.

"Is it work or play?"

"It's hard work, but I still love it." Spike rocked back and threw that special curve, the twister that launched from the earth as if bound for the projects about a half mile behind me. As it sailed over my right shoulder, I turned to take the now-familiar charge down the sidewalk.

10:15 AM

There was a man down the street, and after the customary "sorry," Spike yelled "Help!" The man scooped up the ball and tossed it to me, cutting my run in half. With it in hand, I returned to find another passerby working Spike over about the Knicks. Then another. Then another.

"You should be some sort of spokesman for the team."

"Yeah," he laughed, "I should own it." We got back to throwing the ball and did so without speaking for several tosses. No one came up to ask him for a favor. No one came up to talk about the Knicks. We just threw the ball, and a relatively consistent arc began to creep its way into his delivery. The ball popped into my glove and echoed off the sidewalk.

Spike watched the ball into the webbing on each catch. After several minutes passed, he took a second and glanced at his watch, then quickly looked back up at me.

"One last question," I said, speaking quickly. "What do you think are good words to live by?"

"It's deeds that matter, actions." The ball slapped into his pocket. "You know, doin' the right thing is a deed, not just words." He fingered a grip. "And you oughta be judged by your deeds, so do the right ones." He looked me in the eyes and let the ball fly as the empty mitt fell to his side. It slapped into my pocket a last time as I started walking toward him, crossing the squares of the sidewalk until we were side by side. "You want a ride back to the office?" he asked.

"No thanks," I answered. "I think I'll just walk." We shook hands and as he turned to walk across Cumberland, I reached down to switch off my tape recorder. As I looked back up, he was hopping into the Range Rover.

After packing my glove, I held the ball in the sunlight and inspected it. It was scratched up pretty good, having made more than the usual number of trips down the sidewalk. Spike couldn't throw a curveball to save his life.

1:15 PM

After a long ride on the subway, I got off the Q line at Brighton Beach. As a hot dog with double relish protested in my gut, I walked south toward the Atlantic Ocean. As I drew near the sand, a mix of seagulls, calm surf, rap music, and Ukrainian billboards filled my senses.

Stopping at a bank of pay phones to make a call, I noticed a small anthropological study at my feet: a banana peel, wilted and black; five cigarette butts in no particular pattern, two of them smudged with lipstick; a torn Trident gum wrapper; and a dirty Burger King bag, rolling up the sidewalk at the insistence of ocean breezes. With the receiver in hand, I made plans for dinner back in Manhattan and then went down to the water, wading around barefoot with my duffel tossed over my shoulder.

After playing catch with a journalism grad student and the wife of a famous jazz violinist, I decided to call it a day. Sitting in a cafe, I planned my drive north before heading back to the subway station on foot. As I passed the bank of phones, a man in a blue maintenance suit swept up the last of the butts.

VERMONT HIGHWAY 100

The following morning, after weaving through commuter traffic in Grand Central Station, I hopped on a train north to Larchmont. Once there, I was treated to hot grilled cheese sandwiches and slices of garden-fresh tomato by the woman at whose home I had left my car. By noon, after bidding her profuse thanks and a farewell, I hit I-95 bound for Boston, stomach full and Springsteen blasting on the stereo.

I had been on foot for five days in New York City and it was sheer heaven to be back behind the wheel, America darting by on all sides. I arrived in Newton, a western suburb of Boston, where I spent the afternoon putting together notes from New York City and then tossing the ball with a professor from Harvard Medical School. He was an unbelievably generous man, inviting me back to his home for the night. There, I discovered his wife to be equally charitable—she allowed me to call her Fran all evening long while in reality her name was Helen.

Early the next morning, I drove through Newton to meet up with Eddie Ginsberg, a family court judge and aspiring commissioner of major league baseball. It was an enchanting experience, throwing his bright orange baseball on the lawn as Pumpkin, his poodle-shitzu mix, darted between our legs. With his radiant smile and bow tie, Eddie went on at length about the state of the world and baseball in it. "I decided to become a lawyer," he said with a smile, "the day I knew I couldn't replace Ted Williams."

By midmorning, I was driving northwest on State Highway 119, a road that lifted away from the infinite congestion of Boston toward quiet towns like Groton and Townsend. Farther down 119, Ashby rose from the landscape with its uniform white buildings and aged headstones beside the local community parish.

I pulled off there and threw a brand-new ball with a cosmetics saleswoman on the commons at the church. Two questions into our chat, she began crying, tears flowing freely down her cheeks. We sat down and I tried to comfort her as she told me about her son who had died at the age of nineteen. Had he lived, he would have been thirty-eight.

Highway 119 curved into New Hampshire, rising and falling through marshes, lakes, and towns like Fitzwilliam, a place so insulated from the world that a store I discovered there was wholly unstaffed yet open for business. A handwritten sign on a table near the cash register read: "If we're not here, please leave cash or a signed check in the jar. Deduct 25% from prices marked 'sale.'"

After crossing into the southwest corner of New Hampshire on 119, I pulled into Brattleboro, Vermont, where I played catch with a 72-year-old director of a funeral home. He mentioned that wearing trifocals made it challenging, but he insisted on throwing the ball, despite my concerns. No more than five tosses later, a throw of mine glanced off the heel of his glove and hit him squarely in the mouth, freeing a front tooth. As he was carted off to the dentist, I left town, feeling terrible.

North of Wilmington, I turned onto Vermont Highway 100, a road that curved often, twisting its way up the mountains only to release itself and snake back down the slopes into West Wardsboro and the sleepy main street of Wardsboro proper. It was beautiful country, silent save for the hiss of the humidity and enthusiastic trills of the birds.

I pulled into a hostel south of Jamaica still feeling a bit blue about the fellow back in Brattleboro. After a couple of hours and a pot of macaroni and cheese, however, I began to let it go and took measure of my surroundings: I was the only occupant in the entire building, and for the first time since before New York City I was surrounded by utter silence.

In the same fashion that the New Jersey Turnpike had delivered me into the chaos of New York City, Vermont Highway 100 had put me back out into the country, where I could slow down. I awoke refreshed the next day and put the car in gear. I was on the homestretch.

Stopping in Jamaica, I spoke with the chef/co-owner of the Sweet Woodruff Tavern & Grill, a man who grew up in Michigan not all that far from Mark Haxer. Between drags on his cigarette, he told me about his bout with alcoholism and his handful of cooking appearances on national TV.

Turning off Highway 100 further north, I detoured to Bridgewater and spoke with a man who worked at a furniture factory. He took great care with his words, trying to relate the immense pride he put into his handmade chairs. "I guess it's like this book that you're writin'," he said. "Each chair that gets my stamp makes me immortal."

I continued at about 45 mph up through gorgeous towns tucked off Highway 100 to Rochester, where a hot dog stand caught my attention. Just off the road, at a curb near the town park, stood "D's DOGS." I parked about fifty yards up the street and walked back, duffel in hand. His daughter was there to help handle the lunch hour, so I convinced "D"—Dennis—to take a break with me in the park.

Walking under the shade of trees on the trimmed grass, I fished out the right-handed glove for Dennis—he was a lefty—and paced back until about twenty feet separated us.

The ball I had inaugurated back in Ashby was picking up its first light brown sheen from the oiled gloves, and I put my fingers across the strings, letting it sail. It popped easily into Dennis's glove, the sound muffled by the lush grass. Gripping it in his left hand, Dennis put the ball into an unusually high arc.

"It's Dennis Bad-ness?" I asked. He nodded. "How do you spell Badness?"

"B-A-D-N-A-I-S."

"And you live here in Rochester, Vermont?"

"Yup."

"Tell me about yourself."

"Well, moved here about twenty years ago from Woodbury, Connecticut—it's a small town. The huntin' and fishin' really drew me up here because I love the outdoors. I was born and raised in Woodbury. I don't know. I'm just a country boy, you know." Dennis spoke slowly in a soft voice, his feet planted as the ball arced effortlessly from his fingers. "My mother worked in a trainin' school and I lived with her. I didn't live with my father. Went through high school and stuff down there and then after that, I came up here."

"How did you end up in Rochester?" The ball sailed between us.

"I came up here the first time to do a little bow huntin', and I fell in love with the rivers. Then I came up on a vacation and stayed. I was twenty-five at the time; I'm forty-five now."

"Do you have a family?"

"I have two daughters and a son. Jane, the oldest there, helps with the stand." He pointed over to the sidewalk, where a couple of folks were prepping their dogs. "I have another daughter, Denise, and a boy, Harley."

"Named after the motorcycles?"

"Yup." A simple question got a simple answer.

"Are you married?"

"No, single. My ex-wife lives in Connecticut; I never did remarry. We're still friends though." Spinning backwards, the ball arced from his fingers.

"What have you done during your twenty years in Rochester?"

"Well, I started out bangin' nails in construction, did some foundation work. Then I worked a little on my own—built a few houses—but I had some medical problems so I had to lay off a bit. That's when I started the hot dog stand." When he mentioned the stand, Dennis's voice lightened.

"How's the hot dog business treating you?"

"Been great."

"You get mostly locals or tourists?"

"The locals, pretty much." The ball slapped into his webbing and he turned to check on the stand. "Tourists are like a bonus."

"What would you like to see happen with the business?"

"Well, I'd like to expand it a little bit. I don't want to see it get too big—just make a livin' is what I'm lookin' to do, you know?"

"And I figure you're a Harley rider?" The ball traced a fat parabola from his hand.

"Oh yeah, I rode Harleys all my life. I bought my first one 1968 and then I bought a bunch of 'em as junkers and rebuilt 'em."

"Do you go to rallies?"

"Yeah, I go to Laconia every year and I've been to Sturgis. Went there for their fiftieth anniversary and to Daytona for their fiftieth. . . . " He paused, glancing over at the street. "Nobody lives in South Dakota so it's a good place to ride."

"Do your kids do any biking?"

"Oh yeah, Jane's got her own motorcycle but Harley's a little young for it yet; he just turned sixteen, but he can't wait. And my other daughter doesn't have a bike yet but she's working toward it."

"Do you collect Harleys?" I crunched my fingers on the ball and tried to work the knuckler.

"I did have a collection, but two days after Christmas last year my house burned down and I lost 'em. I lost everything I had."

"Were you insured?"

"Nope." He sighed a small breath and lofted the ball. "Yeah, I'll never forget that one. I was a collector of rare and exotic things so I had a lot of one-of-a-kind pieces. And I had four Harleys. Three of 'em burned."

"What other sorts of things did you lose?"

"Well, I'm a gun collector—or I was a gun collector. They all burned. A lot of fishin' stuff, a lot of—like I say—rare things. I had a beaver sculpture, for instance—things like that." I returned a toss.

"Were you lucky to survive?"

"Well, at the time, you couldn't have told me that and I certainly didn't think that I was. But now I can see that I am indeed lucky to be alive." Dennis held the ball, kneading the strings in his thick fingers.

"Tell me about the fire."

"It was about fifteen below zero and I woke up when I heard a pop, but it had started in a back room and it took me forever to find it. I went outside and my dogs—I have a couple of rabbit dogs—were going crazy and I couldn't figure out what the hell was wrong with 'em." He continued to thumb the strings. "So I walked back into the house and opened the door to the back room and it was like in the movies—you know—when I opened the door—Christ! The flames come outta there and knocked me on my ass." Dennis shook his head slowly, staring at the grass near his feet. "It wasn't good, it wasn't good at all." Shaking his head a last time, he raised his eyes to mine and lofted the ball. We threw three, maybe four times before I spoke.

"Are you religious?"

"Naw." Pop. Into his glove.

"I was just wondering because sometimes something like that tends to click people over to faith."

"That's a strange thing," he chuckled, tossing the ball. "A good friend of mine was just telling me that's what I need—some religion. 'That's what's wrong with you,' he was sayin'.'"

"What do you think about that?"

"Naw. My religion is what I believe in, you know? I've got my kids, you know, I'm a big family man."

"Is that what you're happiest about in your life—your kids?"

"Oh yeah," he said, the ball popping into the mitt. "They're great."

"What would you like to be remembered for?" I worked my fingers over the hide of the ball, trying another knuckler.

"The best hot dogs," he said with a laugh. "I mean, it's great work. You definitely get to meet a lot of people." Feet planted, Dennis arced the ball with his effortless motion.

"Did you play baseball as a kid?"

"Naw, I kinda hated sports. My sports is huntin' and fishin' and the likes, you know."

"Oh yeah?"

"Yeah, I get most of my food from huntin' and fishin'. If it's out there and can be eaten, it's in the freezer.

"What do you think are good words to live by?"

"Good words? Oh, I don't know . . . " Mirroring his words, the ball arced with a plain gracefulness. "Just be honest, I guess."

"What do you think of America, Dennis?"

"Oh, America's the best, definitely. I wouldn't want to be anywhere else. I would like see America 'cause I'm sure there's a lot in it that's fascinating. I've traveled the East Coast quite a bit, but not much else. Went to Arizona on a rabbit-huntin' trip once, but I've never been to any other country and I have no wants to. I'm sure there's nothing out there that we don't have here." Gloving my toss, he nodded conclusively. "Somewhere in the United States, I'm sure you can find the beauty that's in wherever else you'd want to go, as far as I'm concerned."

"Any final thoughts?"

"Just that D's Dogs are delicious." He smiled as he lofted the ball.

"What makes a good hot dog?"

"The grill, I think—getting that cookout taste. I always thought that was the best. I've got a good product, you know. I figure every hot dog I make for somebody else is exactly the way I'd make it for myself, and that's a good way to be. I see other people doin' other things and everybody tells me I should do this and do that and do things different, but I do it like I like."

"How many dogs do you sell on an average day?"

"Oh, you never know. Some people come every day, been comin' every day since I opened. But it's like any other business—one day up, one day down."

"What's your season?"

"It's debatable, but usually May to October, through the end of foliage. It's a good season, lots of people. That's when the leaf peepers come up."

"Leaf peepers?"

"Yeah, the tourists that come up to see the leaves changing. We call 'em leaf peepers."

"What do you do the rest of the year, when you're not running the stand?"

"Well, last year I worked in a bike shop, did a little wrenchin' on Harleys. I'll probably do the same thing this year." Dennis arced the ball and I returned it. We continued throwing as conversations from the hot dog stand drifted through the park. Knowing I should let him get back to work, I framed one last question.

"What do you think the best quality of people is?"

"The best quality? I don't know if there is one. People are people, you know. They're all right, for the most part. I mean . . . there are a chosen few that are gonna be no-good, rotten people. Then there's the good people, and then there's the ones in between, you know? Just gotta get lucky and meet the good ones."

"Do you think you meet the good ones, mostly?" I fingered across the strings and threw.

"I meet 'em all."

"Yeah?"

"Hey," he said, lofting the ball a last time near the leafy canopy. "I sell hot dogs."

By midafternoon, I was back on 100, tallying miles toward Montpelier. The road was a relaxing one, smooth asphalt curves through verdant agricultural valleys in a landscape completely void of billboards. Turning east in Montpelier, I got onto Route 2, which I took as far as Plainfield.

Stopping there, I threw the ball with an administrator at Goddard College, a woman who, as a child, had been a dancer in Hollywood. Her thoughts were a myriad of fond memories and liberal passions, and as for her baseball, she had deadly accuracy with the fastball. Toward the end of our chat, twilight was mounting and I decided to stay in the area for the night.

I had dinner at the Maple Valley Inn, then drove outside of town to watch the moon rise. It incandesced over the landscape, turning the firs and fields—green by day—into silver silhouettes framing the golden lights of the hamlet.

Shortly after, however, storm clouds gathered, filling the sky with rain. Returning to the restaurant for some coffee, I met a young couple, David and Ailyn, who invited me to stay at their home for the night. I followed them through horizontal rains to Lower Cabot, where we talked about racing vintage Saabs—something Ailyn did; swimming in abandoned gravel quarries—which David had done; and being alive in America. The rain beat against the door while we sat cozily inside, shooting words like arrows into the night.

THOMAS GAGE   RETIRED POLICE CHIEF – *Lancaster, New Hampshire*

I awoke in Lower Cabot at around 8 AM to an empty house—David and Ailyn had already headed off to work. When I stepped outside, the air was thick with the scent of cool fog and dark, moist earth. After packing up my things and leaving a note, I pulled their door shut and ventured back down the road to Route 2, where I signaled left and resumed progress eastward.

Following a stop at a bakery in Marshfield, where I ate cheese danishes fresh from the oven, I proceeded up the road, blankets of fog massaging my car as I closed in on New Hampshire. By the time I reached the border, the fog had acquiesced to a simple overcast sky, its flat gray light spreading from horizon to deep green horizon.

Harkening back to my technique out west, I pulled into the courthouse in Lancaster looking to speak with the sheriff's dispatcher. Five feet past the door, however, I realized that wouldn't be necessary. As soon as the words, "Excuse me suh, may I help you?" broke across the hallway, I didn't take another step.

The man I turned to was Thomas Gage, sitting at a desk near the main entrance in full sheriff's regalia. After a brief description of my purpose for being in Lancaster, New Hampshire, on this overcast morning, he pulled up an extra chair and we began talking. Within five minutes, I had extracted my MacGregor and Tom was studying it. "This is a beautiful glove. It's really great," he said, turning it over in his hands. "The finger goes out the back? Super." He pushed his index finger through the hole and slapped the pocket with his other hand.

"A couple of weeks ago, I went to a friend's birthday party and he and his grandson were out playing catch. It seems to inspire people," he said, opening and closing the glove, "and relax them." He leaned back, stretching a leg out under the table and staring at the lofted ceiling of the courthouse's spacious lobby.

"I remember when I was a kid, we used to hitchhike into Boston, me and this buddy of mine. We'd just leave a note for our mother. We'd make a couple of bean sandwiches and go down to Braves Field and see the Boston Braves play. Then we'd sleep out in Boston Common. One time, a policeman came and banged on our feet and got us out, just like a coupla hobos." He smiled wide with a twinkle in his eyes, his hand still opening and closing the mitt.

———————————

Five minutes later, Tom stood in the doorway about fifteen feet in front of me. We wanted to throw further, but given that we were inside the main entrance space of the Coos County Courthouse, we decided to play it conservative.

"I was born in Dover, New Hampshire, on 9/27/32," Tom began, his thick New England accent weighing down his words. "Graduated from Somersworth, New Hampshire, High School in 1950, enlisted in the military—the Army—for the Korean War, but I ended up in Germany for a few years. Then I came back from the Army and decided I wanted to be a policeman." Moving his left foot slightly over the polished floor, Tom brought the ball up near his ear and tossed. The ball traveled a short way and popped in my webbing, the sound echoing off the interior surfaces of the building.

"I like to tell the story about my qualifications to be a police officer. You know, I got out of the Army and went down to see one of my neighbors who was the police commissioner, and I told him I wanted to be in the police department, City of Somersworth. And he said, 'Well, you haven't registered to vote yet, have you?' and I said, 'No, I just got out of the service,' and he said, 'Well, if you would decide to join the police force, you'd probably register Republican, wouldn't you?' And I said, 'Oh, I'm sure I would.' Well what happened was, the city of Somersworth was all Democrats—the city council, everybody in the city, almost, were Democrats. . . . And if I signed on as a Republican, then there'd be two Republicans and one Democrat on the force. So a little while after that, I got the job, because of my 'qualifications.'" The ball moved between us methodically, the slaps into the webbing amplified by the shiny floor and paneled walls.

"And at that time, you didn't have to get certified and go to school and all. So I just went to the police department, they give me a gun, a club, and a badge, and I went out onto the street as a policeman. And I've been in police work forty years now." Tom's accent was prominent—department came out "depahtment" and army was pronounced "ah-mee."

"I was in Somersworth, New Hampshire, for about three years, and then one winter, I took a drive up through the mountains and got to Whitefield, Coos County." That's Coos—pronounced coe-oss. "Well, I was down at the common, where there's the bandstand, and at that time they'd flood the area and make it into a skating rink. So anyway, I saw kids skating there and I thought that it'd be a nice place to bring up the kids. Well, I read in the paper that the police chief there was retiring so I applied for the job and got it. So I moved up here with my family and I've been up here ever since." The ball moved between us, popping loudly in the gloves.

"I always took the tests for state police and applied, you know, to advance to bigger departments, but when the opportunities actually came I always declined them to stay in Whitefield.

"Then in 1963, I started in on the real estate business on weekends and nights. And after I retired from full-time police work in 1975, I did some sheriff work. I worked as a sheriff up here in the summer and the fall and then I worked as a security chief down at a hotel in Florida during the winter and spring."

"Do you still?" I tossed.

"No, I did that from '75 to '85. It was at the largest occupied wooden building in the world, actually, a resort hotel just outside of Clearwater, Florida, in the town of Belleair. It was the craziest job I ever had but it was fun. I lived in the hotel and was in charge of security and my wife was in charge of all the cashiers so we'd work together. Then the hotel got sold in '85 and I didn't want to work year-round under the new management, so I quit." Tom adjusted the glove, wiggling his index finger out the back with a grin.

"Did you enjoy police work?"

"Well, it made for an interesting life in that I was always out, you know, never was confined to a factory job and stuff and uh, I enjoyed serving the public, you know." When he got going with a thought, Tom's accent weighed on his words like sourdough, something that's always there but in a pleasant sort of a way. "Whitefield was a great place and I had a good rapport with people, you know. Doing things for them was rewarding. And I don't think I was your typical police officer in that I think I was more of a PR person—you know—I wanted to help people. I think a lot of the modern-era policemen tend to treat the public as the enemy, but the public really isn't the enemy because, you know, if you want to solve burglaries or any crime, if you get the public on your side and they like you, they'll help you, tell you stuff. If you're going to treat them like they're the enemy all the time, they're certainly not going to help out." I gloved a toss at my waist.

"You mentioned your wife. When did you marry?"

"I married after I got out of the service and was married for forty years. We were high school sweethearts."

"And you got divorced?"

"Yeah, August of last year. We, you know, we're still friends and we still get along good. We had no real problems with the divorce." His fingers laid across the strings before sending the ball through the lobby.

"Do you have a family?"

"Yeah, I had four kids and lost a son, Steven, in '73."

"Oh." I froze, thinking I had asked too much, but Tom continued throwing and talking.

"He drowned—hit his head on a rock in a big pool at the base of Mt. Washington, at the Upper Falls of the Ammonoosuc River. It really was turbulent that day—thundering in there so loud you couldn't hear yourself talk. He just had a little more courage than he should have that day and it caught up with him."

"Did that change your life?" Pop. Into the MacGregor.

"Well, I don't know. I mean, I think about him every day. Fact, the ex-wife and I went to the cemetery day before yesterday. It's a little one down in Whitefield. And I think, you know, you think about him every day, but it doesn't bother me to talk about him 'cause I have nothing but good memories." The ball continued moving, pacing his words. "I just have great memories, fantastic memories of Steven. He loved the mountains. Actually, he died in a place he loved, and he was there with his girlfriend.

"And Steven's funeral was wonderful in that it was in our backyard. The whole town just sort of walked up to our place and gathered, and the school band played. We had his hiking boots out there where everyone could see them and it was just special, you know?" I nodded and threw.

"But really, God gave me another Steven." Tom motioned to me and I walked toward him as he pulled out his wallet, tucking the glove under his arm as he sifted through small portraits. "This here's Michael—that's my grandson—and there's Steven. Don't they look alike?" The likeness was uncanny; both smiling faces fixed in my mind's eye as I backed up.

"How old would he have been now, if you don't mind my asking?"

"No, not at all. Let's see . . . thirty-eight." The ball popped and Tom nodded, "Yeah, thirty-eight, this year."

"And you have three daughters?"

"Yeah, one's in South Carolina and two of them are in this area." We returned to a rhythm, the ball flying its short course through the lobby before echoing a pop into the webbing.

"What do you think about America, Tom?"

"Well, it's gotta be the greatest country in the world. I mean, I got up today at 5:30 or 6:00, like every day, and listened to the news on the radio. You hear all the things happening in Rwanda and Somalia and all those places and it's gotta be awful there, you know? When you think that there are children that'll know nothing but famine and war—just thinking about that—we're so lucky to be able to be here and live as we do." We threw the ball without speaking several times before Tom continued.

"And you know, I don't know if it's true, but I always thought if I was traveling with others in a foreign country and for some reason or another we were taken prisoner or captive, I always thought that, you know, the whole U.S. Army would come get me out." He chuckled, kneading the ball in his fingers. "I'm not sure that's the case, but I'd like to think it would be." I smiled at the notion of Tom being held hostage, his captors wondering why he added r's to the end of words like "Carolina" and "Somalia."

"What do you think it's all about?" I held my glove up to catch.

"What do I think it's all about? Life in general?" I nodded as the ball flew. "Well, I think life is what you make it, really. There's a lot of opportunity in this country, you know. You talk to people who've lived here all their life and they have trouble gettin' by and so forth, and then other people come over on a boat and open up a restaurant or whatever and only in America could it happen that they'd become millionaires. Mind you, not from luck but because of their work and their knowledge and stuff. I just think we're fortunate to live here."

Moving his foot forward smoothly, Tom let the ball sail. "Did you play sports growing up?"

"Yeah, I played football. I was the captain my senior year. Also played first base on the baseball team and center for the basketball team." The ball popped, echoing off the linoleum.

"Were you sort of a big stud on campus?"

"Well, I was big," he answered, smiling with that same twinkle in his eyes. "I don't know what sort of stud I was."

After shooting a few pictures of Tom on the front steps of the courthouse, I hopped back behind the wheel and drove through Lancaster, where the gray skies lightened as the sun pressed behind them.

Thirty-seven miles down Route 2, I paralleled the wide waters of the Androscoggin River before crossing the border and leaving New Hampshire behind. At the state line, a sign greeted me: "Maine—The Way Things Should Be."

The road was beautiful toward Rumford, curving through mountainous terrain thick with evergreens. Pulling into Mexico, Maine, I stopped at a beauty salon and threw the ball with the proprietor. After skidding the quickly aging ball along the asphalt parking lot one too many times, she gave up and we went inside to chat. Before I could finish, however, she had to clear me out: perm appointment at 2 PM. With my hands full of free samples of some sort of mint foot lotion, I got back into the car and headed for Bangor.

The countryside between Dixfield and Skowhegan was agricultural, an area that seemed more in tune with the twang and crooning of country music than with my preconceived notions of "the rugged Northeast." East of Skowhegan, the land flattened out, the rolling hills and valleys giving way to more straight-shot ribbons of pavement that drew me speedily into Bangor.

Once there, I followed directions given to me by the professor back in Boston to the home of some of his friends. We spoke at length over an evening meal about my experiences thus far, the people of America, and the magic the journey had imprinted on my life.

I shared with them the quote from Opa—about fearing what we don't know—and we discussed tossing a baseball as a means to finding out more and fearing less. Indeed, we hadn't even played catch, yet the simple idea of doing so had opened a seat at their table, transforming the three of us from strangers to friends in the space of a couple of hours.

R U S T Y   M Y E R S   CONFLICT RESOLUTION SPECIALIST – *Somesville, Maine*

U sing Bangor as a home base, I spent the next two days making excursions into the Maine countryside, tossing the ball with everyone from a sixth grader in Corinna to a birthing coach near Orono. Around noon the third day, after loading up my cooler with ice, I said a fond good-bye to the folks in Bangor and got on Alternate Route 1 headed for Acadia National Park.

After an hour in too much traffic with too little patience, I left Acadia and its natural beauty for the small peninsula town of Southwest Harbor and its lobster rolls. As I leaned against the weathered wood of the concession shack and talked with the man inside, he suggested I track down a woman named Irma Jo Gott, whom he said had been around as long as he could remember.

Navigating the small streets of Southwest Harbor, I kept my eyes peeled for her home, a small structure tucked among many summer cottages. After I rapped on the screen door several times, she opened it and let me in, steering me through the narrow channel of free space amid all the clutter. Her home was an eclectic explosion: three pianos, six birds, an organ, two small dogs—yipping constantly—and a doll collection arranged haphazardly about the cramped abode.

Her life story was colorful enough to match. Irma Jo was the former postmistress of Southwest Harbor, a dear woman who had married thrice and divorced the same number of times because, as she confessed, "I can't help falling for men." I didn't question the phone she held in her hand, however, until I was about to leave. That's when, holding it out, she suggested I use it to call Rusty Myers. "Now *he's* a character," she said.

A short drive later, I pulled into a forested area near Somesville, following the directions I had been given to a small A-frame home surrounded neatly by a whispering forest of evergreens. I approached the entrance and knocked on the door as the wind moved through the open space. After I'd waited a while, a bespectacled man opened the door without a word and motioned me to a chair inside. With bright eyes studying me, he let a moment pass before pointing at a tree out front and asking me what I saw in the moss growing on the bark. I answered, "A face," and he uttered a calm "Oh." He then pointed to a painting hanging on the wall opposite me that depicted some Indians engulfed in a cloud and asked me what I saw. I answered, "They're going away," and again he said, "Oh."

We spoke for what felt like an hour, my words gradually slowing in pace until they nearly matched his own. At that point, he smiled, and I suddenly felt welcome. I arranged to stay the night and then drove to the rocky coast, where I spent the remainder of the afternoon taking pictures of a lighthouse near Bass Harbor.

After dark, I returned to Rusty's. He and I piled into an old pickup truck, heading through hill and dale toward Blue Hill to pick up tipi poles. On the drive there, Rusty and I swapped thoughts and ideas in words that barely registered over the whine of the engine. In between topics, I stared forward, mesmerized by the dim field of gold pushing forth from the headlights into the unfamiliar, inky night. Pulling up to a home in the middle of another forest, we secured about twenty tipi poles to the truck's roof. After Rusty made arrangements with the owner of the poles, we drove back through Blue Hill, where we stopped for a drive-thru dinner at McDonald's.

By a quarter past midnight, I stretched out in my sleeping bag in the permanent tent erected off to the side of Rusty's home. It had been over ten hours since I first came to his door and I was exhausted. Such was our introduction.

The next morning, after a light breakfast, I squared off about thirty feet in front of Rusty as the sun broke through the trees. Raising the ball to throw, I began.

"Tell me your biography."

"Well, I was born in Salina, Kansas, in August 1945. My parents were both raised on the farm and moved to the city. My dad was in partnership with a man in the retail shoe business. My mom was a housewife and involved in all kinds of civic activities—church and so on. I had one sister, five years older." Rusty spoke with a steady calmness, a word or phrase occasionally dredged in his light Kansas twang.

"You mentioned last night that visions played a big part in your life, even at an early age." He nodded. "Tell me about those."

"Well, some of my first experiences came around the age of six when we moved into a new house and I had a room to myself. My walls were papered in a cowboy-and-Indian design and lying in bed, not having to strain, I could observe one of these Indians up in the corner, and on one such occasion, lying there before I went to sleep, the room started to expand or seemed to be going away, which frightened me. And I yelled out to my parents, you know, 'the room's going away!' I'm not sure how many nights this experience happened, but after a while I began to realize they were talking about taking me to 'a person.'" Rusty tossed with ease, the movement of the ball mirroring the unhurried cadence of his words.

"At the time, I didn't know who 'the person' was, but it was the local child psychologist, and my gut told me that wasn't a place to go—that it might be more advisable for me to live with the room going away. So when it happened again, I didn't cry out. And the walls did seem to go away and disappear, and it blackened. But what came were basically light forms in the forms of friendlies—chickens, cows, pigs, dogs, cats—things that brought me a great deal of peace.

"And in the background, somewhere off to the right, as best I can recall, was a face. I didn't pay much attention to the face—more just paid attention to the feeling of peace. And as I was going through elementary school, I could go to that place just about anywhere I was." Pop. Into the webbing.

"As I got older and got more involved in the culture, however—competition, sports—that experience faded. I went there less and less. And as I went on to become a fairly decent athlete—I was an all-state guard on the state championship basketball team and got a scholarship to play basketball at college and those kinds of things—it faded altogether." We threw the ball several times; only the wind spoke through the trees.

"Where did you go to college?"

"I went to K-State and married there early on. My wife got pregnant and we got married, which made it pretty much impossible to pursue basketball like you needed to make it at the college level." Rusty watched his fingers as he gripped the strings. Then he stepped on the soft ground and let the ball arc.

"After college, I taught elementary physical education in the inner city in Denver for two years, at Gilpin Elementary—30th and Stout—which was probably more of an education for me than for the children." He lifted an empty glove and chuckled. "Taught me a lot about city life, taught me a lot about abuse, deprivation, problems that almost seemed unsolvable—and some of them were."

"And you taught there for two years?" He nodded, gloving my throw.

"Then moved back to my hometown and went to work for the bank."

"Why the move?"

"I was burned out. There were seven hundred children in the school. Some of them were migrant workers' children who would come in the first of October and leave the end of March, a lot of the children were really not aware of who their parents were, some witnessed murders in the streets at a very young age." He held the ball. "They were crying out for love and I tried in some fashion or another to fulfill that, but I had my own family and I wasn't being a very good father to them."

"So you ended up back in Kansas at the bank." The ball resumed its flight between us.

"Well, I was twenty-five or so when I returned to Kansas and I stayed there for eleven years as a banker, during which time I really stacked up a lot of activities in my life. I was the president of the school board; vice president of the YMCA board; president of the Central Kansas Foundation, which dealt with alcohol and chemical dependency; treasurer for the State Fellowship of Christian Athletes; treasurer for the Presbyterians of Northern Kansas; chairman of the allocations committee for the United Way, which put me on the board of directors as well; and I was also an elder deacon at the church at that time, involved in raising money for an elderly home. And, on top of all that, I was a full-time banker. Then, one morning when I got up, I realized that I was just totally overextended." The wind sped momentarily through the pines.

"Tell me about leaving Kansas."

"Well, I was pretty numb at that point. I was running ten to fifteen miles a day, five to seven days a week. I was working a lot of hours . . . sick." Rusty held the ball, shaking his head slowly while his eyes seemed to gaze through the ground at his feet. "And as I was doing some career counseling, my wife came to the realization, I think, that our marriage was not as healthy as it should be. Plus there was another man who came into her life. So she filed for a divorce. And divorce in the state of Kansas is a no-fault thing, so there was a settlement and that's how things happened."

"Did the career counseling lead anywhere?"

"Well, I had gotten into it in about 1980 to find out what I was basically about in terms of career or vocation and the guy really said, you know, 'You're about spirituality.'" Rusty had raised his eyes to mine and the ball flew. "And the nearest I could come up with out of that was either psychology or the ministry, so I went to seminary. And in seminary, I discovered that what I was doing in the banking business was creating an aura, or an illusion, of power about myself. Unfortunately, the ministry was the same thing for me—just putting myself in a position where I felt powerful, but not very authentic. I found myself falling back into the same traps that I had decided to take myself away from in the first place." I threw, stepping forward onto the soft leaves and soil.

"So I left seminary and basically, that has led me to discover my own reality and my own sense of call. So today, I'm more interested in what the call is than in setting goals and achieving them. I have a sense of peace. I have become conscious, paying attention, aware of my teachers."

"What do you mean by teachers?" The ball slapped into his webbing.

"Well, one such teacher came to me through a vision rather than through physicalness. It was the face of a man that occurred to me about three and a half years ago when I was facilitating a process with a group of people. There was a guided spiritual experience happening, and at the height of the process the room got exceedingly bright—blindingly bright—and I closed my eyes and this face was right there, a very vivid face." Rusty's voice was vibrant, recounting the details as though it had occurred yesterday.

"And through some real help from many people—most significantly my wife—I came eye to eye with this face within a week. He was a Native American by the name of Pete Catches on the Pine Ridge Reservation in South Dakota. I'd say I was with him three and a half to four hours, in that first meeting, and he gave me a message. And it's not just my message; I think it's a universal message." I threw the ball and Rusty held it, his Kansas twang waxing with the energy in his voice.

"What he said to me was, 'It's not about knowing, it's not about what you know, it's not about what you don't know, and it's not about what you may learn. It's about trust, it's about faith, it's about always following the call.'" The ball rested in Rusty's fingers as a fresh breeze whispered through the boughs.

"And after the meeting with Catches, I started paying more attention to what's flowing through me, and I've come to realize that there's a purpose for all of life and each human being has a gift, just as the grass has a gift, the tree has a gift, and the rock has a gift. There's a message each one of us has that's part of the total package." After finishing the thought, Rusty looked down, rediscovering the ball in his fingers. Raising it to his shoulder, he stepped forward and tossed.

"What do you do now?"

"Well, I've been trained in and work with people in facilitating a process called community building—conflict resolution, if you will—and I work with the Foundation for Community Encouragement. That seems to be my call." Extending his glove low and away, he wrapped the soft leather around my toss.

"What do you think it's all about?" The ball slapped rhythmically as the breezes raced after one another through the trees.

"Trust. Faith. Following our call. Realizing there's a higher power—God, Great Spirit—that's with us. Trusting in that."

"What would you like to be remembered for in the world?"

"Being a real human being." Rusty's words matched the simplicity of our actions—the ball moving back and forth, one man to another.

"Do you think you're on that path, to being a real human being?"

He laughed, a wide smile parting his beard. "That's my hope."

"Do you have any words for America?"

"Whatever we're going through, I think we're going through it for a reason, and there are lessons to be learned. All of our technology is valuable and important—if it's done consciously and sacredly." Pop. The sound drifted into the trees.

"It's the unconsciousness—getting caught in things like alcohol, getting caught in things like money, getting caught in things like cars. Anything that we give greater value than we give ourselves is a danger. And those are all around us in this culture. That frightens me a bit.

"But I think there definitely is hope, I think a consciousness is happening. Some people call it 'New Age,' though I don't know what 'New Age' is. Most of what it draws on is old wisdom. So I think whatever's happening—and it's happening globally—is significant. And important." The ball continued, riding the light breezes that moved between us.

"And a human being has a lot to do with it. We've created a lot of mess. But we can clean up our mess. As the crow comes, the crow says, 'It's dawn, it's time to wake up, it's time to discover our gift, it's time to share our gift, and it's time to receive the gifts of others.' The beauty of the crow is that it will eat the dead things and clean up after them. A great lesson, you see, from the crow. There isn't a species that doesn't have something to teach." From somewhere overhead, a bird whistled a melody. "The mourning dove that we hear right now has something to teach." The bird finished its song and the sound of the breeze returned, given meter by the pops of the ball.

"What do you think of the book idea, Rusty?"

"Well, I think your idea is probably part of your calling. I mean, as you've explained it to me, it came through you somewhat visionary and that's a call. As I said to you yesterday, your main purpose, if it's from a vision, is to make a paradigm shift with your writing. And that means that for the person who reads this, their normal way of doing things will be different as a result of reading this book. And that has to come from your essence. It's not something that I believe anybody can set a goal and achieve. It's something that comes from an acceptance of who you are and what your gift is." He rocked his shoulder, putting the ball in flight.

"Tell me about Native Americans, as you see them."

"Well, there's a great deal there for people of Western civilization to learn. They're a kept people who want to be a part of the nation, but because of the way treaties were written, it's as if they live under a separate law from even our national law. So in some ways, they are Americans. They fight our wars; a whole battalion was lost in World War II that was made up of indigenous native people. But the real battle for them is to bring forth their teachings, their wisdom—things that are really tied to our Mother Earth. And if Western civilization could come to the same consciousness that these people have lived with for thousands of years, we wouldn't be so destructive." The ball spun into the air. "We would be slower to think that our latest discovery is the best, and maybe take a look at its impact seven generations down the road." Rusty finished the thought with a nod.

"What do you think are good words to live by?"

"If somebody wanted my advice, what I would say is to pay attention. However, I understand that this is just my own journey and I can only tell my story. If somebody relates to my story and it's useful to them, that's part of my gift." The ball moved between us a few times without words and then stopped in Rusty's glove.

"I've found that now—as I'm paying attention and not trying to avoid what I seem to be called to—I have a lot of déjà vu. It's like, 'Oh, I've seen this scene before.' In fact, this is one of those moments."

"This is?"

He nodded, tossing a final time.

Somehow, the nearer I got to the eastern end of the country, the fewer miles I covered in a day. I pulled out of Rusty's forested enclave, and after spending some more time down by the lighthouse near Bass Harbor I headed back toward Ellsworth. With french fries resting warm in my stomach, I stopped at Tank Lake off Highway 182—a bypass of the coastal route—and watched pale-skinned teens in denim cutoffs swing on ropes and splash triumphantly into the cool waters.

By evening, I was reclining on the grass in Cherryfield, munching on hot biscuits while a marching band blasted brassy tunes from the new stand. It seemed as though all of southern Washington County had turned out, filling the lawn surrounding the stand with a collective picnic that made me wish twilight would never fade. I camped later that night south of Deblois on County Road 193.

I awoke the following morning with a start as a large truck rumbled past a thicket of trees that separated my tent from County Road 193. After a cup of coffee and some oatmeal off the top of my camp stove, I tossed my gear into the back of the Honda and headed back onto the road.

Passing Deblois, I drove up the Blueberry Highway to Route 9, where I turned right. It's called the Blueberry Highway—or so I had been told in front of the bandstand last night—because it lies in the middle of the area where Maine blueberries are harvested. Not far up Route 9, I stopped at a prefabricated structure that housed the Guptill Farms Blueberry Packing House. Inside, in a low rumble, the belts churned as millions of berries danced to and fro on the conveyors. I tossed the ball with a few of the truck drivers out front, then hopped back into the car and progressed.

I drove as far as Wesley before making a U-turn and heading back the way I'd come. I decided that while the sparsely populated semitundra of Route 9 was beautiful, it would be better to invest my last miles across the United States on the coast, where I might run into more people. Passing back through Cherryfield, I saw that the lawns near the bandstand had been thoroughly groomed, the blades of grass standing in uniform attention as the sun splashed upon them.

Three miles later, I saw a storefront so colorful that it jerked my eyes off Route 1. Signaling quickly, I pulled onto the sandy gravel of the shoulder and brought my car to a stop. Behind a Schlitz sign and an American flag, a blackboard had been hand-painted in bright orange letters that read: "Blueberry rakes for sale." One layer deeper, I saw a large shingle that advertised the store: The Mill River Antiques and Salvage Company and the Downeast Museum of Natural History.

On the approximately forty feet of grass that separated the facade from the side of the road rested the single most stunning collection of goods I've ever seen: a Gulf Oil sign and an old Gulf gas pump, little fishnets and a top of a cab for a pickup truck, some steel wheels and an old porcelain sink; a push lawn mower, three motorcycles, a table umbrella, and a set of four pink wicker chairs. Then there was the old sorting table—similar to the one loaded with crabs back in Maryland—that was piled with picture frames. The items were all in various states of disorder, but were all up for sale.

On the storefront, a smaller miscellany was nailed up: two Maine license plates, a pot, a steak knife, a rusty horseshoe, an oyster shell, a cream pitcher, a watch, an old wrestling shoe, a muffin tin, a snow shovel, a wooden ladder leaning up against an old tractor light, a Big Bird doll, an eight-inch piece of bicycle chain, an old, rusty teapot, and a Florida license plate from 1973.

Behind me, as my eyes wandered in fascination over the place, I heard the squeal of dry brakes and turned to see a man hustling out of the driver's side of a late-model wagon. He was a burly guy, swaying as he paced quickly toward me. Extending his beefy, wrinkled fingers and giving me the firmest handshake in America, he spoke in a gravelly voice: "Name's Jerry Blackburn, pleased to meet ya." His blue eyes sparkled beneath his bushy, blond eyebrows as he welcomed me and turned to unlock the door.

Inside the store, the sensory overload continued. The record player—one of the old box setups—alternated Bob Dylan and Kenny Rogers selections. The shelves were like the outside facade, only infinitely more dense in treasures: a cow-shaped milk pitcher, a bubble gum ma-chine, an old brown fedora, a couple of Barbie dolls, a double-barreled shotgun, a leopard-skin jacket, an old pair of ice skates, an old coffeepot, mud boots, about eighty glass bottles of all shapes and sizes, and an ammunition belt from Vietnam.

I heard things being moved near the entrance, and by the time I traced my steps back to the front of the store, Jerry had placed two chairs a couple of feet apart and mounted a video camera on a tripod in front of them. "You don't mind if I start by taping some of the interview, do you, Nick?" His coarse, spirited voice shot out an infectious laugh as I shook my head.

"Not at all. We can throw the ball later."

Jerry nodded and we sat down, the red light from the video camera peering at us.

"Where are we, exactly?"

"Sittin' here in Cherryfield, Maine. But you go back there to the house, which is con-nected here—ten feet—and you're in Harrington. The town line runs right through the store. Cherryfield's three miles that way, Harrington's three miles that way." With a thick finger, he pointed toward Route 1.

"Tell me about the life and times of Jerry Blackburn."

"I'm forty-five. I moved to Maine in 1983. I was born and raised in Sioux City, Iowa; went through a divorce." His words were void of Atlantic accent, he shaped his words like a midwesterner.

"Did you have a family?"

"Well, I had seven brothers and sisters and grew up Catholic—Catholic schools and such. And hung out in town—you know—and liked huntin' and fishin'. My father worked in a meat-packing house and my mother was a housewife. I've got two younger sisters and all the rest are older." Jerry got up and checked through the viewfinder on the camera, then sat back down.

"So I went to school there—like I said—and in '76, my sister got run over."

"Oh yeah?"

"In Iowa City, as a matter of fact. Er, uh, Marshalltown, which is close to Iowa City. And of all the family, I was the only one who was able to go down and take care of her business and her four kids."

"She died?"

"No, as a matter of fact, she's alive now. Paralyzed from the waist down. Lost her index finger, but she does everything me and you do. Except walk." Jerry turned away and reached for a pitcher of ice water, offering me a Dixie cup and filling it. "So I went down to Marshalltown, Iowa, and she was in the hospital—intensive care for about six months. But anyway, put a long story short, I took care of her business. It was a junk shop like this, and I started buyin' and sellin' for her—you know—takin' care of her business, and it mushroomed."

"When did you finish high school?"

"Actually, I only went to the seventh grade. I have dyslexia but I didn't know it, and back then they didn't know how to diagnose it, so I played AWOL a lot and didn't do very good in school." Jerry's hand shifted on the arm of the chair. His stubby fingernails were lined with grit.

"So I cut meat. I started cuttin' meat when I was about eighteen and savin' my money. I'd go out partyin' with twenty bucks and give my mom the rest of my check. And when twenty dollars was gone, I was done partyin'.

"Then, I bought my first house when I was twenty years old—paid cash for it. In Sioux City. I was working for Swift's at the time. Course everybody's heard of Iowa beef, by now." Jerry's words were engaging and his pace kinetic, one topic piling onto another like the assorted wares stacked on the shelves.

"And while I was there, I also collected Harleys. I bought my first Harley—a 1942 WR—when I was sixteen years old. Paid fifty bucks for it. Then I bought a 1929 JD with a sidecar.

Paid seventy-five for that. And then I bought two 1934 VLs. I paid a hundred and fifty bucks for the pair. These are Harleys. That's dirt cheap. But this is back in the '60s when everybody was choppin' their Harleys and makin' choppers, you know—*Easy Rider* come out about then. And they'd throw away the gas tanks and the fenders and all that garbage. Well me being the collector I am, I started saving all that stuff. Then, in 1980, I sold my collection out for about thirty thousand dollars." Jerry smiled at me before glancing at the camera.

"How long did you stay in Iowa?"

"Well, let me back up a little bit. I sold my Harley collection and I bought a school building—four stories, thirty-three-thousand square foot—and turned it into a pawnshop. See, there was only one other pawnshop in Sioux City besides myself, and that was Eagle, who was an old Jewish fella who'd been in business for quite a while.

"But anyway, I did real good, and then I went through a divorce. I was married to a gal and had two kids—a girl and a boy, two real nice kids. The boy is, I think he's eighteen, and the girl is twenty-two; they're back in Sioux City. So I went through the divorce—it was pretty mean—and packed up and moved up here in 1983."

"Were you planning to open another store?"

"Well, I semiretired when I moved up here. Had a big auction. Sold my school, sold all my personal property, you know, but after two years of huntin' and fishin' and sightseein', I got bored. So I went back to my old ways—into the antiques and salvage, you know, junk, antiques, collectibles, whatever you want to call it.

"But anyway, I've since remarried, three years ago, and my new wife has come into the picture. She likes the business and in fact, I've got another store down the road a piece. Full of stuff. Up that way." Raising his forefinger, he pointed to the east.

"Sounds like a busy life."

"Yeah, I've got forty-five acres up the road a piece and I also build low-income houses for people. And I sell real estate on the side." He picked up the ice water, offering a refill.

"A man of many hats."

"Well, I've got a disability and I've turned my disability around and found little things I can do and I found I love to help people. I build little one-bedroom houses, two-bedroom houses, whatever the family needs. Right now, there's a family that's paying three hundred fifty dollars a month and the rent's going right down the tubes. I can sell them a house for forty thousand dollars where they'll pay three hundred dollars a month and have their own house." Jerry nodded contentedly and I seized the break in conversation to ask if he wanted to play catch. "Oh sure," he said, scrambling out of his chair to turn off the video camera. "How about right out front?"

A few minutes later, we stood on the wiry field grass just to the south of the goods sprawled across the lawn. Jerry's right hand dwarfed the ball. He tilted his head toward his throwing shoulder as his left foot moved forward, and he let the ball fly.

"Do you consider yourself a Maine person?"

"Oh, no, no," he said, shaking his head. "You're never a Mainer unless you're born and raised here, you know. Maine people are gen-u-ine." His voice rumbled as he split the syllables. "But when you get to know Maine people, they welcome you into their house and such. The folks up here really enjoy life." The ball flew from his fingers.

"How did you succeed in the antique business?"

"Well, let me tell you, I'm thinkin' about doin' a tape—a video—on buyin'. I'm gonna go out and buy stuff and then look up each item, appraise each item, for what it's really worth, you know. Then I'm gonna try marketing it—to help people out." Pop. Into the MacGregor.

"I mean, Nick, let me share this with you: I bought a telescope—a spy telescope—this long." He held his hand and glove about two feet apart. "I don't know if you saw it in my shop. I bought that thing for ten bucks. And it's worth—minimum—I was offered two hundred for it and turned that down. Well, let me back up. I bought it and there was another dealer right behind me. I paid for it and he said, 'I'll give you forty-five for it right now.' And I says, 'No, I appreciate it, but—' I like to look it up and do some research on it and find out what it's really worth." The ball flew from my hand.

"I just sold a Pee-Wee Herman doll for twelve bucks. It's worth sixty; if I would've took the time and looked it up, I coulda got forty out of it."

"What did you buy it for?"

"Twenty-five cents."

"And that's how your business works."

"Exactly. Buying and selling. I mean, some days you don't sell anything, but another day you sell a carved bear for five hundred. Well, you've got two hundred in it, so you just made yourself a three-hundred-dollar profit." Behind Jerry, a car whooshed down Route 1 as he stepped into a sharp throw.

"Now once, I was workin' for a guy down in Florida and I was buyin' and sellin' stuff for him—which is unusual 'cause I love to work for myself—but this guy was Benny Wells. He's got one eye and he stutters but he's one hell of an entrepreneur. I mean, this guy's an entrepreneur before they ever heard of entrepreneurs. I used to go down and see a girlfriend down there, and one time I ran into a guy with a truckload of roofing stuff and I asked him what he'd take for the whole truckload. Then, I got on the phone with Benny and said, 'Ben, this guy's got a whole Ryder truck load of shit that's probably worth seven thousand. I think we can buy it for a thousand, deliver it, and clear a profit.' So Benny helped with the money and we did great." The ball landed in his glove and Jerry held it a moment in conclusion. "You wouldn't think the junk business would be that profitable, but it is."

"Are you living the American dream?"

"Yeah, I am. I mean, I get up at probably five-thirty or six—you know—do a few exercises. My wife goes for a walk—in fact, she just come face to face with a bear a couple of days ago." I raised my eyebrows. "Yeah, Miss Tina—must've been about from here to your car. Bear jumped out, took one look at her and hit the road. I told her not to be afraid of bears, you know. Just stick your tongue out, flap your hands and they'll run." Jerry waved the ball and glove around as another car sped past on the road.

"What are you happiest about in your life?" For the first time since the tape started rolling, Jerry tossed a few times in silence.

"Helpin' people, yeah. You get the most rewarding—well you know yourself, you help somebody, it makes you feel good. And times are so bad, you see people dying every day on TV and it just wakes you up. If you do a little bit and you do a little bit and you and you and everybody does a little," he pointed to an imaginary crowd, "that's why America isn't Rwanda—you see what I'm saying? It adds up. And that's what's happening in the cities. The family structure's being torn apart. That's why I'm out here. I'm out here in the middle of nowhere and I feel like I'm startin' something—you know—puttin' the family back where it should be, on their own piece of land where they can grow their own garden, and cultivate self-worth." As he finished the words, Tina came from behind the shop and spoke to Jerry. He introduced me to her and said he and I would have to jump in his wagon and go pick up a woman who worked in his other shop up the road in Harrington.

I held both gloves and with the recorder still going, hopped into the passenger's seat. The engine whined in protest as we slowly progressed up Route 1, Jerry spurting out a nervous laugh as he shifted into third.

"So you say you get the most out of helping people out?" I held the recorder near his seat.

"Yeah, well, take this old lady we'll be pickin' up, for instance. She appreciates gettin' out of the house, and me bringing her on gives her that opportunity—see what I'm saying? Plus she gets twenty-five percent of whatever she sells," he said with a laugh. Continuing up the road, Jerry pointed at small placards at the roadside. "See my signs comin' down? See there— 'Free Ice Water.'" No sooner had I fixed my eyes on a small, hand-painted sign than Jerry pointed over to the other side of the asphalt.

"And see that property? I bought it. There's two acres right there, Nick. Paid a hundred dollars for it. It's just a narrow strip of land. It's eighteen hundred foot long and it's ninety feet deep. If I built something, it'd have to be something like storage, you see? So nobody else valued that land except me and I'll probably end up puttin' storage lockers in there. Self-storage—you know—and have somebody workin' there and collecting the royalties." I nodded quickly as we closed in on the halfway point to Harrington.

Then, unannounced, the dashboard emitted a noise—ding-dong-ding-dong—as the engine cut and the wheels began to coast. Jerry laughed from deep in his throat. "You ain't gonna believe this," he said, the car rolling to a stop on the shoulder. Jerry figured somebody'd be along before too long who could give us a lift to Harrington, and I seized the opportunity to throw the ball a few more times.

After putting the gloves back on, we backed apart twenty feet and threw, our tosses parallel to the passing cars. "So what do you want to be remembered for, Jerry?"

"Well Nick, my motto is if you live right, and do things right, things'll happen right. If you live like a dog and steal and cheat and everything, it's gonna end up catchin' up with ya, you know what I mean?" Stepping forward, he threw.

I nodded as a car whooshed past, kicking wind where we stood. "What do you think it's all about?"

"Life?"

"Yeah."

"That's a really good question, you know that?" He clenched the ball in his fingers and squinted his eyes toward the sun. "The Mormons got a tape out, and they really did a good job on that—what it's all about—you know? I suppose it's like I said before, if you help people and live right and do right—enjoy life the best you can—then that's what it's all about." Another car drove past, the driver smiling at us.

"Do you want to spend the rest of your life here?"

"Yeah, I think so." Pop. Into the webbing. "I'd like to spend some winters in Florida, once the kids are big enough. Have another house down there." We tossed a few times without words, Jerry looking down the road past me.

"What do you think of America?"

"Oh, I love America." He said, the ball resuming flight, "Only in America can you do what we do, you know what I mean? I mean, there's always negativity in the world. But I find if you're positive, and be good, do the best you can, you're gonna shine." Just as the words finished, a pickup truck pulled in behind me and the driver pointed a thumb for us to hop in back. "Just like this," Jerry said as we sat on the warm metal of the truck bed, "you know what I mean?" I nodded and smiled at Jerry as the wind began to toss our hair.

Two miles later, we had been dropped off and we met up with the woman at Jerry's satellite store in Harrington. After some phone calls back and forth to his wife and a pleasant wait in the noontime sunshine, I was back in front of the Mill River store, loading my things into the backseat of the Honda.

After zipping the All Star bag closed, I shook Jerry's hand and thanked him for his time. He nodded and smiled briefly before realizing someone had pulled up and was walking to the front door. "Pay no attention to prices," he hollered, his gravelly voice booming over the lawn collection to the woman with her hand on the door. "Everything's on sale today."

MAINE ROUTE 1

Easing back onto the asphalt, I kept an eye on the rearview mirror and watched as Jerry walked away from the road, disappearing into the goods in front of his shop. I had spent over two hours with him, every minute of it alive. As I passed through Harrington, a sign advertised a local Sunday gathering: "Bean Dinner—5 PM."

Past Machias, the wind whipped off the Atlantic as my car traveled eastward along the curving blacktop, which several times bridged backwater tidal rivers that rushed to patches of ocean. The river water mixed into the brine in a frothy marriage; seagulls darting above in the wind.

Further up the coast, I detoured to a yard sale under a large tent near Quoddy Village, a reservation town. Unfortunately, my words with a young man were cut short when someone showed up looking to buy something from the pile of coats. "Sorry," he said, flipping me the ball, "but my parents'd kill me." South of Quoddy, I stopped in Eastport to throw the ball with the editor at *The Quoddy Tides* newspaper. The way he kept looking at me suggested he couldn't quite believe what I was doing. All the same, he suggested that I head on up to Calais, a frontier town that he said would give me a more authentic feeling of having reached the end of the United States.

A long half hour later, I pulled into Calais and, lacking any better idea, parked my car in an empty lot behind a bank where I could look across a narrow strip of water and see Canada. In the remaining hours of twilight, I walked along the main street of Calais, a small-town thoroughfare of Norman Rockwell storefronts. I stopped at the Treworgy Pharmaceutical and Cosmetic Center, a drugstore with one of those old orange-and-blue Rexall signs that look like Butterfinger wrappers, before heading up to check out the last minutes of the sidewalk sale at the Newberry Company. After talking with a clerk there, I headed back to my car and pulled out the Road Ramen supplies.

As the sunlight faded, a yellow bulb flickered to life over the parking lot and I hunched down under it, cooking my dinner with care. A narrow strip of grass separated the parking lot from the water that flowed between the United States and Canada, and after extinguishing my stove, I sat eating on the green while reflections of the coastal lights danced on the water.

The water sloshed against the small embankment and an occasional horn honked down at the border crossing as I sat in silence on the grass, leaning back on my elbows. I thought about a lot of things that night, near the undulating water, setting up my sleeping bag slowly, wanting not to bring the 12,000-mile journey too quickly to a close. And the night seemed to understand, giving me an unusual calm as the soft waves lulled me to sleep.

I awoke as the sun burst across the eastern horizon. I sat up in my bag and looked around me. Calais was slowly coming to life and I tossed my things into the car so as to avoid any unwanted interest from the local police. After a last gaze over the water, I drove into town and stopped for a leisurely breakfast of hash browns, scrambled eggs, and coffee.

By midmorning, as the sun began to warm the day, I was sitting on a park bench jotting notes in my journal. In the middle of my writing, I heard a conversation and the popping of a baseball behind me. I folded the pen between the pages and turned to see an older man, a ring of gray hair around his head, tossing a baseball softly to a blond young kid.

The kid seemed to be spinning quite a story, his words racing with a frequent interruption of, "And Grandpa, and Grandpa—" I thought again of Opa.

I was startled back to the present when the ball nearly hit the bench. The kid scampered up, grabbing it in his small fingers and looking at me somewhat strangely. He stopped for a moment, looking at his grandfather, who nodded, then back at me. "Wanna play catch, mister?"

A few minutes later, the three of us were playing three-way, the kid filling up the morning with his aspirations of playing pro ball. I related what I had done over the past three months to his grandfather and he smiled widely. "Well I'll be," he said. "I'll be."

After throwing the last round of tosses, they walked with me back to my car. I gave the boy a salute and the man shook my hand, slipping me a folded bill. "You stop and have yourself a nice lunch today," he said. "You deserve it."

I thanked him a last time and got behind the wheel, humbled at his generosity as I pulled away from the park and toward Route 9. The old man and the boy stood there waving, their arms moving in the rearview mirror, smaller and smaller, until I couldn't see them at all.

Fifteen minutes later, I signaled left onto Route 9 and drove into America.